Securities Lending and Repurchase Agreements

Edited by

Frank J. Fabozzi, CFA
Adjunct Professor of Finance
School of Management
Yale University
and
Editor
Journal of Portfolio Management

Published by Frank J. Fabozzi Associates

Table of Contents

Preface

Securities Lending and Repurchase Agreements is designed to provide not only the fundamentals of loan transactions in which a security is used as collateral, but also extensive coverage of issues that must be understood by any entity intending to use this institutional arrangement. To be effective, a book of this nature should offer a broad perspective. The experience of a wide range of experts is more informative than that of a single expert, particularly because of the diversity of opinion on some issues and the technical nuances in areas such as law, taxes, and accounting. I have chosen some of the best known practitioners to contribute to this book.

In Chapter 1, Kevin Burke and George Martello explain the evolution of securities lending from its early roots in 1602 in Amsterdam to the present time. The fiascos and innovations are described. In Chapter 2, Kenneth Miller describes the U.S. dollar repo market: what a repo is, repo market participants, the types of repos, the attributes of repo trades, and funding and match book trading. Peter D'Amario discusses the nondollar repo market in Chapter 3, providing a case study of the creation of the UK gilt repo market.

In Chapter 4, Mark Faulkner and Charles Stopford Sackville provide an institutional guide to the securities lending labyrinth. The focus of the chapter is on the lending of international equities. A fund that wants to enter the securities lending market has a number of programs from which it may select. They include (1) master trust/custody bank participatory program, (2) broker/dealer managed program, (3) in-house managed program, and (4) outside manager/third party lender program. The advantages and disadvantages of each type of program are explained by Anthony Nazzaro in Chapter 5. In Chapter 6, William Caan, Jr. explains how to manage internal lending programs by evaluating the risk-reward trade-off available from different types of lending programs. An important step in the investment management process is performance measurement and evaluation. In Chapter 7, Mathew Jensen and Robert Scheetz explain how the principles of performance measurement and evaluation can be applied to a securities lending program.

In Chapter 8, Charles Dropkin identifies certain legal and regulatory issues in the United States that securities lenders, lending agents, and borrowers should understand and guidelines that should be followed as part of any effective compliance program. He also discusses contractual measures that should be followed to reduce insolvency risk. Nancy Jacklin and David Felsenthal in Chapter 9 discuss the key legal and regulatory concerns from the perspective of one of the parties in a cross-border collateralized borrowing in which the counterparties or the loaned securities, or both, are in a foreign jurisdiction.

The parties to a collateralized borrowing transaction should understand the characteristics of the collateral. In Chapter 10, I describe the basic features of fixed income securities, their risk characteristics, and the issues associated with valuing these securities. In describing the risk characteristics, focus is on the measurement of a key risk — interest rate risk. A major sector of the fixed income securities market is the mortgage-backed and asset-backed securities sector. It has become increasingly common to use mortgage-backed securities as collateral in a secured lending transaction. In Chapter 11, I describe the various types of mortgage-backed securities (passthroughs, collateralized mortgage obligations, and stripped mortgage-backed securities) and the major types of asset-backed securities. A specialized form of reverse repurchase agreements has been developed for mortgage-backed securities. The arrangement, called a dollar roll, is described by Steven Carlson and John Tierney in Chapter 12. The cost of a dollar roll depends on certain assumptions. The authors explain how to evaluate a dollar roll under different assumptions.

The lender of securities that accepts cash as collateral will either invest the cash itself or use the services of a professional money manager. There is a wide range of investment strategies that can be used with a corresponding range of risk/return profiles. Typically the investment vehicles selected by the recipient of cash collateral or the money manager engaged are fixed income securities. In Chapter 13, Eliot Jacobowitz and I review the various strategies that money managers can and have employed to reinvest cash collateral. The risks associated with these strategies are explained so that a lender of securities who turns cash over to a money manager can understand how that manager will attempt to generate a return.

The tax issues associated with securities lending are explained by Richard Shapiro in Chapter 14. There is coverage of both domestic transactions and cross-border transactions. In Chapter 15, Susan Peters explains the accounting treatment of securities lending transactions. She discusses the key accounting provisions for securities lending transactions for (1) government entities as set forth in GASB No. 28, (2) non-government entities as set forth in SFAS 125, and (3) registered investment companies as set forth in amendments to Rule 6-07 of SEC Regulation S-X.

In the last chapter, Robert Sloan describes how the fixed income repo desk and the equity financing desk have evolved in different ways on Wall Street. In the fixed income market, carry is the key because it affects both how a firm finances its fixed income inventory and the valuation of derivatives. Yet, because of the disorganization of the equity financing desks, carry does not play the same role in the equity market and therefore the true pricing mechanism for equity products is not yet sufficiently explored. The author discusses the implications for an equity lending or financing program.

Contributing Authors

Kevin Burke	Mitchell Hutchins
G. William Caan, Jr.	First Chicago
Steven J. Carlson	Lehman Brothers
Peter B. D'Amario	ISMA
Charles E. Dropkin	Proskauer Rose Goetz & Mendelsohn LLP
Frank J. Fabozzi	Yale University
Mark C. Faulkner	Securities Finance International Limited, UK
David Felsenthal	Clifford Chance, New York
Nancy Jacklin	Clifford Chance, New York
Eliot Jacobowitz	Information Management Network
Mathew R. Jensen	RogersCasey
George Martello	Euro Brokers Inc.
Kenneth Miller	Goldman, Sachs and Co.
Anthony A. Nazzaro	A.A. Nazzaro Associates
Susan C. Peters	State Street Bank and Trust Company
Robert W. Scheetz	Alliance Capital Management LP
Richard J. Shapiro	Ernst & Young LLP
Robert S. Sloan	CS First Boston
Charles L. Stopford Sackville	Securities Finance International Limited, UK
John F. Tierney	Lehman Brothers

Index of Advertisers

Chapter 1

The Evolution of Securities Lending

Kevin Burke
Senior Vice President
Mitchell Hutchins

George Martello
Senior Vice President
Euro Brokers Inc.

EARLY ROOTS

The roots of securities lending run parallel with the development of stock trading which began in Amsterdam in 1602. The first share certificates were issued to capitalize the Dutch East Indies Company which was granted a monopoly by the Netherlands on trade east of the Cape of Good Hope and west to the Straits of Magellan. The Dutch East Indies Company, in fact, is considered the first multinational firm. It was expensive to outfit a ship and the risks, as well as the rewards, were high. Shares were a vehicle for spreading the costs of financing these ventures. They also could be traded. Originally, shares were traded on the street. In bad weather, the participants sought shelter in a local church, St. Olofs, until the first stock exchange was built in 1611.

Where stock trading occurs, the practice of short-selling inevitably arises, and hence securities lending. As James Brooks points out in his book, *The Games Players,* borrowing to support short-sales was already prevalent by 1607: "By that time short-selling — the practice of selling shares one has borrowed but doesn't own, in Amsterdam picturesquely called the 'windhandel' or wind trade — was a well-established practice."[1]

Several attempts were made to ban the practice of short-selling but the wind trade ultimately prevailed. As Brooks observes, "...short selling, whatever its evils, is a mechanically essential element in the fair and orderly operation of any stock exchange."[2]

Under the modern concept of short-selling, shares are actually borrowed to effect delivery. In early Amsterdam, it is unclear whether shares were physically borrowed, at least initially. "In seventeenth century Amsterdam, there arose the concept of implied borrowing to complete a sale. The speculators thought in terms of the 'difference' between what one agreed to pay, to sell at, to deliver stock at, or receive at, and what one found at the stipulated time to have become the prevailing value."[3] It could be claimed that this was really an early form of book entry. As a result, it became more commonplace in Europe to see monthly settlement, over the course of which multiple transactions or adjustments to a deal could occur. It's only in recent years, post the Group of 30, that we have seen Europe move towards more compressed settlement timeframes.

In the United Kingdom, stocklending appears to have its roots in the financing of long gilt-edged positions, which became a common practice in the late 19th century. This financing activity eventually evolved into the form of stock lending we know today where a market-maker or "jobber" borrowed stock to cover shorts, and provided collateral. This appears to have occurred in the early twentieth century, much of it motivated by "bond washing." Bond washing involved moving bonds from one hand to another specifically timed around the record date and ex-date so as to take an untaxed capital gain in lieu of a dividend payment. The tax arbitrage strategies still used by some participants today had their roots in bond washing.It was a gentlemen's business in the early days where the 'old boy' network prevailed. "Whether borrowing and lending stock, or borrowing and lending

---

[1] James Brooks, *The Games Players*, New York, 1989, pp. 78-79.

[2] Ibid, p. 84.

[3] Herman Kellenbenz from introduction to *Confusion de Confusiones* by Joseph De La Vega. John A. Wiley, New York, 1996, p. 142. Kellenbenz's introduction is from 1957 reprint of this title, originally published in 1688.

money, it was all done by men walking about the streets in top hats, buying and selling Treasury bills, and taking a view in gilt-edged stocks."[4] It wasn't until the 1960s that the borrowing and lending of equities occurred in the City of London. Certainly, the dress code has changed. The players are not quite so fashionable these days, hatless and wearing off-the-rack rather than bespoke suits.

In the United States, in its infancy, securities lending and borrowing was associated with short-selling. The great bear raids of the early 20th century revolving around names like Piggly Wiggly, Stutz Bearcat and the Great Northern Railroad all involved the ability to borrow shares to deliver against a short sale.[5] When the shares were not available to borrow, say, they had been "cornered" by another party, the short-seller could be forced to purchase them in the open market at an inflated price. The abuses of the market system, some involving short-selling, eventually contributed to the creation of the Securities and Exchange Commission (SEC). It's not that securities lending and borrowing were inherently bad; these functions are critical to the liquidity of certain markets. Unfortunately, they are functions which underlie a practice (short-selling) that has often, rightly or wrongly, been held in disrepute.

1960s

In the United States during the 1960s, stock lending and borrowing were basically back-office functions existing to support shorts and fails. Securities settlement was a physical process and, with growing volumes, fails became a common problem. Fails could be expensive and left the offending party subject to a buy-in. The market was interdealer, brokerage firms dealing with each other rather than directly with institutional investors, the beneficial owners of the shares. In other words, brokers borrowed from each other's "boxes" and didn't need to resort to outside sources as they do today.   Additionally, the market was largely equity-oriented.

---

[4] David Kynaston, *Cazenove & Co: A History*, Batsford & Co. London 1991.

[5] See Joseph A. Walker, *Selling Short*, John Wiley & Sons, Inc., New York, 1991 for an account of these bear raids.

1970s

The 1970s saw the U.S. market begin to assume the form of what we see today. Rebates began to be offered, the practice of returning a negotiated portion of the cash collateral reinvestment earnings to the borrower. A handful of direct lenders emerged including selected insurance companies, university endowment funds and corporate investment portfolios. These early pioneers enjoyed spreads in excess of 6%, as demand outstripped supply.

One of the first fund managers to take advantage of the wide spreads during the early days of stock lending was Harvard Management. Paul Cabot, who managed Harvard's endowment fund and was always looking for "areas of investment mis-pricing, identified lending as an opportunity before the rest of the crowd."[6] As he observed, "We got a notch up through securities lending. The problem today is that there are too many people doing it, so they have driven down the margins and taken away most of the profit."[7] Or, at least, greater supply has forced lenders to be more creative, more proactive.

From the bank custodian's perspective, lending was still regarded as an ancillary, not a stand-alone, product providing supplemental income. New forms of trading activity such as convertible bond arbitrage and borrowing related to new issues spurred the growth of lending. Finally, the implementation of the Depository Trust Company (DTC) provided the foundation for a vast increase in lending. While dematerialization essentially meant the sharp reduction of fail-related borrowing, the development of other forms of trading more than compensated for the fall-off in these volumes.

Bonds Borrowed

In the late 1970s, and early 1980s, dealer shorts were primarily covered by reverse repo and bonds borrowed. Securities lending versus cash was not widespread since some banks were concerned that this would attract capital charges because it could be construed as reverse repo. So dealers provided bonds as collateral to those who chose not to accept cash.

Dealers must finance their long inventories and cover their shorts. Long positions are financed by repoing out their inventory,

---

[6] John Train, *The New Money Masters*, New York, 1991, p.182.
[7] Ibid, p. 182.

engaging in bonds borrowed, or, as a last resort borrowing from a bank at the broker call rate. By using their long positions to cover shorts, the dealer can satisfy two needs at once. Additionally, they can avoid ballooning the balance sheet.

Covering their shorts by borrowing from an institution on a bonds borrowed basis was very effective for dealers. Bonds borrowed typically cost 50 basis points whereas reversing in a specific issue from another dealer cost 100 basis points, thus producing a 50 basis point savings. In other words, the dealers paid a fee of 50 basis points to institutional lenders on the transaction where they gave up bonds from their long positions as collateral. When they were forced to reverse in from another dealer, their financing costs would run to 50 basis points more, that is, the rebate received on the cash collateral would fall 1% short of the cost of the reverse. Again, this method also avoided inflating the balance sheet.

Matched Books

Both large and small dealers run what are referred to as "matched books." By definition, a matched book involves the borrowing and lending of securities to make a spread between the bid and offered rates. As intermediaries or principals, dealers will take cash from one party and give up collateral, then take the collateral and put it out to another party, all at a spread. In essence, the dealer is engaging in yield arbitrage, always trying to make a few basis points. As an example, a dealer may reverse in or borrow securities at a rebate of 5.50% and then repo out the same securities and pay 5.25%, thus making a profit of 25 basis points. The matching of positions is not always perfect because dealers will selectively unmatch positions to take advantage of yield curve differentials, for example.

Matched books also play an important role in the dealer's financing activities. As the types of securities have proliferated, dealers have looked to their matched books to help finance their growth. The matched book has been key to the financing of inventories of less liquid securities such as GNMAs, Asset-backs, Mortgage-backs, CMOs, Whole loans and corporate bonds. The lender is doing what is referred to as a "spread trade," lending U.S. Treasuries against repo collateralized by these other instruments. The spread is a function of the type of collateral taken with the widest afforded to collateral such as Whole Loans where there is a liquidity premium. By way of illustration and depending on market conditions, hypothetical daily rebates could vary as follows:

Instruments	Rebates
U.S. Treasury	5.20%
GNMA	5.30%
Mortgage Backs	5.40%
Whole Loans	5.60%

As the futures markets has grown, the ratio of dealer shorts covered by the matched book has dropped off sharply. A dealer could be short the futures contract without covering until the contract expires. This is not so in the cash markets. Also, the need to cover off-the- run shorts has fallen off dramatically as well.

But these trends have been more than offset by the continued expansion of matched book activity in new types of instruments and general collateral. Spreads have narrowed but volumes have risen to maintain revenue streams. In fact, balance sheet expansion attributable to the growth of matched books has been extraordinary since the 70s, and securities lending has played a significant role in this growth. A recent study of New York Stock Exchange member firms revealed that assets related to securities lending activities grew increased 73% from the first quarter 1993 through year-end 1995 to $652 Billion. According to the Wall Street Journal, this growth probably represents the "fevered investing, borrowing, trading and hedging activities of an investor base joined in an ever-tighter embrace with leverage and derivatives".[8]

Lending Intermediaries

The natural holders of large inventories of securities, custodian banks began to emerge as lenders in the late 70s. Initially, to protect their customer franchises and to protect the confidentiality of customers who were somewhat reluctant to broadcast that they were participating in something so arcane as securities lending, the banks typically acted in the capacity as an agent for undisclosed principal. Under this arrangement, the underlying lender and borrower were unknown to

---

[8] *The Wall Street Journal*, May 8, 1996.

each other, leading to combinations that never would have existed otherwise. This structure was short-lived as we shall see.

The 70s also saw the advent of ERISA legislation which permitted corporate pension funds to lend their securities. The entrance of corporate pension funds didn't happen all at once but occurred gradually over a ten year period.

Besides banks acting as agent, another type of intermediary emerged in the 70s, the "finder." The finder's function was to assist borrowers in the location of securities, and lenders in locating outlets for their securities. Originally, both the lender and the borrower paid the finder. The number of shops proliferated. As one veteran observed, while some finders performed a valuable service, "they did not screen the counterparties, as some unwitting participants may have thought. There were a lot of small shops with a guy and two blondes, who, while short of M.B.A.s, were amply endowed by nature in other respects."

International Lending

For almost the first 250 years of stock lending, the business was confined to domestic markets. It wasn't until the 1970s that firms began to move beyond their national borders. Ironically, it was an old line English stockbroker, Cazenove & Co., that was one of the early pioneers in the lending of overseas stock. According to a former Cazenove partner, Patrick Mitford-Slade, overseas lending started about 1973 when certain market makers, particularly Wedd Durlacker and Pinchin Denny, began making markets in European securities. Since the U.K. market makers had been accustomed to going short in the domestic markets, it was a natural transition to do the same for international securities. This was a factor in London's eventual pre-eminence in international lending. According to Mitford-Slade, "It also meant that the market in these European securities was more liquid than in the European markets themselves and this attracted further business to London. Arbitrage between London and the local European markets led to the need to borrow for delivery into the local market."

Initially, the main countries involved were Holland, France and Germany. Dutch international securities such as Philips and Unilever, N.V., were frequently borrowed. Institutions like Prudential (UK) and Robeco (Holland) were among the original lending pioneers.

While its early start may have been in London and certain parts of the Continent, International volumes did not take off until the large American houses began trading in these securities in the mid 80s. The emergence of the foreign derivatives market, index and tax arbitrage, as well as the spectacular growth of hedge funds and the globalization of U.S. asset managers certainly accounted for a large share of the growth of these markets over the last decade.

1980s
Drysdale and Other Financial Scandals

The collapse of Drysdale Government Securities turned out to be a watershed event in the evolution of securities lending and repo. Drysdale was a government securities house who had built up an immense book relative to its capital base by doing repo and reverse repo with primary government dealers. Drysdale used finders to execute their repo and reverse trades, and then arranged for clearance through a bank, specifically through the securities lending departments of a handful of New York Money Center banks. The dealers recognized the counterparty as the clearing bank who was acting in a capacity as agent for undisclosed principal. While these were repo transactions for the most part, the fact that the conduits were securities lending departments created the misconception that Drysdale was largely a securities lending problem.

In the end, Drysdale's default did reveal some flaws in the way the business was structured both for repos and securities loan. For example, pre-Drysdale, market convention did not call for the collateralization of accrued interest on government loans. Particularly, in periods of high interest rates, this could lead to significant exposures as it did with Drysdale in 1982. Drysdale overreached and ended up unable to meet coupon interest payments. It was Chase Manhattan who had to step into the breech created by its bankruptcy (with a write-off of approximately $250 Million). While it proved a sobering lesson to the market, it led to serious reforms in the way the business is conducted. Among other measures, contracts were standardized, collateral margins and specifications prescribed, coupon accruals established and counterparties and their balance sheets more carefully scrutinized. Additionally, whereas formerly the business was conducted on an agent for undisclosed principal basis, the custodian banks amended their agreements to act as fully disclosed agents so it was clear who the principals were--and consequently, where principal risk lay.

Several other financial scandals plagued the securities lending market in the early 80s related to repo. ESM, Bevill Bressler, Lombard Wall were names all associated with building up large repo positions by means of the duplicate collateralization of loans (the same collateral was used to secure more than one repo). This again allowed the pyramiding of risky positions which ultimately collapsed.

Understandably, because of these problems sources of securities began to contract in the early 80s even as demand exploded. Since many bank programs were still not geared up to handle volume or their managements were still reluctant to get involved with the product, broker dealers pushed hard to grow by means of "exclusive" borrowing arrangements. Under this structure, also referred to as portfolio borrowing, a lender gave exclusive access to its portfolio to a single dealer. While very important in the 80s, today, portfolio borrowing plays a minor role in most dealer shops relative to other forms of sourcing securities.

Tri-Party Collateral Management

Another innovation introduced in the 1980s that helped support the growth of lending was tri-party repo. In the context of securities lending, this meant that the borrower and lender dealt through a third-party custodian bank, namely a Chemical Bank or a BONY, who served to receive, monitor and maintain collateral held in connection with a securities loan. Besides allowing for the book-entry of these transactions instead of physical delivery, this innovation permitted dealers to finance segments of their inventories which, heretofore, were too expensive to finance. The impact was primarily on governments, agencies, mortgage-backs and whole loans. In a market where spreads were slipping because of greater supply, this product helped keep volumes from slackening and even promoted significant growth.

1990s

The 1990s have seen many structural changes in how securities lending is conducted. Volumes have continued to soar due to the proliferation of hedge funds, the continued ingenuity of traders who develop schemes which involve taking a short, and the continuing expansion of the global markets. It is probably safe to say that lending volumes range from $400 to $500 Billion worldwide.

While volumes have continued to grow, spreads have significantly narrowed. The easy 50 basis points on a government loan in the prior decade has become a difficult 12 or 15 basis points, if that. More exotic markets still command a premium as do shares which are dividend-advantaged, where the beneficial owner is subject to withholding and does not benefit from tax credits to the extent that a resident does. To compensate for narrowing spreads, securities lenders have to be more astute when it comes to understanding what is driving a particular loan, and more focused and proactive in terms of collateral management.

Securities Lending and Custody: A Troubled Marriage

Securities lending has been traditionally linked to custody. When a plan sponsor selected a custodian, lending was part of the package. This marriage worked well during the 1980s and early 1990s. But as custody fees plummeted during the early part of the decade, custodians looked to securities lending fees to offset declining margins. Securities lending became increasingly part of the pricing equation as fees became predicated on specified levels of lending income, with some deals guaranteed for up to two or three years. A variable source of revenue was thus linked with a fixed multi-year fee commitment.

The consequent pressure to perform coupled with the tendency of some lenders to jump at the lowest bid in selecting custodians led eventually to some questionable reinvestment decisions. The year 1994 proved an embarrassing year for those lenders who had seeded their short-term portfolios with exotic structured notes, range notes, and inverse floaters. The Fed started ratcheting up rates in 1994, and by mid-year, several banks, particularly Harris and Mellon, found their portfolios well below sea level. The rates being paid on these notes moved inversely to rebates, resulting in forced bailouts. Those customers of agent lenders who had strayed too far out along the yield curve also experienced negative returns for the first time as short-term rates on which rebates were based shot up above the rates on the longer term investments.

In most cases, customers were made whole, at least in connection with the structured notes, but some beneficial owners had to share the pain of the negative returns on account of term mismatches between rebate and reinvestment rates.

What is Securities Lending?

In the aftermath of the cash collateral snafus of 1994, it would appear that the definition of just what securities lending is has radically changed since the days the business was a back-office function largely associated with settlements. Some voices have been raised to assert that it is an investment management activity, while others say it straddles the fence between trading and investment management, that it is a form of asset liability management. The investment management argument ignores the fact that non-cash collateral is playing an increasingly important role particularly in Europe. Cash is not an inherently superior form of collateral just because it happens to constitute the major share of collateral held for U.S. based accounts. At the same time, one should not ignore the fact that dealers in Europe often finance illiquid and volatile long positions through securities lending. A new product, equity repo, has arisen in Europe and gives promise of evolving into a money market vehicle at some point. In some cases, the ability to evaluate and monitor these vehicles has not kept pace. Certainly a key to the growth of such vehicles is the ability to judge their risk profiles and adjust collateralization and agreement structures accordingly.

Just how should a program be structured? Should lending be a vehicle for extracting "intrinsic" or the natural risk-free spread from a securities loan? Or, should the lender feel free to take on some moderate gap risk by playing the yield curve? Additionally, should one assume an even more pro-active and aggressive approach, leveraging a portfolio and using derivatives? These, in fact, are the questions which must be answered by lenders in the 1990s. They cannot leave the decision entirely in the hands of their agents. Finally, it should be clear that the one-sided focus on lending returns at the expense of just how those were achieved also contributed to the reinvestment excesses of the 1990s.

Unbundling of Securities Lending and Custody: The Future

It would appear that one trend that will clearly affect securities lending in the late 1990s is the separation of the lending decision from the custody decision. The increasing issuance of separate RFPs for securities lending is a signal to agent lenders that they will be judged strictly on their credentials as lenders.

Just as investment managers have discreet styles, so too will securities lending agents be selected for their specialist or, for that matter, their generalist expertise. While no one would envision the microsegmentation one sees today in the investment management business, it would not be unusual to see selections made by investment, i.e., fixed income (international and domestic), equities (international and domestic) and by geographic location, namely North America, Europe and Asia. Another approach may to differentiate various attitudes to risk taking. For example, one plan sponsor may opt for a program focusing only the "intrinsic value" of a portfolio, taking little or no risk on the reinvestment side. Others may select a program where loans are made exclusively against non-cash collateral or one that is very aggressively managed from a cash collateral perspective. In the end, this development means that lenders will have more options, more flexibility in meeting their lending objectives. While the undifferentiated off-the-shelf agency programs will continue to exist, more customized, more segmented programs will almost certainly emerge.

Chapter 2

The US Dollar Repo Market

Kenneth A. Miller
Vice President
Goldman, Sachs and Co.

INTRODUCTION

The global fixed-income markets could not be as large as they are today without the parallel existence of a highly liquid, low credit risk vehicle in which participants can borrow cash and securities. The repurchase agreement (repo) is the foundation for the fixed-income markets. Without repo, the development of a liquid derivatives market, notably swaps and financial futures, would not have been possible.

The overall market for borrowing and lending fixed income securities is often called the "repo market." It includes repurchase agreements, collateralized loans, buy/sells and securities loans, usually used interchangeably. Forms of collateralized lending date back hundreds of years. Collateralized loans or repos are employed so that the rate on the loan more closely reflects the credit quality of the underlying asset rather than that of the borrower. Consequently, an efficient collateralized lending market has allowed borrowers of lesser credit quality to obtain financing at attractive levels.

Repurchase agreements began in the United States in the late 1910s when the Federal Reserve Bank began using bankers acceptances as collateral to occasionally provide liquidity to member banks. Since the late 1970s, the U.S. repo market has grown significantly, becoming the most developed and largest in the world. Current out-standings are in excess of $1 trillion. The US repo market has been the laboratory for developing an understanding of legal, regulatory and credit issues. Indeed, it has been the scene of several spectacular fail-ures. Although painful, these incidents have led to a more complete understanding of the nature of the repo market — or collateralized lending market — and the potential credit exposures which participants face. Continually refined market standards and maturing supportive legislation within the US has provided a strong underpinning for repo.

Although the US market has its unique and often parochial quirks, it has served as a model for the rapid expansion of the interna-tional repo markets. Among the attributes lifted from the US markets, documentation patterned after the United States' pioneering PSA ("Public Securities Association") Master Repurchase Agreement is per-haps the most significant. Some international jurisdictions have enacted legislation enabling US style (often called "classic") repo. Some of the push to develop repo markets came from highly active US-based pri-mary dealers, but much of it has resulted from the recognition of the overwhelming benefits of the repo product to local fixed income market liquidity and safety.

In this chapter, we will look at the US dollar repo market. In the next chapter, the nondollar repo market is covered.

THE REPO MARKET PARTICIPANTS

There are five primary uses for the global repo markets:

1. To fund leveraged traders, notably dealers, in their normal trading and distribution efforts.
2. To provide flexible, highly secure, and high yielding invest-ments for cash rich investors.
3. To lend securities that others need to enhance portfolio yields.
4. To provide an efficient means to borrow securities against short positions.
5. To earn net interest income by trading repos in a "matched book."

The borrowers of cash tend to fall into three major categories:

- Dealers needing to fund inventories.
- Highly leveraged traders and speculators (i.e., hedge funds) needing to fund trading positions.
- Fully paid portfolio holders (i.e., security lenders) that lend securities which are in demand and then reinvest the cash generated at higher yields.

The lenders of cash fall in two broad categories:

- Cash rich accounts such as money market mutual funds.
- Security lenders reinvesting cash generated from lending securities.

THE REPO: A DEFINITION

There are four basic types of transactions utilized by the dealer community to finance inventory or borrow securities. Each is economically similar, but have unique characteristics with respect to documentation, credit exposure, and marking to market procedures. Which type of transaction is used is typically driven by the counterparty to the dealer based on legal restrictions, internal policy, or custom. Specifically:

> A *repurchase agreement* is the sale of an asset under an agreement to "re-purchase" the asset from the same counterpart. Interest is paid on a repo by adjusting the sale and repurchase prices. A reverse repurchase agreement (reverse repo) is the purchase of an asset with a simultaneous resale of the same or similar asset. Market practice defines repo's from the perspective of recognized dealers — in other words, if the dealer lends securities (and borrows cash) the trade is a repo, if the dealer borrows securities (and lends cash) it is called a reverse repo.

> A *securities lending transaction* is the loan of a security while taking collateral — usually cash — as security for the loan.

Interest is commonly referred to as the "rebate." Borrowing the security is normally the genesis of this transaction.

A *collateralized loan* is normally executed for funding purposes, and usually represents a bank lending to a dealer. Interest is paid as with any bank loan. Borrowing cash is the principle purpose of a collateralized or secured loan.

A *buy/sell* (or sell/buy) is similar to an repo, but actually represents two separate outright trades, one for forward settlement. As with a repo, the forward price is set to represent a money market interest rate, but unlike a repo, a sell/buy is normally not executed subject to documentation or the ability to mark the transaction to market.[1] Sell/buys are fairly common in Europe and Asia, but rare within the United States.

We should focus further on repo. As mentioned, a repurchase agreement is the sale of an asset with simultaneous repurchase on a future date of the same, or similar asset, at prices which reflect short term money market rates. The price difference (often called the "drop") between the sale price and repurchase price is determined by setting the sale price at the current market value of the bond, including accrued interest (ignoring initial margin), calculating the interest to be paid at the agreed upon rate, and summing the market value exchanged on the sale date to the interest. This final amount represents the "repurchase amount." To calculate the bond price on the repurchase date, accrued interest on the bond is calculated as of the repurchase date, subtracted from the repurchase amount, with the result, when divided by the face, being the "repurchase price."

In the event of default by the party borrowing the cash, the holder of the collateralizing security is able to sell the security and obtain cash.[2] Although economically a repo is a secured or collater-

---

[1] The PSA/ISMA Global Master Repurchase Agreement includes a Buy/Sell annex which includes mark to market provisions.

[2] In the United States, certain repos have been defined through legislation to be exempt from the stay provisions of the Bankruptcy Code. If a repo is exempt, then securities collateralizing the transaction can be immediately liquidated under the terms outlined in the RP agreement between the two counterparties.

alized loan, the documentation makes it appear as a sale and future repurchase.

The original owner of the collateralizing security retains all the economic risks of the security's value. Price movements and coupon payments are due to the owner. If a security is on repo over a coupon payment date, the party reversing in the security will pay the coupon (a "manufactured" coupon or dividend) to the lender on the day it is received. If the security issuer defaults, the losses are incurred by the original owner. Keep in mind, however, that the bankruptcy of the issuer of the security and the default of the owner of the security may not be unrelated. The failure of an issuer of bonds collateralizing a repo could result in the bankruptcy of the owner of the bonds.

Repos and reverse repos are normally executed under the terms of a Master Repurchase Agreement. Within the United States, the most common repo agreement is the Public Securities Association Master Repurchase Agreement (PSA Agreement). In much of Europe the PSA/ISMA Global Master Repurchase Agreement (GMRA) has gained acceptance. The standard agreements provide both parties with a degree of protection and defined responsibilities for each transaction. These agreements have been developed in such a way as to give the transaction the best elements of collateralized lending and buy/sells. The documents limit credit exposure by netting the risk of all repos and reverse repos between the two counterparts.

THE REPURCHASE AGREEMENT TRANSACTION: AN EXAMPLE

On December 16 a client lends cash to a dealer for one day at 6%, maturing December 17. The dealer assigns $100 million face of the US Treasury 6⅞s of 8/15/25 as collateral. On the 16th the bond was priced at 111. Repo interest is calculated on an actual over 360 day basis.[3] The repo would appear as follows:

---

[3] Actual over 360 is the standard in the US market. Repo is occasionally done on other accrual bases, including discount, bond basis or actual over 365, but these exceptions are normally related to trades that mirror particular assets. In non-US markets conventions differ, particularly day counts.

Start date December 16:
Face:	$100 million
Bond price:	111
Accrued interest factor:	2.29789402
Market value (proceeds):	Price + Accrued × Face
	$113,297,984.02

Repurchase date December 17:
Repo interest: $113,297,894.02 × 0.06 × ⅟₃₆₀ = $18,882.98
Repurchase price: $113,316,777.00 = Initial proceeds + Repo interest
Collateral price   Repurchase price − Accrued interest) /1,000,000
      ($113,316,777.00 − 2,316,576.09)/1,000,000 = 111.00020091

A sell/buy would be constructed if the repo is broken down into two distinct outright cash market trades — selling the 6⅞ of 2025 on the 16th and buying it back on the 17th. In this case, the sale would be booked at 111 and the buy at 111.00020091 (any necessary rounding would slightly effect the money market interest rate earned).[4]

VARIETIES OF REPURCHASE AGREEMENTS

The settlement and custodial arrangements associated with a repurchase agreement are an integral element of the transaction. Depending on these operational choices, a counterpart lending cash could have very little, or conversely significant, credit exposure to the borrower.

As with any securities movement, *the settlement method* may introduce intraday credit exposure. Securities are transferred by two general methods: delivery versus payment (DVP) or non-DVP. Delivery versus payment means simultaneous and irrevocable movement of the cash and securities. Because of the simultaneous movement, neither party is exposed for the value of the asset they are delivering.[5]

Once the transfer has been completed, credit exposure depends upon the custodial arrangement underlying the trade. If the cash

---

[4] A buy/sell with an intervening coupon date is more complex.
[5] It is important to recognize, however, that a $1 million dollar security could be moved DVP for $2 million in cash. If this were to occur, the party giving the cash would be exposed for $1 million at the time of the transfer and thereafter. DVP does not guarantee fair value.

lender's independent clearing agent is the holder of the securities collateral, the transaction is considered "deliver out." If the borrower of the cash also holds the collateral, then the trade is called "hold-in-custody repo" (HIC repo) or "letter repo." If a special arrangement between an independent custodian, the investor, and borrower of cash is executed where the custodian withholds transfer of assets until after value is established, then the trade is called a "tri-party repo." These custodial arrangements are explained in more detail below.

Hold-in-Custody or Letter Repo

A *hold-in-custody* or *letter repo* refers to a trade in which the dealer (the entity requiring the funding) receives cash from the lender and also holds the securities being pledged as collateral in its own account. HIC is also to referred to more cynically as "trust me" repo. Securities are generally moved into a segregated account at the dealer. A term hold-in-custody repo will normally have its collateralizing securities moved back into the dealer's account during the business day to accommodate security settlements by the dealer. At the close of business collateral will be reassigned to the HIC repo.

A term HIC trade carries potential exposure elements of an unsecured borrowing since there is risk that the collateral may not exist or may be pledged to multiple counterparts. If such an event occurred it would constitute fraud by the borrower. The credit losses experienced in the mid-1980s from the failures of Bevill Bressler and ESM were each the result of dishonest and fraudulent collateralization actions by the borrowing dealers.

A HIC repo does have its advantages, however, since hold-in-custody secured lenders would take precedence over unsecured creditors in the event of a bankruptcy liquidation. The failure of Drexel Burnham GSI provides an example of such a liquidation. In this case, the repo lenders were protected by the courts as secured lenders.

There are commercially valid reasons for a dealer to offer a HIC repo trade beyond an unwillingness to deliver collateral. HIC repo is often executed using collateral that is difficult to deliver because it is physical (such as whole loans) or small in size (such as mortgage pools).[6] In exchange for gaining relief from the costs and difficulty of delivery, the dealer may offer a higher rate than on an equivalent deliver-out repo. Additionally, a dealer may only offer HIC settlement on small trades to avoid the expenses of moving and clearing otherwise undeliverable securities.

Deliver-Out Repo

A *deliver-out repo* is exactly what the name implies. Securities are delivered to the cash lender's custodian in exchange for funds. Transfer of securities is normally accomplished DVP, but this is not always the case. Presuming the securities are correctly valued and delivery is made versus payment, intraday credit exposure is eliminated. Term deliver-out transactions are normally subject to a mark-to-market and often have an initial margin amount or *haircut*. There is currently an effort underway to include in the mark-to-market a revaluation of the repo trade itself in addition to that of the underlying collateral. As of this writing, however, the mark remains only on the underlying collateral.

Tri-Party Repo

A *tri-party repo* is similar to a deliver-out repo in that the securities collateral is held by an entity other than the borrower of the cash. In the event the borrower fails to return the cash, the lender can take possession of the collateral and liquidate. A typical tri-party repo arrangement also provides for the custodian to ensure that the collateral meets the lender's requirements (for instance, only US Treasury bills, notes, or bonds) and to value the collateral assigned. Valuation usually includes ensuring daily repricing and executing margin calls. Tri-party repo repricing is often done using a dealer's pricing on more esoteric securities, particularly non-generic mortgages and asset-backed securities. Although the custodian is not valuing the securities, the responsibility may still exist to ensure the existence and segregation of the collateralizing securities.

Tri-party repo is appealing to both dealers and investors since, although dealers pay fees to their custodian banks, these fees are usually small and are offset by the savings from not having to deliver securities and being able to assign collateral after the Federal Reserve

---

[6] Of course, if securities are delivered, the counterparty has to receive them. Many accounts are not staffed in such a way to easily accept securities deliveries, so the demand for HIC may be from the lender of cash as well as from the dealer.

securities wire closes. This savings is usually reflected in a higher yield to investors. US tri-party repo has become the dominant form of repo used for financing by primary dealers.

Four-Party Repo

A *four-party repo* is a variant of tri-party repo. Instead of a single custodian, two custodians are involved. Usually a tri-party repo custodian will be the dealer's clearing agent. A four-party repo will add the lender's custodian bank as a "sub-custodian." In general, the duties and responsibilities of the tri-party custodian remain with the dealer's bank. The sub-custodian simply oversees the custodian's activities and pays and receives cash from the custodian upon notification that the collateral meets the terms of the trade. There is little additional security provided in such an arrangement. The purpose for the added counterparty usually is based on legal requirements to employ only one custodian or to employ only a banking institution located in a particular state or city.

Buy/Sells and Sell/Buys

Buy/sells and sell/buys are an alternative to reverse repos and repos. As mentioned earlier, a repurchase agreement is an agreement to sell a security with a simultaneous agreement to "re-purchase" (or buy) the same security at a fixed future price which reflects money market rates. The same trade could be booked as two distinct outright cash market trades. Although the repo agreement creates a transaction which purports to be a buy and a sale, it also puts in place a series of legal rights and commitments that do not exist with outright trades.

A buy/sell is a simple trade to book and clear. If two counterparts can trade securities they can execute buy/sells. Its operational and legal simplicity make buy/sells common in new and underdeveloped markets. Buy/sells produce four troublesome issues, however:

1. Buy/sells do not allow for a mark-to-market. Because of this, significant credit exposure and capital haircuts can arise from these trades.[7]

---

[7] In addition, in the event of default, the defaulting counterpart or bankruptcy court could exercise only those transactions which are profitable. This can lead to dramatically larger credit exposure than would exist under a repo agreement.

2. Sells/buys may trigger a tax event. In some jurisdictions, the sale will be viewed as a disposition of the portfolio's assets for tax purposes, and result in capital gains/losses being applied to the portfolio.
3. Sell/buys are sometimes employed to reduce balance sheet size by recording such a transaction as a disposition rather than financing. US accounting principles require retention on the balance sheet of securities funded via a sell/buy.[8]
4. Sell/buys can be used to purposely trigger "apparent" favorable tax events. It is extremely important for participants in the buy/sell market to be cognizant of a counterparts' rationale for undertaking a trade. Both participants have been held liable for penalties arising from one counterpart's disallowed tax claims stemming from buy/sells.

Considerations in Selecting a Repo Product

Various rationales drive the choice of repo product. The choice begins with the dealer setting rates: ease in operationally handling a trade will result in offering more attractive rates on hold-in-custody or tri-party repo. Dealers will also pay higher rates on repos collateralized with poorer quality collateral. As a general rule, the harder it is for a dealer to finance its inventory, or the poorer the dealer's credit rating, or the more difficult to deliver securities, the higher the rate. In other words, rates are indicative of four interrelated issues — expenses, initial margin, credit quality of the bond and credit quality of the borrower.

Investors should evaluate the amount of credit exposure they are willing to assume to receive higher rates. Usually rate differences relate to demand, but high rates can also be the first indicator of pending credit problems. If most dealers are paying Fed Funds plus 25 basis points for hold-in-custody repo against whole loans, and another dealer begins paying Fed Funds plus 100 basis points, a potential lender should carefully evaluate the reasons for the difference. In every case of a dealer's failure in the 1980s, the initial warning signal was financing spreads getting out of line with the market.

---

[8] With the exception of "dollar rolls" of mortgages.

A wide spread can be explained by an extremely large position that needs to be funded. A dealer may need to pay wider spreads to accomplish this. It does not mean that a dealer is in trouble, but wider spreads warrant further investigation. Of course, the fact that a borrower is nearing failure may not be reflected by wider spreads. Some credits remain "good" until the night they declare bankruptcy.

ATTRIBUTES OF REPO TRADES: SUBSTITUTION, MARK-TO-MARKET, MARGINING, AND MATURITY

A repurchase agreement has several attributes. These attributes are described below.

Substitution

Repo may be executed with or without the right of substitution. If a borrower of cash has the right to substitute, it means that the collateral in the trade, in part or in whole, can be called back and similar collateral supplied to replace it. Usually this means if the trade was for Treasury bills, the borrower would need to replace collateral with bills; if for CMOs, then CMOs would replace the called back bonds, etc. Better securities could always be given if desired. Rights of substitution can be "limited" to one or two substitutions or unlimited.

Mark to Market

When a trade is booked as a repo under the PSA Master Repurchase Agreement it is subject to a mark-to-market. This means that the collateral may be repriced at market value by each counterparty and if the value of the collateral falls below some agreed upon level to the cash on the trade (including accrued interest), the party in deficit may make a "margin call" and obtain additional collateral or cash. Margin calls on term transactions where the specific security was not borrowed to cover a short is normally met with additional securities.[9] Arrangements are

---

[9] Note that meeting a margin call with cash will upset the initial proceeds of the trade and if rates have moved will impact the economics or profitability of the trade.

sometimes made to pay interest on cash margin payments at then current short-term interest rates.

Margining

Trades are often margined at the outset, meaning the borrower of cash or bonds will give additional collateral (bonds or cash) on a trade to reduce the lender's credit exposure to the counterparty. If trades are originally margined, marking to market will restore the initial margin, as well as reprice the underlying securities.

Maturity

Repo trades can be booked for any maturity, including "open" — terminable on demand by either counterpart. Although transactions are executed for two or three years or longer, repo is normally a very short-term money market product, with the majority of trades maturing within one month. The average duration of most major repo books is 10-20 days. Certain trades tend to be shorter in maturity (specials trading) than others (mortgage-backed general collateral).

HYBRID OR EXOTIC REPURCHASE AGREEMENTS

Repurchase agreements are not unique as fixed-income instruments. Anything that can be engineered into a fixed-income security can be embedded into a repo. This includes options, caps, collars, floors, puts, calls, etc. Although the preponderance of repo trades are simple fixed rate fixed maturity transactions or open trades, certain unusual or special transactions are executed from time to time. The genesis for these trades is usually to match a client's underlying assets or expected cash flows or for a dealer to take on a speculative position on market spreads relationships. The more common trades are discussed below.

"Floaters" or Floating Rate Reverse Repos

As with other assets, reverse repos can be transacted with variable or floating interest rates. In relation to the overall market floaters are not significant, but floating rate term reverse repo volume exceeds several billion dollars. Most floaters are booked to match a security lender's asset. For example, consider the following trade: a fully paid government portfolio holder or securities lending agent will lend US governments to a dealer and use the cash to buy a 2-year medium term note yielding 3-month LIBOR plus 5 basis points. The repo will be structured to exactly match the terms of the asset, with quarterly rate reset based on LIBOR, interest payments made quarterly. If the rate on the repo is LIBOR less 15 basis points, then the portfolio holder has locked in 20 basis points of positive spread. Of course, the transaction heightens credit exposure, but is neutral to the portfolio holder in interest rate risk and reinvestment risk.

Flex Repos and Structured Repo

Flex repo began with issuers of long term debt, usually municipalities or municipal agencies, investing cash acquired through a bond issue. As payments were needed, the funds are drawn from the repo. For example, if the builder of a co-generation plant issues a bond to provide funds for construction, the funds can be invested in a repo at a fixed rate for a long period of time (five years or more). As cash is needed, the amount of the repo is adjusted downwards while the rate remains unchanged. Since invested cash can be obtained whenever needed by the issuer, the trades were called flexible or "flex" repos. Flexes normally do not permit reinvestment of cash.

Recently a new kind of flex market is developing. This transaction is designed to exactly match the terms of a new asset acquired by the lender of securities. In this case, however, the asset purchased by the portfolio holder is a mortgage-backed or asset-backed security which has significant prepayment risk. In other words, depending on the level of rates, the asset's amount and duration may fall or rise. The repo would match these characteristics and the rate basis — which could be fixed or floating. Additionally, if the underlying asset has an interest rate cap or floor, the reverse repo would also replicate this.[10]

Construction of repos or reverses to match the exact needs of an investor are similar to any fixed-income structured product. Repos have

---

[10] However, the level of the floor or cap may be different than the new asset. Discussion of these products is beyond the scope of this chapter.

been transacted which include caps, collars, floors, step ups, inverse floating terms, or indexed against various commodity prices (i.e., foreign currencies, gold, oil). In the case of a structured repo, the risk of the structured transaction may be carried by the dealer's repo desk or it may be assumed by the dealer's derivative desk. In the case of asset related repos it would not be unusual for the dealer to structure both the *asset* the investor acquires *and the repo*.

Structured or flex repo may be collateralized by any securities, although governments and mortgages are most common. They are also settled through any acceptable manner — either tri-party, deliver-out, or hold-in-custody. Since the market risk of a structured repo could be very significant, mark-to-market often includes marking the embedded index or swap.

Cross Currency Repo Trades

Repo is often executed with the collateralizing currency being different from the currency of the repoed securities. This is a very common transaction in the non-US markets, but relatively rare within the US. There are two caveats to cross currency trades: first be cautious to insure DVP can still occur when moving a security denominated in one currency versus a different currency being borrowed. Not all clearing systems accommodate multi currency DVP transactions. The US payment system does not allow simultaneous transfer of different currencies without incurring daylight exposure. Secondly, mark to market is somewhat more volatile than single currency repo since there exist both security and currency price movements. As a result, initial margin on cross currency trades is often higher than on single currency trades.

Collateral Swaps

A collateral swap is a funding trade. The dealer reverses in high quality securities, for example US governments, and repos out lesser quality or hard to deliver bonds, for example US corporate bonds. The dealer then repos out the higher quality securities to generate cash. The counterpart receives a spread for the transaction from the reverse rate being lower than the repo rate, The dealer has financed the lower quality securities at the repo rate on the newly obtained governments plus the negative spread on the program.

Most collateral swaps or *programs* are booked as reverses and repos. This is especially the case when the pledged securities cannot be used as pledge collateral under a securities lending agreement (for example, US corporate bonds.) An example is useful. Assume a dealer reverses in US governments at 4¾% from a client and repos corporates of equal value to the same counterpart for the same maturity at 5%. The dealer then repos out the governments to other investors at 4⅞%. The net effect is that the counterparty to the swap locks in 25 basis points and the dealer finances corporates at 5⅛% (4⅞% government repo rate plus the 25 basis point negative spread on the swap).

FUNDING AND MATCHED BOOK TRADING

The most significant dealer uses for repo are funding and covering short positions. Large volumes of securities can be financed through the repo market at attractive rates with little or no financing haircut. The major users of the repo market for financing are highly leveraged traders or portfolio holders with very short-term cash needs. RP is also used interchangeably with securities borrowing by dealers to cover short security cash positions. As is the case with securities lending, fully paid owners of security portfolios will often lend securities held within a portfolio to dealers, take the cash received and reinvest it at a positive spread, building the yield on their portfolio.

Dealers also trade repo. Since RP is simply a loan or borrowing of cash, if a trader lends cash at a higher rate than it borrows, it can earn a positive spread. The collateralization of the repo market provides high liquidity and limited credit risk, so bid/offer spreads are normally very narrow. Active matched book trading occurs in using US governments, mortgages, non-US sovereigns, and LDC debt. Other repo trading books exist, but are much less liquid and narrowly focused. Dealers trade two distinct books: general collateral and specials.

General Collateral Matched Books
General collateral matched books are money books, fulfilling a financial intermediation role. In a general collateral ("GC") book, the aim is to borrow and lend cash and earn a spread. GC trades often have the

right of substitution and are normally bid based upon the amount, term, and generic type of security underlying the trade. Securities are allocated after the trade is agreed upon. Securities held long in a GC book may cover a firm's short positions, but short covering is not the purpose of the trade. Most GC trades are short duration (three months or less) and of large size. The reverse side of the GC book (the dealer borrowing securities) is always DVP. The repo side may be tri-party, HIC or DVP. Non-government books may be funded through collateral swaps.

Spreads in general collateral matched book trading are not substantial. In fact, a successful book may earn 10-20 basis points. Dollar earnings, however, are substantial, since book size may be extremely large. Return on equity and return on risk measurements for the matched book business are very attractive for high credit quality participants.

Specials Trading

Specials trading is driven by the borrowing and lending of particular or specific securities. Specials trading is normally confined to government markets, with the heaviest volume in the futures deliverable and recently auctioned securities (the current 2-year US Government, for example).

Specials trading tends to be more dealer to dealer than GC trading. Positions may be dictated by the longs and shorts created by the government trading desk of a dealer or from large repo desk positions. Duration of specials trading tends to be much shorter than GC trading with much greater rate volatility.

While GC rates are closely related to the level of money market interest rates, specials rates are determined by a security's supply and demand factors. Because of higher levels of risk, specials trading usually returns higher basis point spreads. A spread of 25 to 30 basis points would not be unusual for a dealer who is running a large US Government specials book to earn.

Chapter 3

The Nondollar Repo Market

Peter B. D'Amario
Vice Chairman
ISMA Council of Reporting Dealers Repo Subcommittee

In the previous chapter, we dealt primarily with the repo market for US government (and related) securities. There are, however, active markets for repo in the bond issues of a number of governments worldwide. Collectively, these are known as the nondollar repo markets.[1] In this chapter we will describe the nondollar repo markets.

ORIGINS

Though the nondollar repo markets differ from the US Treasury repo market in several important ways, they are still quite recognizable and comprehensible. The nondollar repo markets are based primarily in London, a result both of London's traditional role as the financial center of Europe and of the fact that the largest repo players developed the market in London first. Repo is, of course, traded domestically in each individual market. Nonetheless, the preponderance of volume continues to be generated by the London-based repo desks.

The nondollar market is younger than the Treasury market, and as a result is smaller in terms of volume and is not yet as well developed or liquid. The nondollar markets were launched in London

---

[1] The largest nondollar repo markets include those in Germany, France, the UK, Italy, Spain, the Netherlands, Belgium, Denmark, Sweden, the European Currency Unit (ECU), Canada and Japan.

in the late 1980s. At this time, the larger US broker/dealers operating in London began to significantly build their positions in nondollar government bonds. These positions had been until then funded either internally (i.e., through the use of firms' own capital) or via bank lines, both secured and unsecured. These methods of financing proved excessively expensive as inventories ballooned, and the dealers sought liquid sources of funding elsewhere. Given their experience using repo as a funding tool in the US market, it is not surprising that these same firms sought to develop a repo market in London. A symbiotic relationship developed between the US firms and a number of large European "universal" banks, which had access to cheap retail funding, and the nondollar repo market was born. In the early days of the market, virtually all trading was interprofessional.

Adding to the demand for a nondollar repo market were the expenses related to failures to deliver bonds. If a dealer was unable to deliver a bond, it either failed on the trade (incurring a fail cost which might be 400-600 basis points) or it attempted to borrow the bond in question via the autolending programs operated by the global clearers — at a cost of up to 350 basis points. The development of the nondollar markets heightened the chance of a dealer being able to borrow a bond to cover a short at a much less expensive rate.

It bears comment that, unlike the US Treasury repo market, the nondollar markets are not predominately screen traded — trading is generally conducted over the telephone. Certain markets (France and Denmark, for example) have screens which are used domestically, but these screens do not account for substantial repo volume.

DOCUMENTATION

The nondollar markets are, by nature, multicurrency markets. Not only is repo traded in 12-15 currencies, but often trades are done on a cross-currency basis (i.e. cash in one currency, collateral in another). These trades are typically subject to a slightly higher initial margin to take foreign exchange risk into account. One of the results of dealing in several jurisdictions is that the legal situation must be taken into account on a jurisdiction by jurisdiction basis. Given this, a premium is placed on having the proper repo documentation in place. The standard repo agreement used in the nondollar markets is the PSA/ISMA Global Master Repurchase Agreement (GMRA).

The GMRA is already in its second incarnation, having been drafted originally in 1992 at the request of market participants who were alarmed at the prospect of multifarious unique repo agreements flooding the market. The London law firm of Clifford Chance, in conjunction with the International Securities Market Association's (ISMA) repo subcommittee and the Public Securities Association (PSA), created the GMRA under English law, using the familiar PSA repo agreement as a template. The GMRA has met with wide acceptance in the nondollar market, and is used by a variety of different organizations in a wide variety of countries. Certain markets, notably France and Germany, have either developed or are developing agreements which are not necessarily GMRA-based. These "alternative" agreements are typically used between domestic counterparties.

The original GMRA was substantially revised in 1995 to reflect changes in market practice as well as to correct some inconsistencies within the agreement itself. The GMRA may be used for all gross paying securities[2] with the exception of US Treasuries. Annexes to the agreement allow it to be used for UK gilts (government bonds), and work is progressing on an annex allowing the GMRA to be used with equities.

Buy/Sell Transaction Structure

Since 1992, the existence of an industry-standard document has gone a long way toward reducing the number of nondollar repo transactions traded as buy/sells and sell/buys. This primitive structure, discussed in detail in the previous chapter, was a precursor to repo in the nondollar markets. The undocumented, unmarginable nature of the buy/sell type transaction renders them inherently more risky than the true repo

---

[2] Gross paying bonds are those which pay their coupons free of any withholding taxes. Most government bonds are gross paying. Net paying bonds pay coupons net of a deduction for withholding tax. Certain recipients are typically able to reclaim some or all of the tax withheld, depending on a variety of factors specific to the country of issue of the bonds and country of domicile of the coupon recipient. Major markets whose government bonds are net paying include Italy, Spain, and Japan.

structure. Nonetheless, the buy/sell persists, particularly in markets such as Italy and Spain, where buy/sells comprise a majority of trades in the domestic markets. Recent initiatives such as the European Community Capital Adequacy Directive (CAD) will continue the trend toward the reduction or elimination of the buy/sell structure.

SETTLEMENTS AND TRI-PARTY REPO

The multiplicity of countries where nondollar repo trades leads inevitably to the issue of settlements. In addition to being able to settle repo transactions in each domestic market, nondollar repo participants may choose to settle transactions in either Cedel or Euroclear.[3] This places a premium on the trader and the settlements area having a detailed understanding of settlement processes and cut-off times.

Tri-party repo has been introduced to the nondollar markets as a funding/investment tool. Currently, a number of institutions and depositories offer separate competing global tri-party services. In addition, several European banks offer tri-party services tailored to individual domestic markets. Each of these services requires unique documentation and settlement procedures; as a result, many market participants have signed up with two or even three different tri-party custodians. This creates problems, since inevitably cash investors and borrowers may not always use the same custodian. Changing or adding custodians is not a simple or cost-free exercise, given the different systems and documentation used by each of the three custodians.

RATES AND MARGINING

It is difficult to generalize about rates in the nondollar markets since each individual market has its idiosyncrasies. Overall, however, securities lent as specials tend to generate somewhat higher fees compared to the US market. Nondollar fees for bonds lent tend to range from 15

---

[3] Cedel and Euroclear are the two major European automated multicurrency securities depositories.

basis points to — in very unusual circumstances — several hundred basis points. The fees are based predominately on the market or individual firm demand for the individual security rather than counterparty creditworthiness, since collateral for bonds lent is usually cash.

Cash rates vary as a result of a matrix of factors; these factors are the market demand for cash, counterparty credit quality, collateral credit quality, and margin levels. Overall market demand tends to change relatively slowly — in 1993 during the bull bond market overall demand pushed rates of return on cash in the nondollar repo market substantially over LIBOR for many investors. Normally an AA credit borrowing cash by repoing out government debt will pay an interest rate in the vicinity of LIMEAN for the cash. Any drop in credit rating or in the quality of collateral (acceptance of supranational and/or corporate debt with a rating of AAA or lower) will result in an increase on the rate earned on the cash invested.

Margins also affect the rate yielded by cash invested in a repo. Unlike the US Treasury repo market, there are no standard initial or variation margins in the nondollar market. Margins are agreed upon between the counterparties and are a function of creditworthiness. It is very unusual for initial margins to exceed 5% (usually this is in the case of a cross-currency repo transaction), and most margins are taken at 2% or below. Variation margin can be set either as a percentage of outstanding transactions or by use of an absolute money amount. Typical practice in the nondollar market is to allow each party to call margin as it sees fit. This allows one party to a repo to be flexible on margin as its counterparty changes its credit profile (not an unusual phenomenon, given that a repo master agreement may be in place for several years).

EUROPEAN COMMUNITY CAPITAL ADEQUACY DIRECTIVE

On January 1, 1996, the European Community (EC) implemented its Capital Adequacy Directive (CAD). The CAD sets financial standards and affects a wide range of activities in the EC's financial services sector. The effects of CAD are wide-ranging for the entire industry, with particular consequences for the nondollar repo markets.

A key component of CAD, with regard to repo, is netting. CAD allows for repo and *documented* buy/sell style transactions to be netted, dramatically reducing the regulatory capital charge resulting from these transactions. CAD specifies, however, that for cross-border netting to work, counterparties must have obtained legal opinions as to the enforceability of cross border netting. The major industry associations in the London market have commissioned opinions for over a dozen markets. These opinions will then be used by the market to offset capital charges.

One likely (and intended) effect of CAD will be the gradual disappearance of the undocumented buy/sell structure in favor of true repo. Under CAD, buy/sells become prohibitively expensive from a capital point of view.

CASE STUDY: THE CREATION OF THE UK GILT REPO MARKET AND ITS LINKS WITH THE CAPITAL MARKETS

Whether speaking of US government repo or the nondollar markets, repo is an integral and critical part of the underlying capital markets of any country. In early 1996, the gilt repo market was officially opened in the United Kingdom and began to trade. It is instructive to look at this market: an analysis shows how the repo market is an important tool in achieving macroeconomic goals which may at first glance seem far removed from repo.

Typically, nondollar repo markets have grown up in a rather organic way, much as humans evolved from a primordial state. The startup of the gilt repo market, on the other hand, follows a more "creationist" approach: one day (January 2, 1996) the market appeared, effectively fully-formed. This allowed participants in the market to give its creation their best shot towards a repo utopia.

Historical Structure

Traditionally there was no true repo market for gilt-edged securities. The borrowing and lending of UK government debt, and the related borrowing and lending of sterling cash, could only be accomplished through a highly structured and closely regulated system particular to the United Kingdom. Characteristics of the system included the existence of a number of intermediaries (such as the stock exchange money brokers, or SEMBs, and the discount houses) through which counterparties transacted their business. Gilt-edged market makers (GEMMs) and discount houses were the only entities allowed to short gilts as part of their market making activities. This privilege was at least in part granted as a result of the GEMMs' commitment to continuously make markets in gilts.

Though allowed the privilege of shorting "stock" (as gilts are often referred to), GEMMs were required to borrow bonds to cover shorts through the SEMBs, who intermediated bonds without passing counterparty names. Counterparties were content to pass large amounts of trading through them based on the perception of tight regulation of the market by the Bank of England.

On the cash side, money market intervention was effected by the Bank of England buying or selling Treasury bills (or other eligible paper) in the market to either release or soak up liquidity. While generally effective, the concentration of bills in a relatively small number of hands was viewed as imperfectly efficient.

Rumblings of Change

The years 1994 and 1995 saw a number of significant changes proposed for the gilt borrowing and lending market and the sterling market in general. Of primary importance was the Bank of England's Autumn 1994 paper. This document initiated a series of consultations with the various entities in the market on the wisdom of changing the existing structure. With the benefit of consultation, the Bank of England hoped to develop an opinion on whether or not to propose the opening of a true gilt repo market in the UK.

Pressure had been steadily growing for some enhancement in the existing system. Making the UK (and its government securities) competitive in the global market was clearly a factor in the opening of the market. From the point of view of the UK authorities, the institution of an open market was intended to drive down the cost to the UK of funding the Public Sector Borrowing Requirement (PSBR). The rationale was as follows: if the ownership of gilts could be made more attractive to a greater variety of entities globally, then it logically follows that the increased demand would drive down the rate that the government needed to pay on its debt. This downward trend was anticipated to result from the widening of the number of players in the market who would be able to trade gilts freely (including shorting), combined with the gilt market's alignment of structure and practices with other government bond markets worldwide. In addition, it was felt that the introduction of an open market would calm the volatility in the short sterling market. Many policy makers and market participants felt that the volatility tended to keep away non-UK investors. Theoretically, at least, it would also give the Bank of England a means of intervening directly in the market (like many other central banks) via repos and reverse repos.

A wide range of market participants was canvassed for their opinions on the creation of a gilt repo market. These participants included GEMMs, SEMBs, Discount Houses, banks, brokers, dealers, corporates, insurance companies, fund managers, and others. Interested parties such as the Treasury, the Inland Revenue, other regulatory bodies, the Stock Exchange, and other exchanges were also invited to render an opinion, as was a panoply of industry groups and associations. Clearly the introduction of an open repo market would have an impact far beyond the repo industry participants themselves.

Once the UK government had approved the concept of an open gilt repo market, the Bank of England established a number of working parties to focus on aspects of this new market: the Code of Best Practice working party developed a code of conduct for the new market, the Legal Agreement working party determined how best to document gilt repo transactions, the Settlements working party focused on how gilt repo transactions would be settled under the new regime.

The Code of Best Practice

As mentioned above, the start-up of the gilt repo market was unique, since it was the first nondollar repo market that emerged fully-formed, as opposed to evolving over a period of time. Given this unusual characteristic, it was felt advisable to create a Code of Best Practice to establish some guidelines for the market. In a general sense, the Code is an assemblage of common-sense practices that should be used. As a code, it is not a legally binding contract, and it does not carry any explicit regulatory penalties for non-compliance; nor is it a manual on how to trade in the open gilt repo market. Nonetheless, it was expected that all gilt repo market participants would use the Code as a guide for minimum reasonable standards of doing business.

The Gilt Repo Annex to the PSA/ISMA Global Master Repurchase Agreement

At the same time that the Bank of England established the Code of Best Practice working party, it established a separate working party to determine how to best document gilt repo transactions under the new regime. This working party was composed of legal experts from a variety of firms and organizations.

Quite early in the life of the working party it was decided that the most suitable document for the new market would be an annex to GMRA, since the document is a widely recognized document in the international repo markets, used by a wide variety of counterparties in a large number of different countries for trading numerous different securities. By adding a gilt repo annex to the GMRA, the working party reduced the need for market participants to reinvent the wheel with every gilt repo counterparty. Rather than negotiating a new document with each new counterparty, market participants need only agree to the annex as an addendum to existing executed GMRAs. This led to a saving of time and money, and simplifies the documentation process for counterparties.

The need for any annex whatever grew from some fundamental operational differences between gilt repo and other repo markets, especially differences related to settlement through the Central Gilts Office (CGO), the clearing entity through which gilts had traditionally settled and where the majority of gilt repo was initially expected to settle. The annex effectively deals with these idiosyncrasies and tailors the GMRA to the gilt repo market. In addition, the annex specifically refers to transactions entered into as agent in view of particular agency characteristics in the gilt market.

As the annex was being created, it became apparent that there were fundamental changes to the underlying Global Master Repurchase

Agreement which applied to all securities, not only gilts. As a result of this, ISMA, in conjunction with the law firms Freshfields and Clifford Chance, undertook a fundamental review of the 3-year old Global Master Repurchase Agreement with the intention of upgrading it to eliminate inconsistencies and inaccuracies.

Settlements

The ability to easily and efficiently settle gilt repo transactions was critical to the success of the gilt repo market. To this end, the Bank of England created a Settlements working party to discuss what changes needed to be made to the existing system and to make recommendations as to how the changes should be implemented.

Traditionally, and in keeping with the rules of the London Stock Exchange, settlement in the gilts market takes place on the business day following trade date. Gilts are moved versus a simultaneous instruction for a payment of cash; this system is known as the Assured Payment system. The Assured Payment system is based on a three-legged arrangement between the CGO (the book entry transfer system operated by the Bank of England), the member of CGO, and the member's settlement bank. Assured Payment functions effectively as a Delivery Versus Payment system, such as those operated by the global custodians. Using this system, a lender of gilts is effectively covered by the commitment of the SEMB's settlement bank to make an assured payment to the lender's settlement bank. Likewise, the SEMB is protected by the GEMM's settlement bank.

The Tax Situation

The satisfactory resolution of the taxation of gilts was a major issue in the creation of an open gilt repo market. In the past, interest payments payable with respect to gilts (i.e., coupons) had been subject to withholding tax, regardless of status of the holder of the gilts (subject to certain exceptions). With the advent of the repo market, it was made clear by the dealer community that the existing tax treatment of gilts could cause severe problems in the establishment of a liquid gilt repo market. Industry practitioners, both individually and under the umbrella of market organizations such as the International Securities Markets Association (ISMA) and the London Investment Banking Association (LIBA), consulted in great depth with the Inland Revenue to develop a system that would be both revenue-neutral for the UK exchequer and sufficiently flexible so as not to stifle the nascent gilt repo market.

The discussion of the taxation of gilts occurred simultaneously with an ongoing discussion of the treatment by the Inland Revenue of manufactured dividends on other net paying securities. In early 1995, the Inland Revenue, HM Treasury, and the Bank of England released a discussion document on changes contemplated to the market. In July 1995, the new rules were announced. Of key importance to the gilt repo market was the establishment of special "Star" accounts at the CGO, in which institutions are able to keep gilts free of withholding tax. In order to retain the revenue-neutrality of the arrangement, Star account holders are required to account on a quarterly basis for gross interest received. This approach received the general support of players in the gilt repo market.

Outlook

The opening of the gilt repo market thus provides a useful case study of how the repo market is integrated into the overall capital markets superstructure in a country. While the example of the UK is convenient due to its creation-from-scratch nature, it is also indicative of a wider integration of repo in other markets. In the US, Germany, France, and a number of other countries, the "repo rate" has taken on an importance to capital markets overall which goes far beyond the repo market itself. In the UK alone, for example, it has been demonstrated that repo is a key part of an overall strategy to update the entire gilt market. An open market in gilt repo is but the harbinger of other major structural changes, which repo inevitably effects.

Chapter 4

Finding A Route to Market: An Institutional Guide to the Securities Lending Labyrinth

Mark C. Faulkner
Managing Partner
Securities Finance International Limited, UK

Charles L. Stopford Sackville
Managing Partner
Securities Finance International Limited, UK

INTRODUCTION

Finding the most suitable route to market and the issue of selecting a counterpart are at the heart of the securities lending business. In this chapter, we discuss these issues for the benefit of institutions whose core businesses do not include securities lending. We focus on the lending of international equities with regard to both lending and non-lending institutions.

Which Comes First — The Desire to Lend or the Route to Market?

How do explorers plan expeditions? Do they first choose a destination, and then plan the route? Or, do they plan a route and thus reach a destination by default? Explorers have doubtless done both.

How do institutions approach lending? Do they first decide to lend, and then find the appropriate route to market? Or, do they become seduced by the proponent of a particular route and slip into the decision to lend?

Historical precedent suggests that it is ultimately possible to reach a satisfactory conclusion in whatever order these decisions are made. Continents get discovered whether people sail off looking for them or not.

Today, when we want to explore a known place, we usually identify the destination and perhaps the motivation for embarking on the journey, before we select the route. So how should institutions approach the lending market? Before we tackle this question, let us explore whether such a "market" exists and whether it is accurate to call it a market. If it does exist, institutions should understand the kind of market that it is. What are its characteristics? What drives it?

Approaching a peripheral activity, for that is what securities lending is for most institutions, requires caution and patience. Navigating this labyrinth is not easy; nor is it impossible. Despite what any marketer of the business may tell you, it is no more a "rocket science" than it is "free lunch."

Market Characteristics

Any market can be defined as a meeting place for supply and demand. The securities lending business qualifies as a market in its own right, given that definition. Lending institutions and a wide variety of intermediaries provide the supply to meet demands of other intermediaries or principal borrowers.

When we look at the source of the demand, the status of securities lending as a market in its own right is somewhat less obvious. The core market driver is a demand for securities that comes from proprietary traders selling the cash market short, frequently to hedge long derivative positions. If we accept this fact, we see that the securities lending market is subordinate to, and dependent on, the cash and derivative securities markets.

The securities lending market is also tied closely to other securities financing markets in the form of the repo, swaps, and prime brokerage products. The recent use of repurchase agreements ("repo") for equity securities, as well as bonds, in Europe is a case in point.

In the repo market, equity lending desks of brokers, dealers, and banks finance their long equity inventory as if they were bonds. Many of these positions, of course, exist either as a result of financing customer strategies or because securities have been borrowed in anticipation of making onward deliveries. Which comes first, the borrow or the repo?

Securities lending is part of the broader securities financing business. The number of firms renaming departments is clear evidence of this fact.

MARKET SIGNIFICANCE

If the derivatives market is the engine, then securities lending is the oil; it brings much needed liquidity to the marketplace — at a price. This oil is expensive. Some estimates suggest that international securities lending revenues (i.e., excluding those in U.S. domestic market) exceed $1 billion per year. It is the search for a share of this revenue that draws institutions from their core activities toward the less familiar world of securities lending.

Securities lending is a specialist activity with its own conventions, practices, and rules. As in any business, it is most rewarding to be an expert. Pension funds hire experienced managers to invest assets to meet the demands of their pensioners. Insurance companies manage assets to meet their liabilities. Securities lending experts focus upon matching supply and demand of lendable securities.

The key factor distinguishing securities lending from many other areas of the financial services sector is its almost complete lack of transparency. This lack of transparency is to the benefit of the experts.

MARKET TRANSPARENCY

The securities lending market is so opaque that it reminds some observers of the bankruptcy business in the United States during the 1980s. Information and experience is highly concentrated in the hands of a relatively small number of firms and people. There are very few screens on which prices are displayed and fewer still where you can get more than an indicative quote.

The market remains this way because it is in the interests of the dominant players to keep it so. More transparency is not in their interest, or so they believe. This lack of transparency does more than restrict the number of institutions bringing supply to the market. It also hampers the speed of any institutional entry.

Most service providers would agree that an informed customer is a better customer. This is not the widely held view in the securities lending business. Such an attitude has not only held the market back, but also led to the development of numerous myths.

MARKET MYTHS

We can dispel some of the more popular market myths.

- "Everyone should lend." — As our examination will show, this business is not for everyone. That being said, everyone *should be* an informed observer. Portfolios and trading strategies change. What is once an unattractive portfolio, from a lending perspective, may become attractive in the future.

- "Lending is risk-free." — While it is true that the risks can be identified, managed, and minimized, no one should expect to be rewarded in this business without accepting some risk.

- "Cash is the only safe form of collateral." — Cash has to be managed and invested to produce a yield, and cash reinvestment is not without its risks. In Europe, fiscal regimes have historically encouraged using securities and letters of credit as collateral. Recently, equities, convertible bonds, and even equity warrants have been accepted as part of collateral portfolios along with the more typical government bonds. The significant losses in the securities lending business are associated almost exclusively with the taking of cash as collateral.

- "Good collateral makes a good counterpart out of a bad one." — Collateral should be seen as insurance against counterpart default. An unrated counterpart with little capital should be seen for what it is, not what it gives you as collateral. Good collateral, in terms of the type of assets and haircut taken, can provide merely a degree of increased comfort.

- "There is one route to market." — In fact, there are several different routes to market, each with its own advantages and disadvantages. The different routes are not mutually exclusive, as some may have you believe.

- "Indemnification eliminates all risk." — Indemnities vary considerably in quality. Some will eliminate most of the risks associated with participation in this business; others are not worth the paper they are written upon. Ultimately one has to recognize that this form of insurance and protection is not without cost. Furthermore, no matter what the indemnification says, one is always exposed to the risk that the indemnifier will not perform.

- "A level playing field exists." — Irrespective of an institution's sense of fairness and desire to treat all counterparts equally, one has to recognize that they are not equal in all respects. Triple A-rated banks are different from single B-rated broker/dealers and should be treated accordingly. The fact that they are not treated differently is a testament to good marketing on behalf of the disadvantaged and an unwillingness on behalf of many institutions to make difficult decisions. In the money markets, a lender of cash explicitly differentiates between borrowers by setting different rates, margins, collateral requirements, and duration limits. Such differentiation is rare in the securities lending business, with the result that an unlevel playing field is artificially leveled. This is not in the long-term interest of the lending community.

- "The market is mature." — There remains a significant imbalance between international supply and international demand in certain countries and for particular securities. Why else would any potential new lender be courted by so many borrower suitors? New firms continue to enter the market, and certain intermediaries continue to operate profitably. The rise of third-party agent lenders is just the latest phenomenon in a market that continues to develop and change. Even where the market exhibits signs of maturity, such as in the U.S. equity market, there remains significant room for revenue generation.

- "Standardized legal contracts fit all scenarios." — Standardized contracts bring the benefits of consistency, and can save on legal expenditure, but they should be seen more as a starting point than a solution. The vagaries of cross-border securities lending transactions mandate careful consideration before choosing to use one of several standard documents without amendment.

- "Tax arbitrage drives the market." — Fiscal authorities around the globe are, quite rightly, fixated upon the collection of taxes due them. When it comes to securities lending, however, their collecting zeal seems to know no bounds. Rather than see the cost of manufacturing a dividend for what it is, namely, a cost associated with borrowing securities (that borrowers seek to minimize), the tax authorities see a dividend arbitrage behind every trade. This is certainly not the case. While it is true that tax arbitrage does take place, and that the securities lending market plays a role in facilitating it, it is equally true that the largest non-dollar lending market is the Japanese market. Here the historically low dividend yields play a minimal role in borrower motivation.

ORGANIZATIONAL CHARACTERISTICS

Before expending any energy on securities lending beyond your organization, you need to spend some time considering the characteristics that your organization and portfolios exhibit. Working on the assumption that it is unlikely that an institution will reinvent itself or adopt a new trading strategy just to facilitate the lending of securities, this approach could save significant resources and frustration.

To simplify the approach, we divide institutional characteristics into two groups — organizational and portfolio-specific. We acknowledge that all organizations differ but feel that some general characteristics are comon across geographical and sectoral boundaries. For the purposes of this analysis, we assume that the regulatory situation affecting any lending decision is known and clear, admittedly an extreme simplifying assumption.

Management Motivation

Every lender is in it for the money. Some may view lending as a peripheral activity to help offset custody and administrative cost and, whatever the merits of their portfolio, may never change this view. Others see lending as a valuable contributor to revenues and a potential source of competitive advantage, and act accordingly.

It is important that the activity be sponsored by a wide cross section of the organization and that the fund managers are motivated to provide their support. As any operations manager will tell you, running a program without the understanding and commitment of the fund managers is fraught with peril. Senior managers need to understand the motivation behind their organization's potential involvement, and move forward only when a degree of consensus is reached.

Technology

While a variety of vendor systems can alleviate a significant amount of the technological strain associated with participating in securities lending, successful participants commit significant resources to internal systems. Borrowers will want to receive available inventory as frequently as possible. Lenders will need: (1) to avoid lending the same securities twice, (2) to deal with sales of inventory by their fund managers, (3) to process both recalls and returns, and (4) to effect any "buy-ins" as necessary. These are not particularly difficult tasks, but each needs to be recognized and addressed.

Credit

A lender's collateral flexibility, be it in terms of cash reinvestment parameters or the ability to accept lower-grade securities, will be rewarded. Like any other market, the securities lending market is a meeting place for organizations with a wide range of credit quality and collateral capabilities. A borrower's credit rating may be inversely related to its propensity to borrow. If an institution has a cautious approach to counterpart selection and a low tolerance for risk, this must be recognized by management charged with researching securities lending. This is not to say that securities lending cannot be conducted profitably, but rather that the route to market selected has to be consistent with the institution's general risk profile.

Do-it-Yourself or Outsource

Some organizations have a propensity to outsource services; others do not. Understanding this fundamental organizational trait, prior to talking to potential counterparts, will enable managers to identify routes that are not likely to be suitable, and to focus on those that exhibit more of an organizational "fit."

PORTFOLIO CHARACTERISTICS

Our analysis of the characteristics of the portfolio or portfolios that might be available for lending has the dual benefit of further exploration of the viability of participation and, should one decide to take the next step, a start on evaluating the merits of a portfolio.

Size of the Total Portfolio

Size is not everything, but it helps. Borrowers covet large portfolios more than they do small ones. A concentrated portfolio of even $50 million of the right securities, of course, is worth investigating.

Size of Individual Holdings

Individual holdings of under $250,000 are of limited appeal to direct borrowers as the average loan transaction size is in the order of $500,000. Generally, holdings of less than $750,000 are likely to be best deployed through the lender's participation in an efficient pooled lending program.

Investment Strategy: Active or Passive

Active trading, which increases the likelihood of recalls, reduces the attractiveness of the inventory. It is often better for a borrower not to borrow a security than to borrow it and have it recalled. Recalls tend to come at the most inopportune times, and can cause significant strain in a lender-borrower relationship. Passive portfolios are ideal lending portfolios, although if you have the same inventory as everyone else, lending revenues are going to be low.

Geographic and Sectoral Diversification of the Portfolio

A broad geographic and sectoral distribution within a portfolio is a positive factor from a lending perspective. The securities markets of the world are in a constant state of flux, and at any given moment a particular country or sector may become a focus of demand. Borrowers like lenders who offer a wide geographic range of liquidity. They understand that the profitability of lending in certain markets may be marginal, and they direct compensating business toward lenders who provide service in such markets.

Tax Position or Jurisdiction of the Beneficial Owner

Borrowers are responsible for "making good" any benefits of share ownership that would have accrued to the lender had the securities not been lent — excluding voting rights. Borrowers, in the case of dividends, must "manufacture" (i.e., pay) the economic value of these to the lender.

The manufacturing of dividends is a major cost component of borrowing securities. A borrower with $100 million of German securities outstanding that yield an average of 3%, for example, could save $450,000 if the manufactured dividend obligation could be reduced by 15% ($100,000,000 \times 3\% \times 15\%$).

An institution's tax position at a particular time is a given, but understanding your standing compared to that of your peers is valuable when one is researching the viability of lending.

By way of an example, U.K. pension funds would usually reserve 85% of the dividend on a Dutch equity. The U.K. Inland Revenue has decided, however, that if that fund were to lend those securities over the dividend date then a borrower must pay 85% to the lender, and 15% to the Inland Revenue. This rule means that U.K. pension funds are less attractive as lenders than, for example, U.S. pension funds.

Attractiveness of the Lendable Inventory

The definition of a security's attractiveness, like so many things in the securities lending business, made rather inaccessible by the adoption of simple code words. "Hot" securities are those in high demand, and general collateral or "GC" securities are those that are commonly available. Needless to say, the "hotter" your portfolio, the more lending merit it has. "Hotness" is difficult to assess without approaching potential counterparts, but as a rough rule of thumb, non-Japanese Asian securities are hot, as are less liquid and tax-advantaged securities worldwide.

In conclusion, if an institution is revenue hungry, with good technology, passively managing a global inventory of large holdings of hot securities, and domiciled in Bermuda, the lending case is particularly strong.

THE SIX ROUTES TO MARKET

Should the organizational and portfolio characteristics exhibited by an institution seem encouraging, the next step is to assess what routes to market are available. The key thing to remember is that there are options, and, despite what anyone may tell you, the choice of route is not a straightforward black or white decision.

Don't Go to the Market

While not going to the market will not endear a potential lender to the proponent of any route to the market, this may indeed be the right decision for a given organization. If, however, the organizational and portfolio characteristics are favorable, there should be a route or routes that offer the required return for a given level of risk and effort.

Use Your Global/Domestic Custodian as Agent

Using your global/domestic custodian is the least demanding route for a lender, especially for one new to the business. Assuming the acceptability of any indemnifications and confidence in the custodian, this route offers few barriers to getting started quickly. Levels of both risk and effort are low, but so too is the cost, in the form of reduced revenues.

The competitive pressures in the custody business are intense and, in securities lending, banks feel they have discovered a money machine — not unlike their old view of the foreign exchange business.

If banks succeed at securities lending, they will not only generate significant revenues to support technological investments and cross-subsidize their core business, but they will also retain their customers. No wonder they are keen to lend your assets!

Appoint a Third-Party Specialist as Agent

If a lender decides not to lend itself, but at the same time believes that the custodian cannot offer the service required, the answer may be to appoint a third-party specialist. In the United States, the demand for this option is born out of frustration with custodial performance. Elsewhere it is typically a response to the increasingly competitive nature of the business and the propensity for institutions, which could lend directly, to outsource to specialists.

Agent intermediaries are sometimes separately incorporated organizations, but are more frequently parts of larger bank, broker-dealer, or investment banking groups. The third-party agent lending specialists represent the most fashionable and fastest growing sector of the business. For a firm already in the lending business, the low marginal cost of entry and significant potential rewards are two very good reasons for setting up a specialist agent.

Select Intermediary as Principal

Many wholesale intermediaries have developed global franchises and use their expertise and capital to generate spreads between two principals that remain unknown to one another. These principal intermediaries again are sometimes separately incorporated organizations, but more frequently parts of larger bank, broker-dealer, or investment banking groups. Acting as principal gives these intermediaries the freedom to deal with organizations that the typical institution may choose to avoid.

The classic principal intermediary is the prime broker — borrowing from institutions and banks to lend to "hedge funds." The technology required to support such a business is a significant barrier to entry, and without the technology lending would be impossible. Given the opaque nature of these relationships, it is impossible for the lender to determine where the securities are going, in particular if they are being on loan or used by the intermediaries' own traders.

Lend Directly to Proprietary Principal

As institutions understand the market dynamic more, they may wish to consider lending directly to the organizations that are the final end users of the securities they supply. The proprietary borrowers include broker-dealers, market makers, and hedge funds. Some exhibit global demand, while others are more regionally focused.

Choose Some Combination of the Above

Just as there is no one right route to market, neither are the options we have outlined, mutually exclusive. Choosing not to lend one portfolio does not preclude the lending of another, just as lending in one country does not mean one has to lend in all of them. Choosing a wholesale intermediary that happens to be your custodian in the United States and Canada does not mean that you cannot lend your Asian assets through a third-party specialist and your European assets directly to a panel of proprietary borrowers.

TYPICAL MARKETING STRATEGIES

The right route to market is a route that is consistent with meeting your realistic objectives. The challenge of finding the right route is not made any easier by the different marketing messages that institutions receive from the securities lending professionals. Besides marketing their own firm's merits, borrowers will adopt certain arguments to encourage an institution to take a particular route.

While it is impossible to detail all the potential marketing strategies that a gifted professional might select, we can identify some of the more frequently used ones.

Don't Go to the Market

It would be most unusual to hear "don't go to the market" unless the portfolio in question were particularly unattractive, but there are times when an attrractive portfolio, with significant revenue-generating potential, draws this response. It really means: "We can't do it, so you shouldn't." Such a reaction is often expressed as the taking of the "moral high ground," and most frequently comes from custodian banks.

This is not to say that there are not genuine instances when the best advice is not to lend, but rather that an institution hearing this line should question whether it is getting good advice or merely an excuse for an inability to perform.

Use Your Global/Domestic Custodian as Agent

The administrative straightforwardness of using a custodian bank makes it the conservative option. Custodians will argue that they are perfectly positioned to clear, report, and process your lending activity in as near a troublefree and seamless manner as is possible. They will give you directed or discretionary options so that you can effectively select your own principals. They will manage collateral in accordance with your investment guidelines and make a great deal of their indemnifications (but only to the extent that they offer them). They will argue about their global reach, commitment, and risk management controls until any thinking person would view any option other than this route to market with extreme caution.

Custodians continue to reap the benefit of planting the seeds of doubt in many an institutional mind. They do so because it sells.

Appoint a Third-Party Specialist as Agent

Fed up with being a small fish in a large pond? A large fish in a large pond? Fed up dealing with Jacks of all trades who are masters of none? Want a partner to help you get fair value from your lending inventory? These are just some of the lines you might expect from a specialist agent.

They would argue that advances in technology have eliminated many of the administrative and communications barriers that once made this route difficult to navigate. They may suggest furthermore that they can achieve a higher utilization rate for securities, and obtain more income per loan. They will attack custodial programs as inefficient and run by non-experts.

Specialists may also argue that many custody programs are victims of their own success. How they do this is determined largely by the size of your portfolios. If the inventory is small, the argument may be: "The custody lending pool that you are in is so large that you are never going to get the kind of utilization that you might in our smaller pool.

You will be relatively more important to us and, while remaining a small fish, will swim in a smaller pond." Should the inventory be large, expect to hear: "Your lending inventory utilization is being undermined by the custody bank's automated allocation algorithms. There are too many lenders in the custody pool who are getting their fair share of loans at your expense, loans you might be able to satisfy on your own. Why not become a big fish in our smaller pond?"

Select Intermediary as Principal

If you are looking for the wholesale distribution of your assets through a securities specialist who can coordinate the demands of many proprietary borrowers and take advantage of them as a principal, then the intermediary route is for you. This is a real departure point for an institution.

Wholesaling requires establishing a desk, incurring fixed costs, and adopting a professional approach to the lending of your securities, although taking this route without such a commitment is avoidable if you sign an exclusive arrangement with one principal and outsource your collateral management function. This might make sense for an entry level institution that wishes to earn while it learns for a specified period of time, but it is less likely to be the optimal approach for a large and attractive portfolio in the longer term.

Intermediaries will make much of their captive demand, be it from prime brokerage customers or affiliated proprietary trading desks. The key trade-off to assess when exploring this route is whether taking it will generate revenue that will justify the commensurate increase in commitment required and concentration of counterpart risk.

Lend Directly to Proprietary Principal

To identify the final end user of any product, one typically looks for the person whose need is the greatest and who is paying the most for it. The securities lending business is no exception to this rule. The proprietary borrowers will tell institutions that they will pay more to borrow securities, borrow from them as a matter of priority, and borrow for longer periods. If this sounds too good to be true, it often is.

The larger proprietary borrowers are frequently able to borrow at rates comparable to those of the principal intermediaries. They effectively eliminate the intermediaries' spread by keeping it for themselves rather than giving it to the institutions. Should an institution wish to gain spread by dealing directly with a proprietary borrower, it will have to fight for every basis point — and know what is a fair market price. This means being an expert and having a number of counterparts, or executing exclusives only after concluding an extensive bidding process.

Choose Some Combination of the Above

An institution is unlikely to hear any combination strategy advice too often. Very few, if any, organizations active in the lending business have all route options available, and fewer still are likely to recommend other options over their own. This is the kind of argument to expect from an experienced lender who has learned over time that a combination approach makes sense, or a representative of a professional counterpart that is taking a realistic long-term perspective, or a specialist consultant.

There are many more marketing strategies that may be adopted to encourage an institution to follow a particular route. When confronted by what seem like logical arguments, many of them contradictory, institutions are not surprisingly bemused, and some fail to make any decision for fear of making the wrong one. Many institutions are led down a particular path by marketing professionals who could just as readily argue in favor of a competing route.

The challenge for an institution is to distinguish between good marketing and good common sense. An examination of one's organizational and portfolio characteristics prior to exploring possible routes will be helpful in selecting the appropriate route, but being prepared for marketing arguments and understanding the pros and cons of each approach is the best form of preparation.

ADVANTAGES AND DISADVANTAGES

There are as many arguments to be made in favor of each route to market as there are arguments to be made against. The goal here is to provide some objective perspective on each approach. Prior to making a route-specific analysis, we offer some general observations.

General

The choice of a route to market brings with it the need to consider the institution's organizational and portfolio characteristics and, above all, the extent to which it wishes to get involved in this peripheral activity. An institution needs to determine whether it is going to embrace the business fully and set up a desk with all the resources that that requires, or take a more passive role and appoint an agent or exclusive principal to reduce the burden of involvement.

The advantages of the former approach are primarily the degree of control and customization combined with retention of all the revenue. These benefits are not without cost, however. Establishing a desk and equipping it to be an efficient market participant is neither cheap nor speedy. An inefficient desk will not generate the revenue that an experienced desk might from the same portfolio. Keeping all of a smaller revenue stream may well be a less attractive proposition than taking the lion's share of a larger revenue pool, particularly when one factors in the cost of establishing the desk in the first place.

The advantages of the latter approach are that the cost of entry is reduced and that the portfolio is being lent by an experienced desk. While it is true that the selected counterpart will take some share of the revenue, the total revenue accruing to the lender may increase. Notwithstanding the revenue sharing issue, the main disadvantage of this approach is the potential sacrifice in terms of control and customization.

While it is possible to negotiate with the agent or principal counterpart the exact type of service that you would like, it is unlikely that you will be able to achieve lending nirvana. One has always to remember, however, that nothing is forever and one could always choose to reassess the options available at a future date.

Route-Specific

Don't Go to the Market There are two main forms of inactivity to assess — not lending at all, or choosing not to lend selected portfolios or parts of selected portfolios (e.g., those in particular countries). Nothing ventured, nothing gained. If you choose not to lend, the main disadvantage is that you may be forgoing revenue. The amount of revenue that you forgo depends on the merit of the portfolios concerned.

The opportunity cost of not lending is equivalent to the potential lending revenue forgone minus a financial estimation of the effort and risk required to generate that revenue. If the opportunity cost is a significant positive number, then the decision not to lend might not be the right one. If, on the other hand, that cost is a small positive or even negative amount, then the decision not to lend is justified.

Use Your Global/Domestic Custodian as Agent   The main advantage of using a custodian is administrative ease. You deal with an entity that you know and trust. Custodians may provide some enhanced security by means of indemnification. There is no need to set up a desk, and the level of management involvement and resources required is minimized.

This is the convenient and conservative way to lend, but convenience does not come without a price or conservatism without missing opportunity. The share of the revenue given to custodians varies from account to account, with a typical range of 20% to 40%. The question the institution must answer is whether this represents value.

Custody lending is conservative or, to put it another way, least common denominator lending. Banks will be banks, and should an institution hanker to be on the leading edge or prefer a customized program, using a custodian is unlikely to be the optimal route.

Some custodians have been so successful at marketing their securities lending programs that some of their customers have become victims of their bank's success. Small and large portfolios alike may be missing revenue opportunities by virtue of the way that the bank allocates loans. Both might lend more securities and generate higher revenues if they were to leave the massive custodial pool and find another route. This might involve appointing another custodian with a smaller pool, or taking another route altogether.

Custodians will make much of their cash reinvestment capabilities. Yet did not certain custodians experience reinvestment problems in 1995?

When you choose this route to market, you are putting all your eggs in one basket: selecting a single organization to be custodian, securities lender, and cash manager. What is the likelihood that one firm is superior at all disciplines?

Appoint Third-Party Specialist as Agent

Using a third-party specialist is the first step away from the custodial route. The principal advantage for the customer is that securities lending-focused organizations and personnel ought to lend effectively.

One reason we see increased use of this choice may be that specialists are newer operations without a lending backlog. As they become successful, however, specialists' customers may suffer the same lack of attention that custodial customers complain about. One consideration is that, as every custodian trots out its agency lending programs, the customer may simply move to another custodian, although the assets remain immobile, unless loaned. There may be situations where regional or product specialization mean that this is nevertheless the right decision.

The unbundling of this product is a double-edged sword. Separating lending from custody brings with it operational disadvantages if the technology is not adequate. Being able to appoint an independent third party to reinvest cash (as some specialists do) allows a further degree of specialization.

Taking this route is something like getting a tailor-made suit rather than one off-the-rack. Finding a good tailor takes some time, and a store-bought option can fit just as well. Using your custodian may be a compromise, but for many it works.

Select Intermediary as Principal

Now we're getting serious. Lenders wishing to receive gross lending fees revenues could choose to deal with an intermediary as principal. The potential gross revenue increase is the main advantage of selecting this route. There are costs, however. This route is essentially only for those for whom the fixed costs of starting a business are less than the variable costs of paying an agent to do it.

Perhaps the major disadvantage of this choice is that you need to establish a business with a desk capable of dealing with the securities lending professionals. A lender's counterpart is rewarded no longer by getting a percentage of the earnings from a portfolio, but now by borrowing securities at the lowest cost. There is, moreover, a potentially combative relationship to be managed. Lenders taking this route need personnel who can extract "fair value" from lendable assets.

Lend Directly to Proprietary Principal

When proprietary principals have similar credit quality as the principal intermediary group, lending directly presupposes that lenders retain even more of the lending fees because they are closer to the market. Taking this route entails only marginally higher fixed costs, because there are likely to be more counterparts. Little else changes, unless the proprietary borrowers are themselves "hedge funds." Dealing with these counterparts requires a sophisticated approach to risk management. The process almost inevitably means, for most lenders, having a principal relationship with various "prime brokers." This is the same as having a relationship with a principal intermediary as lenders have no contractual relationship with the hedge funds themselves.

Some Combination of the Above

Most lenders will find the optimal solution via some combination of the routes described. This can be accomplished in one of two ways. Lenders can make entire portfolios available for loan to both agents and principals on some kind of "first come, first served" basis. Perhaps a better alternative is to segment the lendable inventory. Lend some segments of the portfolio through a custodian, some through an agent, and some on an exclusive or panel basis to selected principals.

COUNTERPART SELECTION CRITERIA

Many lenders are now recognizing securities lending as a stand-alone business and no longer as a peripheral activity. They are demanding access to relevant business information on which to base securities lending decisions. There is a practical need to know one's counterparts and to understand both their capabilities and requirements.

Exhibit 1 identifies some of the key information that a lender should use to select a counterpart.

Exhibit 1: Key Information a Lender Should Use to Select a Counterpart

Financial Strength:
Understand the legal entity that is your counterpart, its relationship with affiliates, and any parental guarantees.
* *Credit ratings – Short- and long-term*
* *Profitability*
* *Balance sheet size*
* *Regulatory capital*

Commitment:
* *Personnel involved in management, marketing, desk negotiation, operations, and administration*
* *Number and locations of desks around the globe capable of servicing local customers (demand and supply)*

Experience:
* *How long has counterpart been in the business?*
* *How experienced are its key personnel?*

Geographic Focus:
* *Location of global head*
* *Does geographic demand or distribution capability correlate with your inventory?*

Size of Program:
* *Is counterpart a niche player with a small book of specials?*
* *Is it a bulge-bracket-borrowers with massive borrowing or distribution capabilities?*
* *Will an organization of your size be significant to this counterpart, or will you get lost in the crowd?*

Collateral Flexibility:
* *Will counterpart be able to give you what you require, without constantly trying to get you to accept what you don't want?*
* *If it is an intermediary, is it taking what the market wants to give?*

Legal and Regulatory Framework:
* *Who regulates the counterpart?*
* *Which legal framework does it favor?*
* *Are its personnel registered?*

Technological and Operational Capabilities:
* *Which system does a counterpart use?*
* *Will it supply you with any technological support, excluding the "auto-fax"?*
* *How will you communicate with each other?*
* *What reporting will you receive?*

Exhibit 1 (Continued)

Route-Specific
All Intermediaries: Distribution Capability:
• *How capable are they of wholesale distribution?*
• *How many borrowers do they have?*
• *Where are they located?*
• *Which market sectors do they occupy?*

Agent Intermediaries:
Allocation Algorithms:
• *How do the formulas work?*
• *Under what circumstances, if any, will the algorithms be overridden?*
• *How will the agent prioritize any guaranteed accounts?*

Indemnification:
If the agent provides indemnification, which of the following exposures are
  covered?
• *All financial loss*
• *Borrower default*
• *Collateral default*
• *Consequential damages*
• *How much, in terms of the percentage of revenue forgone, does indemnifica-*
  tion "cost"?

Transparency:
• *Disclosed or undisclosed?*

Can a lender receive on-line information about:
• *Loaned securities (in aggregate and per borrowing principal)?*
• *Collateral portfolios (as above)?*

Can a lender direct its portfolio to a select group of borrowers?

Collateral and Reinvestment Policy
• *Is the agent capable of managing a wide variety of collateral?*
• *Does it have a triparty/escrow capability?*
• *Is it a capable cash manager?*
• *Can a lender stipulate its own cash reinvestment guidelines?*

Custody
Does a lending agent insist that assets be moved to a designated custo-
  dian?

Principal Intermediaries:
Demand Drivers

What percentage of demand is driven by:
• *"The Street"?*

Exhibit 1 *(Continued)*

- *Proprietary traders?*
- *Prime broker customers?*

Proprietary Principals:
Trading Strategy

What percentage of demand is driven by the following trading strategy?
- *"Naked" shorts?*
- *"Pairs" trading?*
- *Convertible bond arbitrage?*
- *Fail coverage?*
- *Index arbitrage?*
- *Market-making?*
- *Risk arbitrage?*
- *Warrant arbitrage?*
- *Other?*

Source: The Register of International Securities Financing Counterparts

SAMPLE PORTFOLIOS

No two portfolios, even when controlled by the same organization, exhibit identical characteristics. The simplified portfolios we describe are designed to show that the route to market varies by portfolio as well as by organization. Lenders may need to adopt a flexible approach — they may need to have multiple routes available to them in order to do full justice to their inventory.

Small, Active, and Diversified Fund

Characteristics of a small, active, and diversified fund could be:

Portfolio size	$250 million
Average size of individual holdings	$250,000
Investment stance	Actively managed
Geographic/sectoral diversification	Global equities and bonds
Tax position/jurisdiction	U.S. pension fund
Lendable "specials" or "GC"	10% "specials" and 90% "GC"

This portfolio is almost certainly unlendable on a direct basis. Apart from anything else, the individual holding size is just too small and unstable. As part of a custodial or perhaps a third-party agency pool, some percentage of the 100 lines of specials might be lent. It would probably be imprudent to lend more than 50% of any holding. On a lender/agent split of 60/40, at an average fee of 50 basis points (bp), this route might generate $37,500 per year for the pension fund. This is about a 1½bp contribution. If this is an organization's sole fund, the lending case is probably marginal.

Medium, Passive, and Geographically Focused Fund

Characteristics of a medium, passive, and geographically focused fund could be:

Portfolio size	$500 million
Average size of individual holdings	$10 million
Investment stance	Passively managed
Geographic/sectoral diversification	German equities
Tax position/jurisdiction	U.S. pension fund
Lendable "specials" or "GC"	>90% "specials" (seasonal)

This portfolio would set any agent or principal to do cartwheels. Assuming an 85% dividend entitlement and an average 3% dividend yield on the securities held, the lender could expect gross revenue estimates on this portfolio to be in the region of $2.5 million. This represents a 50bp contribution. Even if the lender/agent split were 80/20, the "cost" of the agency route would be $500,000.

Some may believe this is too expensive. A direct route, perhaps even a guaranteed exclusive with a well-rated principal counterpart, might make more sense.

Large, Passive, and Regional Portfolio

Characteristics of a large, passive, and regional portfolio could be:

Portfolio size	$1 billion
Average size of individual holdings	$5 million
Investment stance	Passively managed
Geographic/sectoral diversification	Far Eastern (ex Japan) equities
Tax position/jurisdiction	U.S. mutual fund
Lendable "specials" or "GC"	25% "specials" and 75% "GC"

This is another attractive portfolio from a securities lending standpoint, although there are some operational challenges that need to be overcome. Any lender's first priority is investment performance, and the lending of securities should not impede that objective. Fails, buy-ins, and recalls are to be avoided if at all possible.

If a 25% buffer were considered appropriate, given the passive nature of the portfolio, and fees averaged 75bp, gross lending income could be about $1.5 million. This represents a 15bp contribution.

It is advisable to deal with a regional expert, be it agent or principal. An agency "cost" of $375,000 based on a lender/agent split of 75/25 might be entirely reasonable, but only if the agent is an expert.

MAINTAINING PERFORMANCE

Things change. Just as an institution evaluates its suppliers of custody and asset management services, so it should, we would contend, evaluate the lending performance of its chosen route and counterpart/counterparties. Having expended considerable effort making the original selection, it is essential to allocate some resources to checking whether that choice is as appropriate today as when it was first made.

Exhibit 2 provides recommendations for doing so.

Exhibit 2: Suggestions for Maintaining Performance

Keep Up To Date
- *Obtain regular updates of market developments*
- *Use independent advisors where appropriate*
- *Make your counterparts understand that you are the customer*

Organization: Should your organizational characteristics change, finding a new route may be necessary

Portfolio: Portfolios change over time. Check to ensure that these changes do not require a change of route

Counterparts: Just as your organization changes, so do securities lending counterparts.
- *Are they still suitable?*
- *Are others now more so?*

THE WAY FORWARD

What to do now?

Non-Lenders

Adopting a logical approach to the lending decision will save time, money, and frustration. Lending is not for everyone.

Examine your organizational and portfolio characteristics before approaching counterparts. When gathering information from the market, do so in a structured manner so that results do not add more confusion than they resolve.

Active Lenders

To ensure that your lending performance remains optimal, you should regularly revisit the lending route decision. Conduct this process with as open a mind as you approached the initial lending decision. Despite what many counterparts may tell you, the barriers to changing routes are less daunting than they would have you believe.

CONCLUSIONS

Navigation is not straightforward. There are often many routes to a particular destination, and it is not always easy to find the best one. It is also difficult to determine what is meant by "the best." Does it mean "the quickest," "the easiest," or "the most profitable"?

Finding the best route to the securities lending market can be as difficult as embarking on an arduous journey. There are no maps, and along the way various vendors will attempt to lure you down their favored path.

The approach we have outlined in this chapter can be adapted to suit any institution's particular circumstances. Should the approach be adopted, it will enable an institution to achieve a better result quicker. The key thing to remember is that while there are many possible routes to take, you should set the pace, and embark on this journey only if you believe it to be worth your while.

We would suggest that institutions focus on the lending decision first and the route second. In reality, lenders are likely to be attracted to the lending decision because of the persuasive powers of a particular route proponent. We would advise taking a step backward to consider in the first place whether participation is really appropriate, and what other routes are available. We would not discourage lenders from calling on the services of an independent specialist's assistance in this endeavor. Then again, we would say that, wouldn't we?

Chapter 5

Evaluating Lending Options

Anthony A. Nazzaro
Principal
A.A. Nazzaro Associates

A fund seeking to enter the securities lending market has a number of options from which to choose. In this chapter, we shall attempt to identify and review the various types of programs available to the current or prospective institutional lender. We shall look at each of these programs in some detail and assess them upon their merits.

The following are the primary types of lending programs:

- the master trust/custody bank participatory program
- the broker/dealer managed program
- the in-house managed program
- the outside manager/third party lender program

Since it is the responsibility of the fund to decide which type of program best fits its needs as a lender, there will be a particular emphasis upon reviewing a set of criteria enabling the fund to evaluate itself as well as its lending options. It is important for the fund/lender to assess its own status and review its profile in order to determine which of the above types of management may be best suited for its securities lending program.

Exhibit 1 provides a list of some of the factors and variables that we will consider and reference as we explore the four primary lending programs.

Exhibit 1: Fund Profile

Type of fund:

 Public/private pension fund
 Non-profit endowment or foundation
 State or municipality
 Mutual fund
 Insurance company

Size of lendable assets:

 Less than $250 million
 $250 million to $1 billion
 $1 billion to $3 billion
 $3 billion to $5 billion
 Greater than $5 billion

Asset allocation ($ value of lendable assets by type of security):

 U.S. government securities
 Domestic equities
 Corporate bonds
 Foreign fixed income
 Foreign equities

Custodial relationship

In-house management of assets or outside

Personnel available:

 Degree of knowledge and understanding in securities lending
 Overall experience and level of comfort in this activity

Degree of control or oversight desired:

 Management of short-term investment fund
 Investment guidelines
 Approved borrowers and limits
 Reporting requirements

THE MASTER TRUST/CUSTODY PARTICIPATORY PROGRAM

The master trust/custody participatory program is by far the largest and most widely chosen option among current participants in the securities lending market, and with good reason. The master trustee bank has custody of the fund/client's assets and provides easy entry into this marketplace. The bank is in the best position to know the client's assets, lend the assets, mark to market the loans, coordinate the purchase and sale activity of other managers of the portfolio, monitor corporate actions, and basically handle all of the operational needs of a lending program for its clients.

Securities lending, by its nature, is an operational activity since it essentially involves the movement of securities and the monitoring of collateral. The bank program is the most widely chosen because it is the best choice from a logistical perspective. Most importantly, the bank has the systems and the personnel with knowledge and expertise in securities lending.

Many funds, in their profiles, do not have any expertise in this area and look to their custodians to provide it. The main caveat here is to avoid becoming too passive. The fund that participates in the bank program has an important fiduciary responsibility which it cannot delegate entirely to the bank. The fund must know and understand the terms of the agency agreement which is the controlling document authorizing the bank to lend the fund's assets. The agency agreement delineates the responsibilities of the custodian, and the guidelines and rules under which the program will operate. The fund/client should be aware of any risks under the program and the limits of its liability and exposure.

Since the bank program is the dominant and most logical choice, why are there other options to consider? Two factors have kept securities lending from being the exclusive domain of the banks. The first factor has to do with sheer size. A very large master trust bank may have as many as 100 to 200 participant clients with aggregate lendable assets exceeding $200 billion. If a typical institutional client, responding to the earlier profile, has lendable assets of $200 million to $300 million, there is a significant dilution effect when pooled with lendable assets of this magnitude.

To illustrate this point with a simple example, let's assume borrower XYZ wishes to borrow 50,000 shares of IBM. Our hypothetical client owns 100,000 shares of IBM. However, the bank may have five million shares of IBM available to lend and held by 40 different accounts. Which participant client will get the loan? Loans are automatically allocated within the system in an equitable manner based upon ownership, demand, size, and position in the queue. The point is that the relatively small fund/clients may realize only a minimal incremental return from their participation in this program. The large portfolio of lendable assets of the bank are attractive to borrowers, but there is a law of diminishing returns applicable to the participant. In the aggregate, the bank program may be very large, well managed and successful, but the individual participant is part of a large pool of assets and a long list of clients.

The second factor to be considered is the fee-split. Banks offer a great deal to their participant clients since the bank essentially does everything and offers the client a turnkey program. Also, many banks offer some limited form of indemnification against certain types of losses, i.e. borrower default. In return, the bank expects to be compensated accordingly, and this is reflected in a generous fee split. Today, due to increasing competition, many banks are willing to negotiate their fee in the client's favor. The size and attractiveness of the client's portfolio will dictate the leverage a particular client may have in the negotiation of a fee-split arrangement. In the final analysis, the bank program remains a prudent choice and a wise route to securities lending for many institutions.

THE BROKER-DEALER MANAGED PROGRAM

A second option for participating in securities lending is a contractual arrangement with a major brokerage firm for the lending of the portfolio. This normally involves a custodial relationship with the brokerage firm whereby the firm has custody of all or part of the assets of the fund.

Some brokerage firms are willing to pay a guaranteed fee to the fund for the exclusive rights to the securities lending revenue of the portfolio. The fee may be a flat fee or a small percentage rate based upon the market value of the portfolio. The term of the agreement is usually one year. The major benefit to this approach is the certainty of cash flow or guaranteed income. Also, fluctuations in interest rates or lending demand will have little effect upon the earnings in this type of lending program.

Similar to the banks, brokerage firms offer a turnkey operation with qualified personnel running the program and little active involvement by the client. The major drawback is the concentration of credit exposure to one broker-dealer if the dealer is acting as principal as opposed to being an agent. The fund is essentially lending its assets to one borrower. The key considerations should be the size of the portfolio being allocated to the broker-dealer, the supervision of collateral, i.e. marks to the market, and the creditworthiness of the broker-dealer.

Some lenders have contractual arrangements with broker-dealers to manage their lending in only a specific segment of the lending market such as foreign equities. This limited arrangement enables the lender to utilize the strength and expertise of certain brokerage firms while maintaining diversification and control over the rest of its program.

THE IN-HOUSE MANAGED PROGRAM

The third securities lending option is the in-house program. This type of program is ideally suited for funds with large portfolios of assets and an in-house staff of investment professionals with expertise and experience. Examples of this type of profile would be mutual funds and insurance companies. These institutions may have $10 billion or more in lendable securities, manage their own assets, possess strong personnel and systems capabilities, combined with overall market savvy.

The in-house managed program gives the lender ultimate control with full supervision of its lending policies and investment guidelines. In addition, there is no dilution of assets or sharing of income as previously described. Beyond the initial cost of systems, the primary expenses are the salaries of the lending personnel, office overhead, and the bank transaction fees generated by the lending activity.

The securities lending revenues generated by large, in-house programs that are well managed are the highest in the industry. However, along with the benefits of full control and supervision come the full responsibility and commitment necessary to remain competitive in the business. The program cannot be managed as a sideline or ancillary activity. The in-house program requires a full commitment to all facets of the operation, including the maintenance of proper levels of loan collateral, credit analysis of borrowers and investments, implementation of sound lending policies, investment guidelines, and internal reporting to senior management. This last point is especially important. Oversight by senior management is critical to a successful in-house program. The group responsible for the lending and investment activity should be part of a well defined reporting structure within the organization. As stated earlier, if the in-house program is well managed, the rewards are great.

THE OUTSIDE MANAGER/THIRD PARTY LENDER PROGRAM

The fourth option is the independent or outside manager, sometimes referred to as a third party lender. The securities lending manager is not the principal/ lender and not the custodian bank, but an independent third party, hence the name. This mode of lending is a hybrid of the bank and in-house programs, and attempts to provide the best attributes of both. The outside manager seeks to provide the expertise of the bank program, but without its portfolio dilution, while maintaining the control and profitability of the in-house program.

For the fund that is not large enough to command a stand alone in-house program, but has an attractive portfolio and seeks to maximize its lending potential, the independent manager provides an alternative. Outside managers seek to provide the relatively small client/fund with enhanced portfolio visibility and greater loan opportunities. This is a reasonable expectation given the fact that the manager may have only a limited number of clients. In addition, the fund can dictate specifically tailored investment guidelines, a segregated investment portfolio, approved borrowers, reporting detail and frequency, and an overall high level of supervision.

A good manager with strong client communication and participation can simulate an in-house program, although this requires a much more active and involved fund. The profile of the fund/lender using an outside manager is generally one who has an in-depth knowledge and understanding of securities lending, experience, and a willingness to be involved in the activity. Typically, the custodian bank still plays an integral role in this mode since all activity and instructions must flow through the custodian. This can provide the lender with another layer of reporting and supervision over the lending program. Also, fee splits are more negotiable and heavily weighted in favor of the lender.

A drawback to the outside manager route may be the overall size of the manager's base of lendable assets. Whereas the bank managed program may be too large, the outside manager program may be too small, resulting in an inability to compete effectively. One must find a manager that strikes the right balance in terms of the number of clients, size of lendable assets, and compatibility since the relationship takes on partnership-like qualities. This can be a very rewarding route to securities lending given the right combination of fund and manager.

CONCLUSION

The menu of securities lending options available to the prospective lender is varied and diverse. The analysis of options begins at home with a solid assessment of the individual fund's profile, including its characteristics and goals. A thorough review may act as a helpful guide in finding the perfect match. Although the purpose of this chapter was to introduce and describe the various modes of securities lending, an evaluation of these options will require a more in-depth study not only of each category but also of the individual entities within each type of category. Within each peer group there are better banks, stronger brokerage firms, and more competent managers.

The single most important issue to keep in mind is that all types of funds, within the purview of the prudent man rule standard, have a heavy fiduciary responsibility to learn and understand as much as possible about their securities lending program under any type of management. It is written in the Book of Proverbs, "Every prudent man acts out of knowledge."

Chapter 6

Managing Internal Lending Programs

G. William Caan, Jr.
Product Manager
First Chicago

In today's marketplace, securities lending programs come in all shapes and sizes. Banks, trust companies, investment banks, insurance companies, and lending boutiques all compete for the opportunity to lend an account's securities. Although the custody bank has traditionally filled the role of securities lender, the evolution of the marketplace has brought about a gradual decoupling of these services. Plan sponsors and account administrators have slowly accepted the notion that the best custody bank is not necessarily the best securities lending bank.

Within this competitive marketplace, lending programs exist in a variety of forms and sizes. As each lender's situation is different, there is no clear right or wrong way to develop and manage an internal lending program. In analysis consistent with the tenets of the Capital Asset Pricing Model, there is a risk-reward trade-off in securities lending program development. This trade-off is derived from several different aspects of the lending program and is manifested in the day-to-day operations of the program. In lieu of the elimination of all risk, the management of a lending program should seek out and quantify risk, and then determine an appropriate expected return for the assumption of that risk.

The focus of risk management in securities lending has shifted in conjunction with market events. In the wake of the Drysdale scandal and the demise of Drexel Burnham Lambert, risk management techniques focused on the evaluation of counterparty risk. Risk management techniques then shifted focus to the risk of collateral investment default, in a response to publicly announced debt defaults. Currently, risk management techniques have reacted to the adverse short-term interest rate market of 1994 by focusing on the investment risk inherent in cash collateral instruments used in securities lending cash collateral portfolios. In each case, the risks were neither unknown nor unquantifiable; rather, the general lack of risk management technique utilization by the securities lending industry created a misinterpretation of the risk/reward trade-off. The excessive returns by securities lending programs in the early 1990s were created through the assumption of various investment risks, not through the inefficiencies of the market.

The goal of a securities lending program is the assumption and management of risks for which one is appropriately compensated and can control, combined with the mitigation or elimination of risks for which one is not compensated, cannot measure, or cannot control. Whether the issue is indemnification, approved broker/dealers, or approved cash collateral investments, the onus of risk management falls on the lender and its agent. Consider the issue of indemnification. In the current marketplace, a lender can receive a variety of forms of indemnification from a lending agent. Usually the issuance of indemnification comes at some cost, whether it be a percentage of the revenue or a straight fee on the value of the outstanding loans. All parties must fully understand the terms of this indemnification and their responsibilities under it. As a participant in a lending agent's program, a lender must evaluate the economics of indemnification, as indemnification most resembles an insurance policy. It is also crucial that a lender fully understand the terms of the indemnification policy. Clearly, indemnification is just one example of the scope of different securities lending services that one can purchase.

SCOPE OF LENDING SERVICES

The critical ingredients in a successful securities lending program are a diversified pool of assets, an experienced cash collateral manager or investment vehicle, a sophisticated risk management group, competent legal and marketing staffs, and a dedicated securities lending infrastructure. The largest lending banks have developed these capabilities over time, while the mid-size and smaller banks have integrated existing capabilities with the purchase of external services. Whereas the larger banks have dedicated legal resources for securities lending, smaller banks may be inclined to use outside counsel on securities lending issues. The development of internal capabilities comes with increasing economies of scale.

The development and direction of one's lending program will hinge of the pool of assets from which lending will occur. The most basic rules of supply and demand influence, to a large degree, the attractiveness of one's lending portfolio. A portfolio of readily available securities, regardless of size, will not provide a sound base for the development of a quality lending program. In contrast, a portfolio of illiquid equities, in combination with a portfolio of readily available securities, will provide a sound base for a lending program. The difference, though subtle, is extremely important. The portfolio of lendable assets must create an attractive alternative to the borrowing community. A lending program is built on the gradual increase in scale of the amount of securities on loan. To increase this amount, the lender must provide his sole source of demand, the broker/dealer, with an incentive to develop the business. It is extremely difficult to create a competitive securities lending program without the benefit of securities in high demand. With only readily available securities in his portfolio, the lender does not offer value to the broker/dealer. However, with the enticement of access to the illiquid equities in its portfolio, the lender now can offer an incentive to the broker/dealer. In essence, a lender gets better performance from its portfolio when it can leverage its low demand securities loans with high demand securities loans. Taken a step further, a lender with an excessive amount of international securities can use leverage to get maximum performance from its other securities.

The developmental years of the securities lending market was a period of excess profits for the brave but few participants. However, securities lending has grown into a commodity business with many participants. Excess profits have been competitively eliminated and securities lending programs have responded to the new landscape. Securities lending programs differentiate themselves by creating either competitive advantages or comparative advantages. The larger programs in the country have the competitive advantage of larger asset pools and larger illiquid asset pools than their smaller counterparts. They create these large asset pools through aggressive custody bids, rated service and performance, and reputation. This competitive advantage is then used to dictate the relationship between lender and borrower. It is both necessary and profitable for borrowers to maintain tight relations with the larger lenders, even if the terms of this relationship are skewed in the lender's favor. These terms can include a minimum balance expectation or a slightly uncompetitive rebate structure. This balance of power resembles an oligopoly more than a monopoly. The smaller lending program does not capture this power imbalance and is thus disadvantaged competitively. To become competitive, the smaller lender must create comparative advantages with his larger competitors.

Comparative advantages can be created in a variety of forms. For instance, a lending program which has a highly competitive cash reinvestment program can offer above market rebate rates to the borrower to incent him to increase the quantity of loans. Likewise, a lender with a broad range of acceptable non-cash collateral offers more flexible financing opportunities to the borrower and can increase the quantity of loans. However, both examples included the acceptance of additional risk by the lender on behalf of its clients.

Cash collateral investment management can provide a lending program with a competitive advantage. Through the early 1990s, the stable to declining short-term interest rate environment, coupled with a flat to sloped yield curve created an environment where simple investment approaches yielded solid securities lending returns. However, the sudden change in the short-term interest rate environment in 1994 placed a greater emphasis on the ability to manage cash collateral for a lending program. Interest rate sensitivity analysis, gap analysis, shock analysis, and duration risk analysis became buzz words in the lending industry. Investment risks within a collateral portfolio presented real problems for the lending industry. The risks were always present, yet the fundamental shape of the yield curve and the stability of short-term interest rates concealed these risks. This lead to a misconception in the marketplace that securities lending could be risk free. Additionally, custodians misinterpreted the risk-reward trade-off in securities lending because they did not truly appreciate the risk factor.

In today's lending market, lenders and lending agents have a better understanding of the risk potential of a cash collateral portfolio. Armed with this knowledge, both parties can make educated decisions regarding acceptable risk parameters. Without some form of risk, it is extremely difficult to achieve returns on a host of security types. However, the decision to accept risk can, in turn, provide generous returns. Gap risk investing, defined as the difference between loan maturity and investment maturity, can produce excess profits in a steeply sloped yield curve environment. The risk taken in this investment approach is an increase in the floating interest rate on liabilities (loans) without a concurrent increase in the fixed interest rate on assets (cash investments). Sophisticated investment managers can effectively manage gap risk, a fact which becomes apparent in a changing interest rate environment. This competitively advantage is not always immediately discernible, as it takes an adverse market to differentiate the sophisticated from the unsophisticated.

Credit risk investing also offers lending programs the opportunity to produce excess securities lending returns. The lender of one asset type can generate revenue by investing in a security of lesser credit. This revenue opportunity increases as the investor goes down the credit curve. Matched duration loans (no gap risk) with credit risk may offer the lender an appropriate risk-reward trade-off. Once again, this risk may be quantified. Statistical data allow the lender to develop an approximate risk-reward trade-off. For instance, A2/P2 overnight commercial paper may trade at a yield 20 basis points above the fed funds rate and 15 basis points above A1/P1 commercial paper. By taking the default rate of A2/P2 overnight commercial and applying it to a portfolio, one can achieve an expected rate of return for the portfolio. This will quantify the risk in strict dollar terms. However, the adverse publicity associated with security default may override the economics of the transaction. Additionally, a statistical default average for a security type is meaningful when a portfolio consists of the entire universe of that security type. Clearly, this is not a practical portfolio management approach.

The acceptance of broker risk can offer, in specific instances, a superior risk-reward trade-off. In the discussion of credit risk, a lender was compensated for taking on default risk. This same compensation opportunity is available by assuming broker risk, especially when it is disguised as credit risk.

The following example should help to illustrate this opportunity. Assume that a lender desires to lend securities at a fee in exchange for different securities. The securities received as collateral will dictate the fee which the lender can charge in the transaction. Once again, fees increase in conjunction with the declining credit of the collateral. The lender decides to lend shares of IBM to a borrower and accepts D-rated Corporation Y 10-year bonds as collateral for the loan of shares. The lender will be compensated for allowing the borrower to pledge non-investment grade bonds as collateral. The primary risk associated with this transaction is not the quality of the collateral. Instead, it is the quality and solvency of the borrower. The collateral only becomes an issue should the borrower become insolvent. The lender, upon borrower insolvency, still has the bonds, albeit D-rated, as collateral in the transaction. However, if the bonds default and the borrower is still solvent, the lender merely returns the insolvent bonds for different bonds. This form of borrower risk is relatively misunderstood, which tends to result in excess profit for those lenders capable of exploiting it. In an apparent dichotomy, many lending agents will require U.S. Treasury securities as collateral for loans with broker/dealers, while purchasing unsecured short-term investments in the same dealer's name.

A lending program's ability to manage risk and receive appropriate compensation for the acceptance of risk will provide a competitive advantage. In addition to risk management abilities, the lending program must have the skills to market this risk management. Many lending programs have adopted an educational approach to the discussion of securities lending with current and prospective lenders. Likewise, lenders have achieved a heightened awareness to the nuances of securities lending through consultants, trade journals, or their own mishaps. With the competitive nature of the securities lending market today, there are no "free lunches." Lending programs which manage expectations and risk will differentiate themselves in this market.

A securities lending program can also develop a comparative advantage through a proactive lending desk. The developmental style and approach to managing a lending desk can provide a value-added component to a program without changing one's risk tolerance. The current source of borrowing demand is concentrated among a finite list of broker/dealers. The creation of this demand is widespread, involving parties ranging from hedge funds to options trading firms to securities houses. However, because the broker/dealer community acts as an intermediary between end user and lending program, it should not be difficult for lending agents to develop an understanding of their source of demand. Once developed, this understanding can provide lending agents with a blueprint for structuring a plan to meet this demand. The approach to meeting demand varies across programs, resulting in different levels of performance from similar asset bases.

One approach to generating demand for loans is a systematic delivery of available assets to borrowing parties. This information link allows a lending agent to broadcast its lendable position to the borrower community, eliminating borrower search time. Additionally, borrowers can initiate loans at a predetermined rate based on this availability. The result of this systematic link is greater loan volume in marginal securities for the lending agent.

Alternatively, or concurrently, a lending program can format its approach to lending in a pro-active style. Rather than waiting for calls from borrowers searching for specific securities, a lending desk may initiate calls to borrowers. In this fashion, the lending agent is attempting to generate additional demand, or fill demand for which it otherwise may be excluded. In a competitive marketplace, the borrower has multiple locations of securities supply. A pro-active lending desk can provide a lending agent with alternative methods to maximizing the use of its supply. In marketing terms, a pro-active lending desk utilizes these methods as cost-effective advertising. However, the effectiveness of pro-active lending should be kept in perspective. It is not a substitute for aggressive cash collateral or a sizable asset portfolio. It is merely an opportunity for a lending program to provide value at the margin for its lending clients, given a static portfolio and risk parameters.

PRODUCT VARIABLES

Each and every organization that offers securities lending services must in some fashion provide critical functions for its clients. Additionally, all lending programs must address some very basic variables to the lending product. These variables include legal counsel, marketing, risk management, collateral reinvestment, and trading. A competitive lending program may provide all of these services or may in fact hire specialists to perform specific lending tasks.

Participants in securities lending activity have undoubtedly turned to legal professionals for aid in the interpretation of either borrower agreements (typically "PSA") or client lending agreements. In both instances, there are a series of legal issues which require legal interpretation. It is essential that all lending programs have extreme comfort with the legal rights and obligations dictated in their contracts. The specificity of lending often precludes internal general counsel from rendering decisions within internal comfort levels. Although the instances where parties have needed to invoke legal contracts in a court of law have been limited, the exposure level created with lending can be large. Several of the larger lending agents have dedicated securities lending counsel to address the ever changing legal landscape. Regardless of program size, expert legal counsel, whether internally developed or externally purchased, is an essential element of an effective lending program.

Risk management and analysis techniques, coupled with expert legal advise, provide the framework for liability and exposure management within a lending program. Each lending program addresses risk management in different fashions with differing levels of sophistication. The vulnerability of several lending programs to sharp interest rate rises in 1994 detailed the effectiveness and ineffectiveness of such management. However, the approach to risk management should provide each lending program with the means to measuring risk. Once measured, acceptable risk can be managed and unacceptable risk can be eliminated. Across lending programs, acceptable risk and unacceptable risk can vary widely. Likewise, risk acceptance can vary within a program, depending on the appetite of any individual lender.

The development of an integrated trading desk is crucial to a competitive lending program. Despite the technological advances within the industry, securities lending is still a relationship-oriented business based on people. Lending agent traders need not fit a specific characterization. Formal education, personality, financial market experience, and general "street savvy" play a role in the development of a trader. However, there is no clear recipe for success. It is important for a manager to staff a desk with the type of trader who can implement a specific approach to the business. A pro-active approach requires people with sales skills, while a reactive desk requires people with financial skills. Within all traders, it is crucial that there is an understanding of demand and its source. One need not know the specifics of a convertible bond arbitrage as they relate to financing, delta-neutral hedging, and currency hedging. Rather, a trader should know that these opportunities exist and approach the market to determine the appropriate terms of a prospective loan.

HURDLES TO INTERNAL DEVELOPMENT

The decision to internalize some or all variables in one's lending program requires a strict business case study. In most instances, the decision may on the surface appear clear cut, yet after careful analysis of the aforementioned variables, this decision may become clouded. First and foremost, the decision to internalize any aspect of a lending program should be a positive net present value product. It just does not make rational business sense to invest $500,000 in systems and technology for an annual revenue stream of $50,000. Similarly, it does not make sense to invest the same $500,000 in systems and technology if there is not a company-wide commitment to remain in the business. This issue remains an integral issue in the current state of consolidation and exit strategies. Likewise, for the plan sponsor community, the internalization of securities lending activity requires similar analysis. The sponsor must ask itself the following questions: "Am I receiving services from my lending agent commensurate with the fees I pay?" "Do I have the necessary capabilities and desire to run my own securities lending program?" "Do I have the required risk management tools to insure that I can measure and quantify my risk tolerance?"

In the market, there is not an absolute size that a portfolio must be to support an internal lending program. Obviously, a cost/benefit analysis needs to be considered for all the variables. However, rule of thumb dictates that a mid-sized portfolio ($250 to $500 million) of securities with an underlying benchmark of the S&P 500 or the Lehman Government Bond Index will generate its best securities lending revenue when it is a part of a much larger overall lending portfolio. The increase in portfolio utilization as part of a larger lending program can and should offset the accompanying agent lending fees. However, it is important to evaluate the factors which create revenue for assets in a securities lending program. An aggressive cash collateral investment strategy can add more revenue to the bottom line than a good lending desk. A portfolio of high demand international securities can add more value than an aggressive cash collateral investment strategy. All lending participants need to search out the true sources of value-added activity within a program. Theoretically, one can view the lending agent's split as a fee paid for services. In that light, the analysis then becomes an issue of percentage variable costs for an agency program versus fixed costs for an internally developed program. The analysis is not quite so straightforward, as it assumes that gross lending revenue generation will remain constant.

A major impediment to implementing an internally run lending program is the fear of foregone revenue. Revenue is traditionally stable to lenders who participate in an external lending program. One can measure revenue over time and market cycles to determine a mean average. Further statistical analysis can determine expected returns within one, two, or three standard deviations, assuming normal distribution. However, a new, internal program has no past history from which one can draw revenue conclusion. It is not difficult to hypothecate revenue under various market scenarios, yet these hypothecations have no historical validity. Each lending program will operate differently and produce different returns. It is often the fear of trading a known revenue stream for an unknown revenue stream which keeps larger lenders in a lending agent's program.

Additionally, the move from an externally lending agent's program to an internally managed program requires some degree of change. Areas of change can include operating activities, cash collateral investment activities, loan negotiation activities and various other activities. A detailed business plan can address each and every change, yet it does not diminish the psychological impact of "change" within an organization. It is often difficult to sell the concept of "change," regardless of the financial impact. Securities lending activity requires the involvement of several areas within a bank, trust company, or other potential lender. These groups may not see an immediate impact from increased lending revenue: however, they will feel the immediate impact of a changed daily routine which may include heightened responsibilities. It should not be surprising to find that these group often inhibit the process of changing the scope of one's lending program. The changing competitive nature of the custody business should help to alleviate this hurdle, as each custodian must place greater emphasis on the creation and maintenance of existing revenue flows.

In addition to increased functionality in the development of an internal lending program, a company eliminates a level of risk management when it leaves an external lending program. The layer of risk protection offered by the external lending agent no longer exists. Whereas the decision to lend to a specific broker/dealer previously required lender and lending agent analysis and approval, this dual approach becomes a singular approach. Lending agent contractual agreements with borrowers, which offered a layer of protection, are replaced by internally developed lending agreements. Cash collateral management and its associated risks now become the sole responsibility of the lender. Many lenders have found great comfort in the sharing of responsibility. Safety in numbers provides one with the assurance that he is not alone in troubled times. It should not be surprising to see many lenders remain with an existing external lending agent. Despite the adverse revenue environment, the shared responsibility approach lends credence to the argument to continue in the current environment.

Successful lending programs can function effectively in a variety of structures. It is important to understand the profit dynamics of one's program to determine the appropriate approach. The decision to change a current program requires a solid cost-benefit analysis under a variety of different market scenarios. The securities lending market will continue to reward those participants who maximize their advantages. It is apparent, however, that the commodity nature of this business has eliminated the ability to produce excess profits just through involvement.

Chapter 7

Performance Measurement For Securities Lending

Mathew R. Jensen
Associate Director
RogersCasey

Robert W. Scheetz
Vice President
Alliance Capital Management LP

INTRODUCTION

Securities lending is an investment management function. In this context, the institutional investor will recognize the importance of performance measurement for securities lending. It has been only recently that institutional investors have focused on measuring the performance of their securities lending programs, though securities lending services for ERISA plans have been in use since the early 1980s. Historically, the measuring of performance for a securities lending program has been done on a lender by lender basis without any uniform definition. The following are just a few of the methods that lenders currently use to determine the success of their securities lending program.

- Dollar earnings versus estimate or budget — measured either quarterly or annually

- Dollar earnings used to offset plan or corporate expenses (custody or consulting, etc.)
- Positive dollar earnings, where any earnings are considered beneficial and incremental to overall value of fund
- High utilization rates versus history or competitive bids
- Above average yield or return on reinvestment of cash collateral versus money market or other short term funds
- Average rebates versus fed funds or LIBOR

While each of these methods are simple and provide the lender with a form of "personalized" performance measurement assessment, none of them capture the total return on an absolute or comparative basis.

Comparative results are particularly valuable but currently elusive. The industry, until recently, has never desired or developed a consistent approach to comparing performance across various lending programs. There are many possible reasons for this, but some of the reasons might be:

- The relative difficulty of producing "fair" cross-time and comparative performance and risk statistics due to the many variables influencing return.
- The economically small impact that securities lending has on overall plan performance — typically measured in basis points on total assets.
- Revenue from securities lending has been positive and somewhat predictable, until recently.
- The securities lending industry has come under increased scrutiny from a few high profile losses.

Measuring of performance in securities lending is admittedly a more complex process than investment manager performance. The advent of new alternatives to lending (third party and principal lending programs) have created a more competitive lending market and caused the industry to reassess how performance is being measured. To continue with our investment manager analogy, one can think of the attention that securities lending is receiving today as the same attention that investment manager performance measurement received in the late 1970s and early 1980s.

This chapter proposes a simple set of formulas that capture the component and aggregate results of securities lending in a few statistics. The simplicity of the calculations highlights the real issue: performance measurement is as much a process as it is a series of formulas. Once familiarized with the calculations, you should concentrate on getting the information from your lender and establish a process of regular .reviews and evaluations. As recent events have shown, the risk of not monitoring the lending program is entirely yours.

PERFORMANCE MEASUREMENT — THE GENERAL THEORY

Our philosophical approach to the process of measuring the results, whether for an investment management account, securities lending program or an administrative service provider, involves separating the outputs of the program into three related, but distinct measurements:

1. *Performance measurement* — the *combined* effect of decisions on the economic results of the program
2. *Performance attribution* — attribution of the economic results to specific decision types
3. *Risk exposures* — ongoing measurement of program risk versus guidelines and restrictions, and the general market

This chapter focuses primarily on performance measurement and risk exposures since one cannot be done without the other, and a simple attribution process. In general, these measures must meet the following criteria:

- Utilize available data
- Control for non-decision factors
- Allow for cross time comparisons
- Simplify for non-practitioner use and more frequent calculation

It is important that these measurements are standardized and comparable across time and products. Performance measurement should gauge the *cumulative economic results* of all decisions made by the securities lender. The process should not penalize or reward the lender for uncontrolled factors such as portfolio composition or turnover.

FORMULA FOR REVENUE

Before we go further, a brief review of the basic formula for securities lending revenue is helpful:

$$\text{Revenue} = [\text{Utilization} \times (\text{Collateral Return} - \text{Rebate Rate})] \times \text{Split}$$

where:

Utilization is commonly calculated as average dollar value of loans outstanding divided by average lendable assets.

Collateral Return is the percent earnings on cash collateral and net earnings or fee on non-cash collateral.

Rebate Amount is the percent rebate (or interest) paid to the borrower in the case of cash collateral.

Split is the percentage of revenues accruing to each party in the case of an agent or principal lending relationship.

For example, given a lender with an average utilization of 20% that earned an average return of 5.5% on collateral and paid an average rebate of 5.0%, the revenue after splitting the proceeds with the lending agent 50%, would be 0.05% or 5 basis points, as shown below:

$$[0.20(0.055 - 0.05)](0.5) = 0.005 = 5\text{bp}$$

The formula can also be used on a dollar basis, though the utilization factor would be removed since it is already captured in the dollar earnings and rebate.

The collateral return is determined by two factors: maturity or duration and credit quality. The rebate is determined generally by market rates and the demand for securities. Utilization is determined by market demand and rebate or fee attractiveness. Utilization and rebate are linked on a loose inverse basis; for a given security, the higher the rebate the lower the utilization. The aggregate and marginal results of all of these factors is the ultimate responsibility of the lender and lending agent/principal.

Reviewing the securities lending general formula, there are two important decisions taking place:

> *Spread:* maximize collateral return within investment guidelines and minimize rebate rates while maintaining a maximum utilization.
>
> *Utilization:* maximize volume of securities on loan while minimizing rebates.

SPREAD PERFORMANCE MEASUREMENT

The basic method for measuring spread performance is as follows:

Market Benchmark (MB) = Fed funds, repo, LIBOR or other appropriate rate

Rebate Result (RR) $= \dfrac{\$R_i}{\$DLO_i}$

Collateral Results (CR) = Time weighted rate of return on the collateral portfolio

where:

i = 1 day

$\$R_i$ = The cumulative dollar rebate paid and accrued for period i

$\$DLO_i$ = Daily Loans Outstanding for period i

Ideally, the RR and CR would be calculated daily. If daily calculation is not feasible, DLO would become Average Daily Loans Outstanding (ADLO) for longer time periods. We expect that non-daily calculation would have a minimal impact on results. For daily periods, if pricing is not available, the yield on the collateral portfolio could be substituted for the rate of return. Again, this should have a minimal impact on results if the maturity of the collateral pool is under a year. It is imperative that both $R and CR cover the same time period. For competitor/market comparisons, it may be more realistic to use returns from monthly averages than daily returns given the amount of data collection and processing required.

The expectation for base-line profitability is MB > RR < CR. For example, assume the following:

$DLO = $9,250,000,000
$R = $527,250,000
RR = $527,250,000 / $9,250,000,000 = 5.70%
CR = 5.75%
MB = 5.80%

This is a profitable program, though this gives no indication of the magnitude of profitability since utilization is not included.

For non-cash collateral loans, the formula would be adjusted as follows:

MB = A market synthetic spread, for example Repo-Fed funds

$$RR = \frac{(\$F_i)}{(\$DLO_i)}$$

where:

i = 1 day
F = Non-cash collateral fee received and accrued
DLO_i = Daily Loans Outstanding for period i

The expectation for base-line profitability is MB > RR. Since these measures establish natural benchmarks for rebate negotiation and collateral account performances, standard practices of investment manager performance measurement can be applied.

UTILIZATION PERFORMANCE MEASUREMENT

To measure utilization, we use targets based on expectations, historical observations, and competitive data. These targets should be reviewed and updated at least monthly to reflect new competitive data, or whenever there are major shifts in expectations based on internal or market related events. The process for changing these targets should be formal and documented.

COMBINING THE RESULTS: NET MARGINAL PERCENT EARNINGS

The overall income to the lending program can be expressed as a percentage of lendable assets. The formula is:

$$\text{Net Marginal Percent Earnings} = \frac{(\$CR - \$RR) + \$F}{\$L}$$

where:

$\$CR$ = Dollar cash collateral earnings
$\$RR$ = Dollar rebates paid and accrued
$\$F$ = Non-cash collateral fee
$\$L$ = Dollar lendable assets

With a little algebra you will recognize this formula as simply spread × utilization — the revenue formula for securities lending.

Ideally, this should be calculated daily, but could be calculated over greater time periods using averages. With proper accounting data, this can be calculated by loan, security type, trader, program total, and any number of other sub-classifications. On the plus side, this method is not subject to arbitrary weightings, it can be compared over time, and a risk measure like standard deviation can be calculated. Unfortunately, it does not measure performance relative to a market benchmark so a tracking error calculation is not possible at the aggregate level. However, it is possible to construct a benchmark based on synthetic market spreads (using fed funds versus repo for example) and observed market utilizations. Another issue is lenders have varying opinions on what assets are considered lendable at any point in time. Given this, general rules for calculating lendable assets should be set with the lender in advance.

All three of these measurements, spread, utilization, and net marginal percent earnings, should be reviewed by security type and aggregate program, and compared to historical results. The benefits of these types of measurements are:

- There are fewer requirements for "manual" benchmarks such as budgets or estimates.
- The performance goals of the lending process are reflected — the rebate should outperform the alternative in the market, and the investment of collateral should outperform the rebate.
- It provides a simple breakdown of rebate performance, collateral investment performance and utilization.
- It allows for cross-time comparisons.
- It can be performed with greater periodicity.
- Widely available data facilitate measurement process.

Key assumptions of this process are that proper guidelines are in place and that the lenders, traders, and collateral manager(s) are operating within these guidelines.

COMPARATIVE RESULTS: INCORPORATING DESIGN RISK

A critical factor to comparing performance across lending programs is to be able to quantify and segregate the lending activity by its riskiness as defined in the design of the lending program. Design risk is any risk characteristic that is specified in the guidelines or operating procedures of the securities lending program. This includes items such as guidelines for cash collateral investment, broker loan exposures, or loan/collateral maturity mismatch. For example, the earnings results of a lending program that is allowed to invest in A2/P2 rated securities should not be compared to a program that can invest in only A1/P1 securities. All too often, though, this type of comparison has been conducted, and the result has been that the buyer of the lending services has not properly understood the different sources of risk in a lending program, and how those risks can positively or negatively impact the overall revenue. In order "to level the lending field" a risk analysis needs to be conducted, and only like lending programs that share similar risk postures should be compared against one another.

The question remains, how does one go about effectively quantifying the appropriate risks in order to draw valid comparisons? As it stands today, the market does not have a uniform process of classifying risk. The following is one approach which we have found goes a long way toward achieving this goal. First, identify the dominant risks in securities lending. Next, define and weight each risk based on how it could ultimately impact the potential return of the lending program. Lastly, score each risk (with 1=conservative to 5=aggressive) to determine a standardized risk classification.

Let's illustrate further. Assume that you decide that the three dominant risks in lending are counterparty (or borrower default), collateral (primarily the reinvestment of the cash but non-cash as well) and interest rate (the mismatch between the loans and investments). Next, you decide to weight the risks as 20%, 40% and 40%, respectively. Finally, you score each by its level of riskiness (the scale we have suggested above is 1 to 5). The definition of each risk as to what is conservative and aggressive needs to be clearly described. An example of defining the interest rate risk might be as follows: a matched program receives a score of 1 since it represents a conservative posture, while a program that is willing to take on a mismatch position of 20 days receives a score of 4.

By going through this process for each of the three risks, the end result will be a numerical score that will then enable you to compare one lending program to another on a risk-adjusted basis. We fully concede that this process by no means captures all the risk variables in a lending program, but it does provide some rigor to the process and culminates in a standardized risk measurement analysis that better allows lenders to perform the much desired "apples to apples" comparison.

TEMPORAL RESULTS:
MEASURING PERFORMANCE RISK OVER TIME

A simple measurement of performance risk, or the risk taken within the design parameters of the program, can be derived from the performance calculations presented earlier using the concept of tracking error and the information ratio. *Tracking error* is the standard deviation of excess returns, where excess return is percent of performance above or below a standardized benchmark. This measures the volatility, or risk, of performance above or below a benchmark. For example, you could look at the tracking error of rebates versus repo rates — a high tracking error combined with large cumulative amounts of out performance (i.e. rebates are less than repo) means that the securities lender is consistently negotiating very competitive rebates. Alternatively, high tracking error of CR versus RR may indicate that the collateral manager is taking unnecessarily large bets in the collateral portfolio.

The *information ratio* is the ratio of relative out performance (or alpha) to tracking error. This tells you the unit of excess performance you are getting for every unit of excess risk you are taking. A ratio of 1 means, for example, that the collateral manager is producing returns over rebate that are commensurate with the risks taken in the collateral portfolio. This number is also directional, since it will produce negative results (where as the tracking error has only a positive sign) when there is under performance.

These two risk measures, while not detailed, will highlight the need to further analyze the performance results.

We would recommend that institutional investors regularly review risk trends in the following measures:

- Rebates versus market benchmark
- Collateral versus rebates
- Net percent earnings versus historical or constructed benchmark

Also, systems have been developed based on the process of cumulative sums that can detect trends and provide warnings for both tracking error and the information ratio.

CONCLUSIONS

Viewing securities lending as an investment management function puts the performance measurement process in the proper light. Using the methods for comparative performance measurement described in this chapter, along with a disciplined process of periodic data collection, will allow the lender to establish a basis for comparative evaluation and monitoring of their lending program. Ultimately, though, all the analysis that we have described is dependent upon the buyer of lending services. Each buyer will have unique goals and objectives for the lending of their securities; therefore, depending on the importance of securities lending to the buyer will dictate the focus and emphasis placed on performance measurement. The time has come for lenders to agree upon an approach, advocate the need for an industry wide acceptance of universal standards and make performance measurement a necessary and useful analytic tool for the lending community.

Chapter 8

Developing Effective Guidelines for Managing Legal Risks — U.S. Guidelines

Charles E. Dropkin, JD

Partner

Proskauer Rose Goetz & Mendelsohn LLP

Securities lending, whether viewed as a means of generating incremental income to reduce custody expense or as a means of leveraging a portfolio to generate cash for investment, is a highly regulated activity. Securities owners (such as custody and trust customers of banks, public funds, pension funds subject to the Employee Retirement Income Security Act of 1974 (ERISA), insurance companies and mutual funds), lending agents, and broker-dealers (as borrowers) are each subject to a host of legal concerns and regulatory oversight. In this chapter, we will (1) identify certain key legal and regulatory issues applicable to lenders, lending agents and borrowers which must be understood and followed as part of any effective compliance program and (2) discuss contractual measures available for reducing insolvency risk.

LENDER REGULATIONS

Different categories of lenders are subject to different regulations. ERISA lenders, for instance, must be cognizant of potential prohibited transactions which could result from lending securities to a borrower who provided (or whose affiliate provided) financial, advisory or other services to the plan. To facilitate lending by plans, the Department of Labor in 1985 promulgated a safe harbor.

Prohibited Transaction Class Exemption 81-6 (PTCE 81-6) allows lending of securities by employee benefit plans subject to ERISA, under prescribed circumstances, to domestic banks and registered broker-dealers who are "parties in interest" with respect to such plans. Because the definitional reach of a "party in interest" in Section 3(14) of ERISA is so broad, it is very difficult to be sure that a counterparty is not a party-in-interest. In order to safeguard against the unintentional violation of ERISA, which could give rise to pecuniary penalties in the form of an excise tax on the borrower and strict liability for any losses on the plan fiduciary, an ERISA lender should ensure compliance with PTCE 81-6, as well as general ERISA standards of prudence and diversification of cash collateral investments.

The primary condition of PTCE 81-6 is that neither the borrower nor an affiliate of the borrower has discretionary authority or control with respect to the investment of the plan assets involved in the transaction, or renders investment advice with respect to those assets. In addition, the plan must receive from the borrower (either by physical delivery or by book entry in a securities depository) by the close of the lending fiduciary's business on the day in which the securities lent are delivered to the borrower, collateral (consisting of cash, securities issued or guaranteed by the United States government or its agencies or instrumentalities, or irrevocable bank letters of credit issued by a person other than the borrower or an affiliate thereof, or any combination thereof) having, as of the close of business on the preceding business day, a market value, or in the case of letters of credit a stated amount, equal to not less than 100% of the then market value of the securities lent. Prior to the making of any loan, the borrower must have furnished the lending fiduciary with its most recent available audited statement of the borrower's financial condition, its most recent available unaudited statement of its financial condition (if more recent than such audited statement), and a representation that, at the time the loan is negotiated, there has been no material adverse change in its financial condition since the date of the most recent financial statement furnished to the plan that has not been disclosed to the lending fiduciary.

The loan must be evidenced by a written loan agreement, the terms of which are at least as favorable to the plan as an arm's-length transaction with an unrelated party would be. The plan must receive a reasonable fee that is related to the value of the borrowed securities and the duration of the loan, or has the opportunity to derive compensation through the investment of cash collateral. Where the plan has that opportunity, the plan may pay a loan rebate or similar fee to the borrower, if such fee is not greater than the plan would pay in a comparable transaction with an unrelated party. The plan must also receive the equivalent of all distributions ("in lieu of" payments) made to the holders of the borrowed securities during the term of the loan, including, but not limited to, cash dividends, interest payments, shares of stock as a result of stock splits and rights to purchase additional securities. Marks-to-market must be made daily, and loans must be terminable on demand.

Insurance companies and public funds must determine as a threshold matter, under state law, the extent to which securities lending is a recognized practice, either regulated as an investment or as a loan, and any applicable restrictions thereon, including with respect to cash collateral investment and (in the case of insurance companies) eligibility of securities out on loan for required minimum capital purposes.

The extent to which mutual funds may lend securities will depend, in the first instance, upon applicable provisions in the governing prospectus and constituent documents. Typically, reflective of SEC no-action letters and 6(c) orders under the Investment Company Act of 1940 (which governs both open and closed-end mutual funds), a mutual fund will not have more than one-third of its portfolio out on loan at any one time. Potential investors in mutual funds should review a fund's prospectus carefully, since the proceeds of cash received as collateral in a securities loan may be invested in instruments of a type and risk profile different than that of other fund holdings.

AGENT REGULATIONS

Lending agents, such as banks, are independently regulated in securities lending activities. In 1985, the Federal Financial Institutions Examinations Council (FFIEC) issued a statement on bank activities in securities lending which has been adopted by both the Office of the Comptroller of the Currency (OCC), the regulator of national banks, and the Board of Governors of the Federal Reserve System (FRB), the regulator of state member banks and bank holding companies. The Statement provides guidelines under which bank activities as a lender and as an agent are to be conducted. Those guidelines require the following:

1. The bank's recordkeeping system should produce daily reports showing securities available for lending and those out on loan, as well as the material terms of each loan.
2. Collateral is to be marked to market daily. A collateral margin greater than 100% of loan value should be set on the basis of price volatility, and lent securities should not be released unless collateral is sent simultaneously.
3. A management committee should approve each borrower after independent credit review. Management should establish individual credit limits for each borrower.
4. Lending should be effected under written contracts with the owner of the securities and with the borrower, outlining the bank's responsibilities and fees.
5. If the bank indemnifies lenders, written opinions of its counsel and accountants should be obtained as to legality and proper accounting treatment.
6. Loans and indemnities should be reported on the bank's call report.

Under present risk-based capital guidelines of the OCC and the FRB, banks generally may indemnify customers in securities lending transactions, and incur no risk-based capital charge, if the indemnification is limited to no more than the difference between the market value of the securities lent and the market value of the collateral received, and any reinvestment risk associated with cash collateral is borne solely by the customer.

A lending agent bank with discretion to invest cash collateral on behalf of a customer will be treated as a fiduciary. Lending agent banks, when dealing with mutual fund customers, should be careful to limit investment discretion to avoid characterization as an investment advisor to the fund, which would require separate approval by the fund's directors.

BORROWER REGULATIONS

Broker-dealers are subject to rules and regulations of both the Securities and Exchange Commission (SEC) and the FRB.

The customer protection rules under the Securities Exchange Act of 1934, as amended (Exchange Act), and particularly Rule 15c3-3 thereunder relating to possession and control of customer securities, contain specific provisions relating to the contents of a written securities lending agreement. In brief, any loan of securities must be evidenced by a written agreement that at a minimum:

1. sets forth in a separate schedule or schedules the basis of compensation for any loan, and generally the rights and liabilities of the parties as to the borrowed securities;
2. provides that the lender will be given a schedule of the securities actually borrowed at the time of the borrowing of the securities;
3. specifies that the broker or dealer (A) must provide to the lender, upon the execution of the agreement or by the close of the business day of the loan if the loan occurs subsequent to the execution of the agreement, collateral, consisting exclusively of cash or United States Treasury bills and Treasury notes or an irrevocable letter of credit issued by a bank as defined in the Exchange Act which fully secures the loan of the securities, and (B) must mark the loan to the market not less than daily and, in the event that the market value of all the outstanding securities loaned at the close of trading at the end of the business day exceeds 100% of the collateral then held by the lender, the borrowing broker or dealer must provide additional collateral to the lender by the close of the next business day as necessary to equal, together with the collateral then held by the lender, not less than 100% of the market value of the securities loaned; and,

4. contains a prominent notice that the provisions of the Securities Investor Protection Act of 1970 (SIPA) may not protect the lender with respect to the securities loan transaction and that, therefore, the collateral delivered to the lender may constitute the only source of satisfaction of the broker's or dealer's obligation in the event the broker or dealer fails to return the securities.

Regulation T, one of the margin rules which deals with extensions of credit by and to brokers and dealers,[1] provides that "without regard to the other provisions of this part, a creditor [broker/dealer] may borrow or lend securities for the purpose of making delivery of the securities in the case of short sales, failure to receive securities required to be delivered, or other similar situations." This language does not require that the delivery for which securities are borrowed must be on a transaction which the borrower has himself made, either as agent or principal; one may borrow in order to relend to another for the latter to make such a delivery. However, the borrowing must be related to an actual delivery of the type specified, *i.e.*, delivery in connection with a specific transaction that has occurred or is in immediate prospect. A broker/dealer may not borrow securities merely to enable it or another broker to have the securities "on hand" or to anticipate some need that may or may not arise in the future. A borrower, however, who reasonably anticipates a short sale may borrow securities up to one standard settlement cycle in advance of the trade date. Borrowers may "lock up" a supply of lendable securities for potential future use by paying an up-front commitment fee to reserve particular securities anticipated to be needed for a future borrowing. Regulation T is not violated by such a "lock-up" since the broker-dealer would not be committed to borrowing the securities, but merely would be assured that the securities would be available, if and when needed for a permissible borrowing purpose.

---

[1] Regulation T is applicable to securities lending transactions because of concern by the FRB (which has delegated authority to prescribe margin rules and regulations) that the margin requirements, which would apply to a loan of cash secured by securities, could otherwise be circumvented by restructuring the transaction as a loan of securities secured by cash, thereby permitting the lender of securities to obtain more cash for the securities than could be obtained by borrowing on the securities.

The staff of the FRB has tended to read the borrowing purpose requirement of "other similar transactions" narrowly in the context of bona fide arbitrage. Thus, borrowing equity securities for the purpose of becoming a registered owner to participate in a dividend reinvestment plan has been held to be an impermissible purpose and not "bona fide arbitrage." But borrowing a convertible security and immediately converting it to make delivery on a short sale was permissible where effected as part of a bona fide arbitrage (and where the broker had received assurance that the conversion process would be completed in time to make actual delivery on the short sale). Regulation T exempts those broker/dealers registered with the SEC solely as government securities brokers or dealers and permits creation of a government securities account for customers of broker/dealers to enable transactions in U.S. government securities to be effected without regard to the securities lending provisions of Regulation T. Effective July 1, 1996, U.S. broker-dealers, pursuant to amendments to Regulation T (the July T Amendments), will be allowed to lend non-U.S. traded securities to a foreign person for any purpose that is lawful in the foreign country. In this regard, a foreign security not listed on NASDAQ or a U.S. national securities exchange is not "U.S. traded" solely because American Depository Receipts on the foreign security are traded in the United States. The FRB continues to resist changing its stance on borrowing U.S. securities to take advantage of dividend reinvestment.

Regulation T also prescribes the scope of collateral which can be pledged. As a result of the July T Amendments, a broker-dealer can pledge as collateral cash (which includes any freely convertible currency not limited to the currency in which the loaned securities are denominated), cash equivalents (which include bankers acceptances, negotiable bank certificates of deposit, and money market mutual fund shares), securities issued or guaranteed by the United States or its agencies (which include government-sponsored obligations such as FNMA and FHLMC obligations which are not full faith and credit obligations of the U.S. government), foreign sovereign non-convertible debt securities that are margin securities, any collateral which is permissible under Rule 15c3-3, or irrevocable letters of credit issued by a bank insured by the Federal Deposit Insurance Corporation or a foreign bank that has filed an agreement with the FRB on Form FR T-1, T-2. The FRB's staff has disallowed the use of unlisted corporate debt as collateral, but is considering whether to allow any security that qualifies for loan value to serve as collateral (valued at its regulatory loan value).

STRENGTHENING REMEDIES THROUGH DOCUMENTATION

Failure to comply with applicable legal provisions relevant to the conduct of securities lending can subject participants both to civil and, in some cases, criminal sanctions. Compliance, however, with such provisions, while legally mandated, will not protect a lender against the most significant transactional risk it faces, namely, counterparty insolvency. A well drafted securities lending agreement, however, can be of benefit in seeking to mitigate this risk.[2]

When a broker faces bankruptcy, a lender or agent is usually not taken completely by surprise. The broker may have informed it of financial difficulties, the lender may have deduced it on its own or based on action of the SEC or a national securities exchange, or the lender may have heard rumors in the marketplace.

Ideally, the lender would like to terminate the loan and regain possession of the loaned securities before the broker enters bankruptcy. It can do so in one of two different ways.

First, the lender may call the loan. If a broker has borrowed U.S. government securities, it is required under most securities loan agreements to return the loaned securities the same day it receives the call notice or the next business day. However, if the bank has loaned foreign securities or U.S. equity securities, the agreements typically permit the borrower up to the normal settlement period to return them. Obviously, as the settlement period for return of loaned securities increases, the risk that the broker may file for bankruptcy or be the subject of an involuntary proceeding during that interval is heightened.

Before it calls a loan in advance of an expected termination date, the lender must determine the amount of the damages that the bro-

---

[2] Although the Public Securities Association, a trade association for the broker-dealer community, has promulgated a prototype form of master agreement, the lending community has been slow to embrace the document, preferring instead to tailor the agreement to its particular needs.

ker likely will seek to assess against the lender for early termination.[3] Similarly, the lender must analyze the cost of liquidating any cash collateral it had received from the broker that may have been invested in term instruments. It may be that the total of these costs is higher than the discounted cost to the lender of the risk of a bankruptcy filing by the borrower.

A second way for a lender to obtain the loaned securities is to exercise a buy-in by foreclosing on the collateral and applying the proceeds to the purchase of equivalent securities. Depending on the applicable loan contract, prior notice to a borrower (and an opportunity to cure) may be required. However, as a threshold matter, a lender can foreclose on collateral only if an event of default has occurred under the applicable contract. A lender must be especially careful in determining whether an event of default actually has occurred before it acts — if it improperly forecloses on collateral and triggers a chain reaction in the market in which other lenders foreclose on the broker, resulting in the broker's financial collapse, the broker stands a good chance of winning a suit against the lender and being awarded significant damages.

There are a number of standard defaults that should be contained in loan documentation with the broker to allow the lender to foreclose on the broker.

For instance, the agreement should contain a default for breach of the broker's covenants to provide timely financial statements to the lender and reports with the appropriate regulatory agencies. The broker should covenant to give notice to the lender of any material adverse change in connection with its business or financial condition. It also should be obligated to notify the lender of any stock exchange, Securities Investor Protection Corporation (SIPC), SEC or National Association of Securities Dealers investigation, complaint or proceeding, or any similar action by a state regulatory body. And the broker should covenant to provide the lender with all tax receipts related to any withholding on payments made by it to a lender in respect of borrowed foreign securities (including "in lieu of" payments).

---

[3] While, for U.S. tax reasons, securities loans must be terminable on demand to avoid a recognition event, in practice parties may enter into loans with specified expected termination dates. Any early termination by a lender typically requires it to compensate the borrower for the cost of replacing the loan.

The securities lending agreement should contain a cross default to any other debt upon which the broker is or becomes obligated, including debt owed to the lender in any different capacity. The lender should also insist on defaults related to any breach of representations by the broker, including the Regulation T representation under which it has agreed to use the borrowed securities only for limited purposes, as described above. Finally, the documentation should allow the lender to call a default upon the broker's failure to remit its "in lieu of" payment or failure to respond to requests for additional required collateral. Requiring a broker to furnish adequate assurance of its ability to perform whenever a lender deems itself insecure is also a desirable contractual protection for a lender.

Once a broker has defaulted, the terms of the agreement it has entered into with the lender will either permit the lender to terminate the loan on notice to the broker or will terminate the loan automatically. If the lender gives notice to the broker, it is able to exercise its rights within a reasonable period thereafter. It can foreclose on its collateral and buy-in securities immediately after a securities loan automatically terminates.

To avoid claims that the lender has waived a particular default, the default upon which the lender relies to foreclose on collateral should occur at some time reasonably near the time at which it acts. Very often a lender will not be able to call a loan or realize on collateral and buy-in securities before a broker files for bankruptcy. Under the U.S. Bankruptcy Code, a "securities contract" is defined to include a loan of security. A "security" is defined to include, *inter alia*, notes, bonds, debentures, collateral trust certificates, transferable shares, limited partnership interests, and other interests commonly known as "securities." While ordinarily the right of a securities lender, upon the default of a broker-dealer as borrower, would not preclude the lender from immediately exercising contractual remedies, liquidating collateral and applying proceeds thereof to the buy-in of equivalent replacement securities, the applicable provisions of the Securities Investor Protection Act (SIPA) would override this lender protection in the event of the liquidation of a registered broker-dealer. In the past, the trustee appointed pursuant to SIPA typically, as one of its first acts, would request the bankruptcy court to issue an order staying a securities lender (or repo participant) from immediately exercising available contractual remedies. It may be that until a lender is served with a copy of that order or has knowledge or notice of it, the lender is entitled to liquidate a broker's collateral without violating the court order. If a lender were to so act, though, it is likely that it would be challenged by the SIPA trustee and that challenge would have to be resolved by the courts. How the courts would decide the issue is far from certain.

By letter dated October 30, 1990, the Deputy General Counsel of SIPC stated that, in the future, SIPC would not seek to stay the exercise by a financial institution of its contractual right to utilize cash collateral to cause the liquidation of a securities lending contract with a broker-dealer under liquidation. The SIPC letter, however, intentionally did not address securities loans collateralized by securities and, accordingly, SIPC retains the option to seek to stay liquidation thereof. During the period of an imposed stay a lender may suffer losses if the market moves against it. A lender is unable effectively to hedge its exposure since it cannot predict with confidence when the stay will be lifted. This "stay" risk is also troubling for banks who have indemnified their customers against loss from broker default since the agent banks, upon the insolvency of the broker (which is a normal default under the applicable securities lending contracts), will promptly have to perform upon the indemnity at the time when they are stayed from liquidating the collateral to fund the buy-in. The SIPC letter, as an expression of policy, is subject to change or withdrawal at any time.

There are a number of steps that lenders could take to minimize the damage from an injunction prohibiting close outs. Lenders could expand the scope of defaults contained in their securities lending agreements to increase their ability to call a default and foreclose on their collateral before any bankruptcy filing takes place. Along these lines, lenders may seek to increase the number of automatic loan termination provisions contained in the agreements and decrease the ability of brokers to cure defaults during grace periods.

Perhaps the best course of action for lenders to take is to try to avoid the SIPA risk. To do so, lenders can contract with entities that are not eligible for SIPA protection. The contra-party in a securities loan could be the parent of a broker-dealer, or a government securities affiliate of a broker-dealer that is not subject to SIPA, perhaps with a parent company guarantee. Alternatively, lenders could request letters of credit to support their borrowers' obligations. Because they should not be included in the broker's bankruptcy estate, there is virtually no risk that payment under a letter of credit would be enjoined. A clean draft typically would be honored the day it was presented or the next day.

Where a lender accepts a letter of credit as collateral, it should be careful not to allow the broker to initiate amendments without prior consent of the lender or to sanction a course of conduct whereby the issuing bank, upon request of the account party, amends the letter of credit and then sends a confirmation to the beneficiary. As is its right, the lender should insist that the issuing bank obtain its prior express written approval for any changes to the terms or amount of the credit.

Finally, to shift the stay risk to customers, agent banks may refrain from offering indemnification. If a bank acts prudently during the course of its relationship with the broker, it should not be held liable for any ensuing losses suffered by its customers due to broker defaults.

Chapter 9

International Legal and Regulatory Concerns

Nancy Jacklin
Partner
Clifford Chance, New York

David Felsenthal
Associate
Clifford Chance, New York

Securities lending today frequently involves lenders, borrowers, and agents as well as securities and collateral in more than one jurisdiction. A variety of legal issues are raised by cross-border transactions. This chapter considers such issues from the perspective of one of the participants in a cross-border transaction in which the counterparties or the loaned securities, or both, are in a foreign jurisdiction.

OVERVIEW OF THE ISSUES

A participant in any international securities lending transaction should consider the following legal issues: (1) the capacity and authority of the counterparties; (2) applicable regulations governing the transaction; (3) transfer and timing issues relating to transfers of foreign securities; (4) transfer and timing issues relating to collateral; (5) the impact of insolvency of a foreign counterparty; and, (6) ownership issues arising upon the insolvency of an agent and liability issues involving an agent. Tax issues are also, of course, crucial in international securities lending, but are beyond the scope of this chapter.

CAPACITY AND AUTHORITY ISSUES FOR FOREIGN COUNTERPARTIES

Capacity

Different types of organizations (*e.g.* corporations, municipalities, banks, and partnerships) will have different legal capacities based upon variations in the underlying authorizing statutes. In transactions involving foreign counterparties, a participant should look at the laws applicable to the formation of the counterparty, as well as specific regulatory rules governing the counterparty, to determine the counterparty's capacity to enter into the transaction.

Typically, the legal capacity of corporations and banks to enter into securities lending transactions will be relatively well established within the relevant jurisdiction. In some jurisdictions, well-known problems must be addressed: for example, in certain jurisdictions banks have limited authority to grant security interests, which may affect their ability to post collateral for a securities loan. The legal capacity of entities other than banks or corporations to enter into securities lending transactions may not be as well established. In particular, a municipality or other government entity may be subject to specialized statutes which affect its ability to engage in securities lending. For example, some U.S. state entities are limited in the amount of aggregate debt that they may incur or in the type of transactions that they may perform.

Entities can also be subject to limits on their capacity to engage in securities lending because of restrictions in their corporate charter and by-laws or equivalent documents. It may be appropriate, as part of the due diligence process prior to initiating a securities lending transaction, to examine the charter and by-laws or equivalent documents of a counterparty.

Authority

In addition to having the legal capacity to enter into a securities lending transaction, a counterparty must also properly authorize such a transaction. The steps necessary to obtain proper authority are generally set out in the statutes governing the organization of a counterparty and in its charter and by-laws or equivalent documents. If available, resolutions of the board of directors or other appropriate governing board of the counterparty may clearly establish the authority of a particular officer to execute a securities loan. In the absence of such a resolution, officers of the counterparty may be authorized under the charter and by-laws to undertake transactions that are entered into in the ordinary course of business. Whether securities lending transactions are part of an entity's ordinary course of business would depend upon, among others things, whether the entity is a financial institution that engages in securities investment or dealing as part of its regular business.

In some cases, a securities lending participant may feel comfortable with regard to capacity and authority of its counterparty after examining corporate resolutions and other documents of the counterparty. In other cases, particularly involving a foreign jurisdiction with an unfamiliar legal regime, a participant may wish to obtain an opinion of counsel from a counterparty as to the counterparty's capacity and authority.

REGULATIONS

U.S. Regulations

Any securities lending transaction must conform to applicable regulatory requirements. In the United States, these requirements generally arise in connection with regulation of different types of institutions, such as the U.S. supervisory policies for banking organizations issued by the Office of the Comptroller of the Currency and the Board of Governors of the Federal Reserve System (the "Federal Reserve") for banking organizations, Regulation T of the margin regulations issued for brokers and dealers, SEC Rule 15c3-3 for brokers and dealers, exchange rules applicable to members of an exchange, and ERISA rules applicable to pension plans. These requirements are discussed in Chapter 8.

In the international context, it is worth noting that, effective July 1, 1996, the Federal Reserve adopted amendments to Regulation T which allow U.S. broker-dealers to lend "non-U.S. traded foreign securities" to a foreign person (or borrow such securities for the purpose of relending them to a foreign person) for any purpose legally permitted in the foreign country. The loan of securities must be fully secured with collateral having at all times a value of at least 100% of the market value of the loaned securities, but no restrictions are imposed on the type of collateral. A non-U.S. traded foreign security is a foreign security that is not registered, or otherwise traded, on a U.S. exchange or listed on NASDAQ.

Foreign Regulations

The transaction must conform to applicable foreign regulations, which may apply to a foreign counterparty engaged in securities lending or specifically to securities lending activities involving foreign securities. In the United Kingdom, for instance, in order to achieve favorable tax treatment, securities lending activities of a U.K. institution must be approved by the Inland Revenue.

TRANSFER OF SECURITIES

In any transaction involving foreign securities, both borrower and lender (or the agents acting for borrower or lender) need to be aware of the requirements for legal and effective transfer of the foreign securities from the lender to the borrower. Such a transfer should be examined to determine (1) what steps are legally required in order to give the borrower the right to freely sell the security and (2) how such steps are to be carried out in practice.

Transfers of foreign securities may also raise timing issues in that transfers of foreign securities will not always be simultaneous with transfers of collateral. Collateral will often be denominated in a different currency than the loaned securities and, if so, transfers of the loaned securities and collateral will not settle at the same time. If there is a time lag between the transfer of the loaned securities and the transfer of the collateral, the party making the first transfer will have an unsecured exposure to the other until the completion of both transfers. Typically, securities lending agreements provide for collateral to be delivered before (or at the same time as) the loaned security is delivered, and to be returned after (or at the same time as) the loaned security is returned. As a result, the risk of loss during the time lag between transfers will typically fall on the borrower, unless specific provisions in the relevant agreement state otherwise.

In addition, for loans of foreign securities, the parties should understand that transfers of the loaned securities and collateral can only occur on a day on which banks and securities markets are open for business generally in the places where the relevant securities and collateral are to be delivered, which may not be the same days on which the parties are open for business. The securities lending agreement should reflect this.

TRANSFER OF COLLATERAL

Transfers of collateral in international securities loans should be reviewed to determine (1) the legal requirements for the transfer to create a perfected security interest and (2) the practical steps needed to meet such requirements. (A perfected security interest in this context is one which gives the lender rights in the collateral that are superior to those of the unsecured creditors of the borrower even if the borrower is insolvent.) The legal issues raised by collateral transfers are often more difficult than those that arise in connection with transfers of a loaned security.

In a transfer of collateral, the first legal issue is what law governs the perfection of the lender's security interest in collateral. Generally, the law governing the perfection of the collateral will be the law where the collateral is located or, if the collateral is held in book-entry form at a financial intermediary, the law of the intermediary's jurisdiction. Under the New York choice of law rules, for example, the law governing the perfection of collateral in a physical security is the law of the jurisdiction where the security is located. Having determined which law governs perfection, the next issue to be determined is whether creation of a security interest and perfection is possible at all under such a law. For example, under English law, it is not possible to create a valid security interest over cash deposited with the secured party. If the security interest can be created and perfected, the issue then arises as to what steps are necessary under the relevant law to create and perfect the security interest. In some cases, it may not be feasible as a practical matter to take the steps needed for perfection. For example, under English law, security interests in the form of a floating charge created by a U.K. corporation must be registered by filing at a public registry within a strict time limit. This is impractical given the relatively short duration and high volume of securities lending arrangements. Moreover, registrations are open to the public and parties may not wish to disclose their securities lending activities.

Another issue that must be confronted with respect to collateral transfers is what use the lender can make of the collateral. In many instances, particularly if the lender is a broker-dealer and the collateral consists of securities, the lender will want to have the right to freely sell or pledge the collateral. The sale or pledge of collateral, often referred to as rehypothecation, may be permissible under New York and other U.S. state law, but often raises problems under the laws of other countries. For example, German law does not generally permit rehypothecation of collateral.

In some cases, the difficulties of creating a security interest in collateral and in arranging for rehypothecation have led parties to transfer collateral by granting full ownership rights, instead of only a security interest, to the lender. For example, the standard form English securities lending agreement provides for outright transfer of ownership of the collateral to the lender during the securities lending transaction, and return of ownership of the collateral to the borrower upon the termination of the lending transaction.

INSOLVENCY OF THE FOREIGN COUNTERPARTY

If a foreign counterparty in a securities lending transaction becomes insolvent, the court overseeing the foreign counterparty's insolvency may review the terms of the transaction. Typically, the court overseeing the insolvency will be in the jurisdiction where the counterparty is organized. The review of the securities lending transaction by such a court gives rise to two sets of legal issues. First, the court may consider whether the securities lending arrangement complies with the laws of the court's own jurisdiction, even if the securities lending agreement is governed by a different law. Second, the permissible procedures for closing out a securities lending arrangement against an insolvent counterparty will depend upon the relevant insolvency laws. Certain insolvency laws may impose a stay, for example, under which the counterparty of the insolvent entity cannot liquidate collateral without court approval.

AGENCY

In international securities lending transactions, agents often act on behalf of lenders. One crucial issue that arises in connection with such agents is whether securities held by the agents will be part of the property of the agent in the event of the agent's insolvency, thus exposing the principal to credit risk with respect to the agent. In the international context, the determination as to whether the securities become part of the property of the agent will generally be determined by the law of the jurisdiction where the agent is organized.

Another issue to be addressed with respect to international securities loans is that of the undisclosed principal. In certain cases, agents may act for lenders without disclosing to the borrower the identity of the lender. This raises issues as to whether or not the agent will be liable as principal to the borrower. In the international context, the issue is further complicated, if the parties are in different jurisdictions, by the need to determine which law determines the liabilities and rights of the agent. An additional issue is the extent of discretion of the agent, particularly with respect to investments of cash collateral, and the liability of the agent for losses resulting from such investments.

These matters should be addressed in the agency agreement, but the laws of the jurisdiction in which the agent operates may establish minimum standards of care for the agent, which may affect the agent's liability for losses incurred as a result of the agent's exercise of discretionary powers.

CONCLUSION

The legal issues that arise in connection with international securities lending, as discussed above, are not fundamentally different than those that arise in the domestic context. For purposes of legal analysis by a participant, the crucial difference between domestic and international transactions is that international transactions require the participant to consider familiar legal issues, such as due authority of a counterparty and appropriate transfer of collateral, under the laws of the various relevant jurisdictions and not only the laws of the jurisdiction where the participant is located.

Chapter 10

The Fundamentals of Fixed Income Securities

Frank J. Fabozzi
Adjunct Professor of Finance
School of Management
Yale University

A participant in the securities lending business should understand the characteristics of the collateral. The collateral can be classified as either equity securities or fixed income securities. In the latter category is a wide range of products with varying risk characteristics. The purpose of this chapter is to threefold. First, we describe the basic features of fixed income securities. Second, we look at the risk characteristics these securities, emphasizing the measurement of one key type of risk. Finally, we look at the issues associated with valuing fixed income securities.

FEATURES OF FIXED INCOME SECURITIES

The features of a fixed income security affect its value and how the security's price will change when interest rates change.

The Maturity of a Bond

The term to maturity of a bond is the number of years over which the issuer has promised to meet the conditions of the obligation. The maturity of a bond refers to the date that the debt will cease to exist, at which time the issuer will redeem the bond by paying the amount borrowed. The maturity date of a bond is always identified when describing a bond. For example, a description of a bond might state "due 12/1/2000."

The practice in the bond market, however, is to refer to the "term to maturity" of a bond as simply its "maturity" or "term." As we explain below, there may be provisions in the indenture that allow either the issuer or bondholder to alter a bond's term to maturity.

There are three reasons why the term to maturity of a bond is important. The most obvious is that it indicates the time period over which the bondholder can expect to receive the coupon payments and the number of years before the principal will be paid in full. The second reason is that the yield on a bond depends on it. Finally, the price of a bond will fluctuate over its life as yields in the market change. The price volatility of a bond is dependent on its maturity. More specifically, with all other factors constant, the longer the maturity of a bond, the greater the price volatility resulting from a change in market yields.

Par Value

The *par value* of a bond is the amount that the issuer agrees to repay the bondholder at the maturity date. This amount is also referred to as the *principal, face value, redemption value*, or *maturity value*. Bonds can have any par value.

Because bonds can have a different par value, the practice is to quote the price of a bond as a percentage of its par value. The par value is taken to be 100, which means 100% of par value. So, for example, if a bond has a par value of $1,000 and the issue is selling for $900, this bond would be said to be selling at 90. If a bond with a par value of $5,000 is selling for $5,500, the bond is said to be selling for 110.

Coupon Rate

The *coupon rate* is the interest rate that the issuer agrees to pay each year. The annual amount of the interest payment made to owners during the term of the bond is called the *coupon*. The coupon is determined by multiplying the coupon rate by the par value of the bond. For example, a bond with an 8% coupon rate and a principal of $1,000 will pay annual interest of $80.

When describing a bond issue, the coupon rate is indicated along with the maturity date. For example, the expression "6s of 12/1/2000" means a bond with a 6% coupon rate maturing on 12/1/2000.

In the United States, the usual practice is for the issuer to pay the coupon in two semiannual installments. Mortgage-backed securities and asset-backed securities typically pay interest monthly. For bonds issued in some markets outside the United States, coupon payments are made only once per year.

In addition to indicating the coupon payments that the investor should expect to receive over the term of the bond, the coupon rate also indicates the degree to which the bond's price will be affected by changes in interest rates. All other factors constant, the higher the coupon rate, the less the price will change in response to a change in interest rates. Consequently, the coupon rate and the term to maturity have opposite effects on a bond's price volatility.

Zero-Coupon Bonds Not all bonds make periodic coupon payments. Bonds that are not contracted to make periodic coupon payments are called *zero-coupon bonds*. The holder of a zero-coupon bond realizes interest by buying the bond substantially below its par value. Interest then is paid at the maturity date, with the interest being the difference between the par value and the price paid for the bond. So, for example, if an investor purchases a zero-coupon bond for 70, the interest is 30. This is the difference between the par value (100) and the price paid (70).

Floating-Rate Securities The coupon rate on a bond need not be fixed over the bond's life. *Floating-rate securities*, also called *variable rate securities*, have coupon payments that reset periodically according to some *reference rate*. The typical formula for the coupon rate at the dates when the coupon rate is reset is:

Reference rate + Index spread

The *index spread*, often referred to as simply spread, is the additional amount that the issuer agrees to pay above the reference rate. For example, suppose that the reference rate is the 1-month London inter-bank offered rate (LIBOR). Suppose that the index spread is 100 basis points. Then the coupon reset formula is:

1-month LIBOR + 100 basis points

So, if 1-month LIBOR on the coupon reset date is 5%, the coupon rate is reset for that period at 6% (5% plus 100 basis points).

The index spread need not be a positive value. The index spread could be subtracted from the reference rate. For example, the reference rate could be the yield on a 5-year Treasury security and the coupon rate could reset every six months based on the following coupon reset formula:

5-year Treasury yield – 50 basis points

So, if the 5-year Treasury yield is 7% on the coupon reset date, the coupon rate is 6.5% (7% minus 50 basis points).

The reference rate for most floating-rate securities is an interest rate or an interest rate index. There are some issues where this is not the case. Instead, the reference rate is some financial index such as the return on the Standard & Poor's 500 or a nonfinancial index, such as the price of a commodity. Through financial engineering, issuers have been able to structure floating-rate securities with almost any reference rate. These securities are called *structured notes*.

A floating-rate security may have a restriction on the maximum coupon rate that will be paid at a reset date. The maximum coupon rate is called a *cap*. For example, suppose for our hypothetical floating-rate security whose coupon rate formula is 1-month LIBOR plus 100 basis points, there is a cap of 11%. If 1-month LIBOR is 10.5% at a coupon reset date, then the coupon rate formula would give a value of 11.5%. However, the cap restricts the coupon rate to 11%. Thus, for our hypothetical security, once 1-month LIBOR exceeds 10%, the coupon rate is capped out at 11%.

Because a cap restricts the coupon rate from increasing, a cap is an unattractive feature for the investor. In contrast, there could be a minimum coupon rate specified for a floating-rate security. The minimum coupon rate is called a *floor*. If the coupon reset formula produces a coupon rate that is below the floor, the floor is paid instead. Thus, a floor is an attractive feature for the investor.

Inverse Floaters Typically, the coupon rate formula on floating-rate securities is such that the coupon rate increases when the reference rate increases, and decreases as the reference rate decreases. There are issues whose coupon rate moves in the opposite direction from the change in the reference rate. Such issues are called *inverse floaters* or *reverse floaters*. A general formula for an inverse floater is:

$$K - L \times (\text{Reference rate})$$

For example, suppose that for a particular inverse floater K is 12% and L is 1. Then the coupon reset formula would be:

$$12\% - \text{Reference rate}$$

Suppose that the reference rate is 1-month LIBOR, then the coupon reset formula would be

$$12\% - 1\text{-month LIBOR}$$

If in some month 1-month LIBOR at the coupon reset date is 5%, the coupon rate for the period is 7%. If in the next month 1-month LIBOR declines to 4.5%, the coupon rate increases to 7.5%.

Notice that if 1-month LIBOR exceeded 12%, then the coupon reset formula would produce a negative coupon rate. To prevent this, there is a floor imposed on the coupon rate. Typically, the floor is zero. While not explicitly stated, there is a cap on the floater. This occurs if 1-month LIBOR is zero. In that unlikely event, the maximum coupon rate is 12% for our hypothetical security. In general, it will be the value of K in the general coupon reset formula for a floating-rate security.

Suppose instead that the coupon reset formula for an inverse floater whose reference rate is 1-month LIBOR is as follows:

$$28\% - 3 \times (1\text{-month LIBOR})$$

If 1-month LIBOR at a reset date is 5%, then the coupon rate for that month is 13%. If in the next month 1-month LIBOR declines to 4%, the coupon rate is 16%. Thus, a decline in 1-month LIBOR of 100 basis points increases the coupon rate by 300 basis points. This is because the value for L in the inverse floater formula is 3. Thus, for each one basis point change in 1-month LIBOR the coupon rate changes by 3 basis points.

Provisions for Paying Off Bonds

Most bonds are *term bonds*; that is, they run for a term of years, then become due and payable. Any amount of the liability that has not been paid off prior to maturity must be paid off at that time. The term may be long or short. Term bonds may be retired by payment at final maturity or retired prior to maturity if provided for in the indenture.

Many issues have a call provisions allowing the issuer an option to buy back all or part of the issue prior to the stated maturity date. Some issues specify that the issuer must retire a predetermined amount of the issue periodically. Various types of call provisions are discussed below.

An issuer generally wants the right to retire a bond issue prior to the stated maturity date because it recognizes that at some time in the future the general level of interest rates may fall sufficiently below the issue's coupon rate so that redeeming the issue and replacing it with another issue with a lower coupon rate would be beneficial. This right is a disadvantage to the bondholder since proceeds received must be reinvested at a lower interest rate. As a result, an issuer who wants to include this right as part of a bond offering must compensate the bondholder when the issue is sold by offering a higher yield, or equivalently, accepting a lower price than if the right is not included.

The right of the issuer to retire the issue prior to the stated maturity date is referred to as a *call option*. If an issuer exercises this right, the issuer is said to "call the bond." The price which the issuer must pay to retire the issue is referred to as the *call price*. Typically, there is not one call price but a *call schedule* which sets forth a call price based on when the issuer can exercise the call option. When a bond is issued, typically the issuer may not call the bond for a number of years. That is, the issue is said to have a *deferred call*. The date at which the bond may first be called is referred to as the *first call date*. Generally, the call schedule is such that the call price at the first call date is a premium over the par value and scaled down to the par value over time. The date at which the issue is first callable at par value is referred to as the *first par call date*.

If a bond issue does not have any protection against early call, then it is said to be a currently callable issue. But most new bond issues, even if currently callable, usually have some restrictions against certain types of early redemption. The most common restriction is that prohibiting the *refunding* of the bonds for a certain number of years. Bonds that are noncallable for the issue's life are more common than bonds which are nonrefundable for life but otherwise callable.

Many investors are confused by the term noncallable and nonrefundable. Call protection is much more absolute than refunding protection. While there may be certain exceptions to absolute or complete call protection in some cases (such as sinking funds and the redemption of debt under certain mandatory provisions), it still provides greater assurance against premature and unwanted redemption than does refunding protection. Refunding prohibition merely prevents redemption only from certain sources, namely the proceeds of other debt issues sold at a lower cost of money. The bondholder is only protected if interest rates decline, and the borrower can obtain lower-cost money to pay off the debt.

Options Granted to Bondholders

Many securities contain an option that grants either the issuer or the investor the right to alter the cash flow of the security. Such an option is referred to as an *embedded option* — it is embedded within the security as opposed to being a stand alone option. A callable bond is the most common example of a bond with an embedded option. A callable bond is one in which the issuer has the right to alter the maturity date of the bond. There may be a provision that allows the bondholder to alter the maturity. This occurs if the bond is putable or convertible.

Put Provision An issue with a *put provision* included in the indenture grants the bondholder the right to sell the issue back to the issuer at a specified price on designated dates. The specified price is called the *put price*.

Convertible Bond A *convertible bond* is an issue giving the bond-holder the right to exchange the bond for a specified number of shares of common stock. Such a feature allows the bondholder to take advantage of favorable movements in the price of the issuer's common stock. An *exchangeable bond* allows the bondholder to exchange the issue for a specified number of common stock shares of a corporation different from the issuer of the bond.

The number of shares of common stock that the bondholder will receive from converting is called the *conversion ratio*. The conversion privilege may extend for all or only some portion of the security's life, and the stated conversion ratio may change over time. It is always adjusted proportionately for stock splits and stock dividends.

Almost all convertible issues are callable by the issuer. Some convertible bonds are putable. Put options can be classified as "hard" puts and "soft" puts. A hard put is one in which the convertible security must be redeemed by the issuer only for cash. In the case of a soft put, the issuer has the option to redeem the convertible security for cash, common stock, subordinated notes, or a combination of the three.

Currency Denomination

The payments that the issuer of a bond makes to the bondholder can be in any currency. For bonds issued in the United States, the issuer typically makes both coupon payments and principal repayments in U.S. dollars. However, there is nothing that forces the issuer to make payments in this way. The indenture can specify that the issuer can make payments in some other specified currency. For example, payments can be made in French francs.

An issue in which payments to bondholders are in U.S. dollars is called a *dollar-denominated issue*. A *nondollar-denominated issue* is one in which payments are not denominated in U.S. dollars. There are some issues whose coupon payment is in one currency and whose principal payment is in another currency. An issue with this characteristic is called a *dual-currency issue*.

Some issues grant either the issuer or the bondholder the right to select the currency in which a payment will be paid. This option effectively gives the party with the right to choose the currency the opportunity to benefit from a favorable exchange rate movement.

RISKS ASSOCIATED WITH INVESTING IN FIXED INCOME SECURITIES

A lender of securities who accepts a fixed income security as collateral, must understand its risk characteristics. In this section we describe the different types of risk that an investor in fixed income securities is exposed to: (1) interest rate risk, (2) call or timing risk, (3) credit risk, (4) liquidity risk, (5) exchange rate or currency risk, and (6) volatility risk. There are other risks associated with managing a fixed income portfolio that we will discuss in Chapter 13.

Interest Rate Risk

The price of a fixed income security moves in the opposite direction to the change in interest rates: as interest rates rise (fall), the price of a fixed income security will fall (rise). Exhibit 1 illustrates this property for four hypothetical bonds, where the bond prices are shown assuming a par value of $100.

The risk that interest rates will rise and that the price of the security will fall is called *interest rate risk*. The degree of interest rate risk for any security depends on various characteristics of the security such as coupon and maturity, and options embedded in the security.

Exhibit 1: Price/Yield Relationship for Four Hypothetical Bonds

Yield (%)	Price ($)			
	6%/5 year	6%/20 year	9%/5 year	9%/20 year
4.00	108.9826	127.3555	122.4565	168.3887
5.00	104.3760	112.5514	117.5041	150.2056
5.50	102.1600	106.0195	115.1201	142.1367
5.90	100.4276	101.1651	113.2556	136.1193
5.99	100.0427	100.1157	112.8412	134.8159
6.00	100.0000	100.0000	112.7953	134.6722
6.01	99.9574	99.8845	112.7494	134.5287
6.10	99.5746	98.8535	112.3373	133.2472
6.50	97.8944	94.4479	110.5280	127.7605
7.00	95.8417	89.3225	108.3166	121.3551
8.00	91.8891	80.2072	104.0554	109.8964

Exhibit 2: Instantaneous Percentage Price Change for Four Hypothetical Bonds
(Initial yield for all four bonds is 6%)

New Yield (%)	Percent Price Change			
	6%/5 year	6%/20 year	9%/5 year	9%/20 year
4.00	8.98	27.36	8.57	25.04
5.00	4.38	12.55	4.17	11.53
5.50	2.16	6.02	2.06	5.54
5.90	0.43	1.17	0.41	1.07
5.99	0.04	0.12	0.04	0.11
6.01	−0.04	−0.12	−0.04	−0.11
6.10	−0.43	−1.15	−0.41	−1.06
6.50	−2.11	−5.55	−2.01	−5.13
7.00	−4.16	−10.68	−3.97	−9.89
8.00	−8.11	−19.79	−7.75	−18.40

Properties of Option-Free Bonds Exhibit 2 uses the four hypothetical bonds in Exhibit 1 to show the percentage change in each bond's price for various changes in yield, assuming that the initial yield for all four bonds is 6%. An examination of Exhibit 2 reveals several properties concerning the price volatility of an option-free bond.

> *Property 1:* Although the prices of all option-free bonds move in the opposite direction from the change in yield, the percentage price change is not the same for all bonds.
>
> *Property 2:* For small changes in yield, the percentage price change for a given bond is roughly the same, whether the yield increases or decreases.
>
> *Property 3:* For large changes in yield, the percentage price change is not the same for an increase in yield as it is for a decrease in yield.
>
> *Property 4:* For a given large change in basis points, the percentage price increase is greater than the percentage price decrease.

Characteristics of a Bond that Affect its Price Volatility

There are two characteristics of an option-free bond that determine its price volatility: coupon and term to maturity.

Characteristic 1: For a given term to maturity and initial yield, the lower the coupon rate the greater the price volatility of a bond.

Characteristic 2: For a given coupon rate and initial yield, the longer the term to maturity, the greater the price volatility.

These properties can be verified by examining Exhibit 2.

The Effects of Yield to Maturity We cannot ignore the fact that credit considerations cause different bonds to trade at different yields, even if they have the same coupon and maturity. How, then, holding other factors constant, does the yield to maturity affect a bond's price volatility? As it turns out, the higher the yield to maturity that a bond trades at, the lower the price volatility.

To see this, we can compare a 6% 20-year bond initially selling at a yield of 6%, and a 6% 20-year bond initially selling at a yield of 10%. The former is initially at a price of 100, and the latter carries a price of 65.68. Now, if the yield on both bonds increase by 100 basis points, the first bond trades down by 10.68 points (10.68%). After the assumed increase in yield, the second bond will trade at a price of 59.88, for a price decline of only 5.80 points (or 8.83%). Thus, we see that the bond that trades at a lower yield is more volatile in both percentage price change and absolute price change, as long as the other bond characteristics are the same.

An implication of this is that, for a given change in yields, price volatility is lower when the yield level in the market is high, and price volatility is higher when the yield level is low.

Duration as a Measure of Interest Rate Risk The most obvious way to measure a bond's price sensitivity to changes in interest rates is to change rates by a small number of basis points and calculate how the security's value will change. The name popularly used to refer to the approximate percentage price change is *duration*. It can be demonstrated that the following formula gives the approximate percentage price change for a 100 basis point change in yield:

$$\frac{\text{Value if rates fall} - \text{Value if rates rise}}{2(\text{Initial value})(\text{Change in yield in decimal form})}$$

where "value if rates fall" is the estimated value of the security if the yield falls by a small number of basis points, "value if rates rise" is the estimated value of the security if the yield rises by the same number of basis points, "initial value" is the current price, and "change in yield in decimal form" is the number of basis points by which the yield is changed to obtain the values in the numerator.

To illustrate the duration calculation, consider the following option-free bond: a 6% coupon 5-year bond trading at par to yield 6%. The initial value is 100. Suppose the yield is changed by 50 basis points. Thus, the change in yield in decimal form is 0.005. If the yield is decreased to 5.5%, the value of this bond would be 102.1600 (see Exhibit 1). If the yield is increased to 6.5%, the value of this bond would be 97.8944 (see Exhibit 1). Substituting these values into the duration formula

$$\text{Duration} = \frac{102.1600 - 97.8944}{2(100)(0.005)} = 4.27$$

The duration of a security can be interpreted as the approximate percentage change in the price for a 100 basis point change in yield. Thus a bond with a duration of 4.8 will change by approximately 4.8% for a 100 basis point change in yield. For a 50 basis point yield change, the bond's price will change by approximately 2.4%; for a 25 basis point yield change, 1.2%, etc.

It is important to understand that the two values used in the numerator of the formulas are obtained from a valuation model. Consequently, *the resulting measure of the price sensitivity of a security to interest rates changes is only as good as the valuation model employed to obtain the estimated value of the security.* We discuss valuation models later in this chapter.

Dollar Duration Duration is related to percentage price change. However, for two bonds with the same duration, the dollar price change will not be the same if they differ in coupon, maturity, or yield. For example, consider two bonds, W and X. Suppose that both bonds have a duration of 5, but that W is trading at par while X is trading at 90. A 100 basis point change for both bonds will change the price by approximately 5%. This means a price change of $5 (5% times $100) for W and a price change of $4.5 (5% times $90) for V.

The dollar price volatility of a bond can be measured by multiplying modified duration by the dollar price and the number of basis points (in decimal form) and is called the *dollar duration.*

Modified Duration versus Effective Duration A popular form of duration that is used by practitioners is *modified duration.* Modified duration is the approximate percentage change in a bond's price for a 100 basis point yield change assuming that the bond's cash flow does *not* change when the yield changes. What this means is that in calculating the values used in the numerator of the duration formula, the cash flow used to calculate the initial value is assumed. Therefore, the change in the bond's value when the yield changed by a small number of basis points is due solely to discounting at the new yield level.

The assumption that the cash flow will not change when the yield changes makes sense for option-free bonds such as noncallable Treasury securities. This is because the payments made by the U.S. Department of the Treasury to holders of its obligations does not change when yields change. However, the same can not be said for callable and putable bonds and mortgage-backed securities. For these securities, a change in yield will alter the expected cash flow.

The price/yield relationship for callable bonds and mortgage passthrough securities is different from that of an option-free bond. As yields in the market decline, the likelihood that yields will decline further so that the issuer or homeowner will benefit from calling the bond or refinancing a mortgage increases. As a result, when rates decline, while the price of a callable bond or mortgage passthrough security will rise, it will not increase by as much as an otherwise option-free bond. For example, suppose the market yield is such that an option-free bond would be selling for 109. Suppose instead that it is callable at 104. Investors would not pay 109. If they did and the bond is called, investors would receive 104 (the call price) for a bond they purchased for 109. For a range of yields there will be price compression — that is, there is limited price appreciation as yields decline. Because of this characteristic, callable bonds are said to have *negative convexity.*

Negative convexity means that the price appreciation will be less than the price depreciation for a large change in yield of a given number of basis points. For a bond that is option-free the price appreciation will be greater than the price depreciation for a large change in yield (Property 4). A bond with this characteristic is said to exhibit *positive convexity.* The price changes resulting from bonds exhibiting positive convexity and negative convexity can be expressed as follows:

	Absolute value of percentage price change for:	
Change in interest rates	Positive convexity	Negative convexity
−100 basis points	X%	less than Y%
+100 basis points	less than X%	Y%

A valuation model should take into account how yield changes will affect cash flow. Thus, when the values used in the numerator are obtained from these valuation models, the resulting duration takes into account both the discounting at different interest rates and how the cash flow can change. When duration is calculated in this manner, it is referred to as *effective duration.* Exhibit 3 summarizes the distinction between modified duration and effective duration.

The difference between modified duration and effective duration for fixed income securities with an embedded option can be quite dramatic. For example, a callable bond could have a modified duration of 6 but an effective duration of only 2. For certain collateralized mortgage obligations, the modified duration could be 7 and the effective duration 40! Thus, using modified duration as a measure of the price sensitivity of a security to yield changes would be misleading. The more appropriate measure for a security with an embedded option is effective duration.

Exhibit 3: Modified Duration Versus Effective Duration

Duration
Interpretation: Generic description of the sensitivity of a bond's price (as a percentage of initial price) to a parallel shift in the yield curve

Modified Duration	*Effective Duration*
Duration measure in which it is assumed that yield changes do not change the expected cash flow	Duration in which recognition is given to the fact that yield changes may change the expected cash flow

Call or Timing Risk

From the investor's perspective, there are three disadvantages of the call provision. First, the cash flow pattern of a callable bond is not known with certainty. Second, because the issuer will call the bonds when interest rates have dropped, the investor is exposed to reinvestment risk. That is, the investor will have to reinvest the proceeds received when the bond is called at relatively lower interest rates. Finally, the capital appreciation potential of a bond will be reduced. That is, callable bonds exhibit negative convexity. Collectively, these risks are referred to as *call risk* or *timing risk*.

These risks also exist with mortgage-backed securities and asset-backed securities whose cash flow may depend on the level of interest rates. In the case of mortgage-backed securities, the cash flow depends on prepayments of principal made by the homeowners in the pool of mortgages that serves as collateral for the security. The timing risk in this case is called *prepayment risk*.

Credit Risk

Credit risk or *default risk* refers to the risk that the issuer of a security may default, i.e., will be unable to make timely principal and interest payments. Credit risk is gauged by quality ratings assigned by commercial rating companies such as Moody's Investor Service, Standard & Poor's Corporation, Duff & Phelps, and Fitch Investors Service. The rating systems use similar symbols, as shown in Exhibit 4.

In all systems the term high grade means low credit risk, or conversely, high probability of future payments. The highest-grade bonds are designated by Moody's by the symbol Aaa, and by the other three rating systems by the symbol AAA. The next highest grade is denoted by the symbol Aa (Moody's) or AA (the other three rating systems); for the third grade all rating systems use A. The next three grades are Baa or BBB, Ba or BB, and B, respectively. There are also C grades. Moody's uses 1, 2, or 3 to provide a narrower credit quality breakdown within each class, and the other three rating companies use plus and minus signs for the same purpose.

Bonds rated triple A (AAA or Aaa) are said to be *prime*; double A (AA or Aa) are of *high quality*; single A issues are called *upper medium grade*, and triple B are *medium grade*. Lower-rated bonds are said to have speculative elements or be distinctly speculative.

Exhibit 4: Summary of Corporate Bond Rating Systems and Symbols

D&P	Fitch	Moody's	S&P	Summary Description
Investment Grade — High-Creditworthiness				
AAA	AAA	Aaa	AAA	Gilt edge, prime, maximum safety
AA+	AA+	Aa1	AA+	
AA	AA	Aa2	AA	High-grade, high credit quality
AA-	AA-	Aa3	AA-	
A+	A+	A1	A+	
A	A	A2	A	Upper-medium grade
A-	A-	A3	A-	
BBB+	BBB+	Baa1	BBB+	
BBB	BBB	Baa2	BBB	Lower-medium grade
BBB-	BBB-	Baa3	BBB-	
Speculative — Lower Creditworthiness				
BB+	BB+	Ba1	BB+	
BB	BB	Ba2	BB	Low grade, speculative
BB-	BB-	Ba3	BB-	
B+	B+	B1	B+	
B	B	B2	B	Highly speculative
B-	B-	B3	B-	
Predominantly Speculative, Substantial Risk or in Default				
	CCC+		CCC+	
CCC	CCC	Caa	CCC	Substantial risk, in poor standing
	CC	Ca	CC	May be in default, very speculative
	C	C	C	Extremely speculative
			CI	Income bonds — no interest being paid
	DDD			
DD	DD			Default
	D		D	

Bond issues that are assigned a rating in the top four categories are referred to as *investment grade bonds*. Issues that carry a rating below the top four categories are referred to as *non-investment grade bonds*, or more popularly as *high yield bonds* or *junk bonds*. Thus, the bond market is divided into two sectors: the investment grade and non-investment grade markets.

Ratings of bonds change over time. Issuers are upgraded when their likelihood of default as assessed by the rating company improves and downgraded when their likelihood of default as assessed by the rating company deteriorates. The rating companies publish the issues that they are reviewing for possible rating change. These lists are called credit watch lists.

Occasionally the ability of an issuer to make interest and principal payments changes seriously and unexpectedly because of (1) a natural or industrial accident or some regulatory change, or (2) a takeover or corporate restructuring. These risks are referred to generically as *event risk* and will result in a downgrading of the issuer by the rating agencies.

Liquidity Risk

For an individual security, liquidity risk involves the ease with which an issue can be sold at or near its value. The primary measure of liquidity is the size of the spread between the bid price and the offered price quoted by a dealer. The greater the dealer spread, the greater the liquidity risk.

Exchange Rate or Currency Risk

A non-dollar-denominated bond (i.e. a bond whose payments occur in a foreign currency) has unknown U.S. dollar cash flows. The dollar cash flows are dependent on the foreign-exchange rate at the time the payments are received. For example, suppose an investor purchases a bond whose payments are in Japanese yen. If the yen depreciates relative to the U.S. dollar, then fewer dollars will be received. The risk of this occurring is referred to as *exchange rate* or *currency risk*. Of course, should the yen appreciate relative to the U.S. dollar, the investor will benefit by receiving more dollars.

In addition to the change in the exchange rate, an investor is exposed to the interest rate risk in the local market. For example, if a U.S. investor purchases German government bonds denominated in deutsche marks, the proceeds received from that bond if it is sold prior to maturity will depend on the level of interest rates in the German bond market, in addition to the exchange rate.

Volatility Risk

As will be explained in the next section, the price of a bond with an embedded option depends on the level of interest rates and factors that influence the value of the embedded option. One of the factors is the expected volatility of interest rates. Specifically, the value of an option rises when expected interest rate volatility increases. In the case of a callable bond or mortgage-backed security, since the investor has granted an option to the borrower, the price of the security falls because the investor has given away a more valuable option. The risk that a change in expected volatility will adversely affect the price of a security is called *volatility risk.*

VALUING FIXED INCOME SECURITIES

Valuation is the process of determining the fair value of a financial asset. The fundamental principle of valuation is that the value of any financial asset is the present value of the expected cash flow. This principle applies regardless of the financial asset. Here we will explain the general principles of fixed income valuation highlighting the complications involved with the process. It is because of these complications that there can be significant differences in the value assigned to a complex security with one or more embedded options.

Estimating Cash Flow

Cash flow is simply the cash that is expected to be received each period from an investment. In the case of a fixed income security, it does not make any difference whether the cash flow is interest income or repayment of principal.

The cash flow for only a few types of fixed income securities are simple to project. Noncallable Treasury securities have a known cash flow. For a Treasury coupon security, the cash flow is the coupon interest payments every six months up to the maturity date and the principal payment at the maturity date. So, for example, the cash flow per $100 of par value for a 7%, 10-year Treasury security is the following: $3.5 (7%/2 × $100) every six months for the next 20 6-month periods and $100 20 6-month periods from now. In fact, for any fixed income security in which neither the issuer nor the investor can alter the repayment of the principal before its contractual due date, the cash flow can easily be determined assuming that the issuer does not default.

It is difficult to estimate the cash flow for a fixed income security where (1) either the issuer or the investor has the option to change the contractual due date of the repayment of the principal or (2) the coupon payment is reset periodically based on a formula that depends on some value or values for reference rates, prices, or exchange rates. Callable bonds, putable bonds, and mortgage-backed securities are examples of the former; floating-rate securities and structured notes are examples of the latter.

A key factor determining whether either the issuer of the security or the investor would exercise an option is the level of interest rates in the future relative to the security's coupon rate. Specifically, for a callable bond, if the prevailing market rate at which the issuer can call an issue is sufficiently below the issue's coupon rate to justify the costs associated with refunding the issue, the issuer is likely to call the issue. Similarly, for a mortgage loan, if the prevailing refinancing rate available in the mortgage market is sufficiently below the loan's rate so that there will be savings by refinancing after considering the associated refinancing costs, then the homeowner has an incentive to refinance. For a putable bond, if the rate on comparable securities rises such that the value of the putable bond falls below the value at which it must be repurchased by the issuer, then the investor will put the issue.

What this means is that to properly estimate the cash flow of a fixed income security it is necessary to incorporate into the analysis how interest rates can change in the future and how such changes affect the cash flow. This is done in valuation models by introducing a parameter that reflects the expected volatility of interest rates.

Discounting the Cash Flow

Once the cash flow for a fixed income security is estimated, the next step is to determine the appropriate interest rate. To do so, the investor must address the following three questions:

1. What is the minimum interest rate the investor should require?
2. How much more than the minimum interest rate should the investor require?
3. Should the investor use the same interest rate for each estimated cash flow or a unique interest rate for each estimated cash flow?

The minimum interest rate that an investor should require is the yield available in the marketplace on a default-free cash flow. In the United States, this is the yield on a U.S. Treasury security. The premium over the yield on a Treasury security that the investor should require should reflect the risks associated with realizing the estimated cash flow.

The traditional practice in valuation has been to discount every cash flow of a fixed income security by the same interest rate (or discount rate). For example, consider three hypothetical 10-year Treasury securities: a 12% coupon bond, an 8% coupon bond, and a zero-coupon bond. Since the cash flow of all three securities is viewed as default free, the traditional practice is to use the same discount rate to calculate the present value of all three securities and the same discount for the cash flow for each period.

The fundamental flaw of the traditional approach is that it views each security as the same package of cash flows. For example, consider a 10-year U.S. Treasury bond with an 8% coupon rate. The cash flow per $100 of par value would be 19 payments of $4 every six months and $104 20 six-month period from now. The traditional practice would discount every cash flow using the same interest rate.

The proper way to view a 10-year 8% coupon bond is as a package of zero-coupon instruments. Each cash flow should be considered a zero-coupon instrument whose maturity value is the amount of the cash flow and whose maturity date is the date of the cash flow. Thus, a 10-year 8% coupon bond should be viewed as 20 zero-coupon instruments.

By viewing any financial asset in this way, a consistent valuation framework can be developed. For example, under the traditional approach to the valuation of fixed income securities, a 10-year zero-coupon bond would be viewed as the same financial asset as a 10-year 8% coupon bond. Viewing a financial asset as a package of zero-coupon instruments means that these two bonds would be viewed as different packages of zero-coupon instruments and valued accordingly.

Valuation Models

The purpose of a valuation model is to provide a theoretical value for a security. Such models are often used for marking to market securities that are infrequently traded.

Valuation models incorporate the general principles that we discussed above. There are assumptions that underlie all valuation models. Some assumptions can have quite a dramatic impact on the theoretical value generated by the model. Consequently, the user of a valuation model is subject to *modeling risk*. To manage modeling risk, the sensitivity of a valuation model should be stressed tested with respect to the underlying assumptions. One particularly important assumption is the expected yield volatility.

There are two valuation models that are commonly used — the binomial model and the Monte Carlo simulation model. A description of these models is beyond the scope of this chapter.[1] The *binomial model* is used to value non-mortgage-backed products. The Monte Carlo simulation model is used to value mortgage-backed securities.

SUMMARY

In this chapter we looked at the basic features of fixed income securities, the risk characteristics of these securities, and the issues associated with valuing fixed income securities.

We emphasized one particularly important risk, interest rate risk. This is the risk that the value of a fixed income security will decline when interest rates rise. The characteristics of a security that

---

[1] For an explanation of these valuation models, see Frank J. Fabozzi, *Valuation of Fixed Income Securities and Derivatives* (New Hope, PA: Frank J. Fabozzi Associates, 1995).

affect its interest rate risk are coupon and term to maturity. Duration is a measure of interest rate risk. Modified duration is an inferior measure for securities with an embedded option. Instead, effective duration should be used and is a by-product of a valuation model.

Valuing a fixed income security requires that the expected cash flow be projected and appropriate interest rates be used to discount the cash flow. It is not a simple task to project cash flow or determine the appropriate discount rate for securities with embedded options. Valuation models are used to determine the theoretical value. However, these models are dependent on the underlying assumptions.

Chapter 11

Overview of Mortgage-Backed and Asset-Backed Securities

Frank J. Fabozzi
Adjunct Professor of Finance
School of Management
Yale University

An important innovation in the financial market is the securitization of assets. Asset securitization is the process of pooling assets and using the pool formed as collateral for a security. The securities created are referred to as *asset-backed securities*. By far, the largest category of assets that have been securitized in the United States and Europe are residential mortgages. Such securities are called *mortgage-backed securities*. While mortgage-backed securities are a special type of asset-backed securities, market participants commonly refer to asset-backed securities as securities backed by a pool of non-traditional residential mortgages.

The purpose of this chapter is to provide an overview of the various types of mortgage-backed securities and asset-backed securities. Because of the characteristics of mortgage-backed securities and the significant volume of collateralized borrowing using these securities, a special type of repurchase agreement is used called a *dollar roll*. This arrangement is described in Chapter 12.

MORTGAGE-BACKED SECURITIES

Mortgage-backed securities are securities backed by a pool of mortgage loans. While any type of mortgage loans, residential or commercial, can

141

be used as collateral for a mortgage-backed security, most are backed by residential mortgages. Mortgage-backed securities include the following securities: (1) mortgage passthrough securities, (2) collateralized mortgage obligations, and (3) stripped mortgage-backed securities. The latter two mortgage-backed securities are referred to as *derivative mortgage-backed securities* because they are created from mortgage passthrough securities.

Mortgages

A mortgage is a loan secured by the collateral of some specified real estate property which obliges the borrower to make a predetermined series of payments. The mortgage gives the lender the right, if the borrower defaults (i.e. fails to make the contractual payments), to "foreclose" on the loan and seize the property in order to ensure that the debt is paid off. The interest rate on the mortgage loan is called the *mortgage rate.*

When the lender makes the loan based on the credit of the borrower and on the collateral for the mortgage, the mortgage is said to be a *conventional mortgage.* The lender also may take out mortgage insurance to guarantee the fulfillment of the borrower's obligations. Some borrowers can qualify for mortgage insurance which is guaranteed by one of three U.S. government agencies: the Federal Housing Administration (FHA), the Veteran's Administration (VA), and the Farmers Home Administration. There are also private mortgage insurers. The cost of mortgage insurance is paid to the guarantor by the mortgage originator, but it is passed along to the borrower in the form of higher mortgage payments.

There are many types of mortgage designs available in the United States. A mortgage design is a specification of the interest rate, term of the mortgage, and the manner in which the borrowed funds are repaid. The most common type is the fixed-rate level-payment, fully amortized mortgage.

The basic idea behind this mortgage design is that the borrower pays interest and repays principal in equal installments over an agreed-upon period of time, called the maturity or term of the mortgage. Thus at the end of the term, the loan has been fully amortized. The frequency of payment is typically monthly, and the prevailing term of the mortgage is 15 to 30 years.

Each monthly mortgage payment is due on the first of each month and consists of:

1. interest of ¹⁄₁₂th of the fixed annual interest rate times the amount of the outstanding mortgage balance at the beginning of the previous month, and
2. a repayment of a portion of the outstanding mortgage balance (principal).

The difference between the monthly mortgage payment and the portion of the payment that represents interest is equal to the amount that is applied to reduce the outstanding mortgage balance. The monthly mortgage payment is designed so that after the last scheduled monthly payment of the loan is made, the amount of the outstanding mortgage balance is zero (i.e., the mortgage is fully repaid).

To illustrate a fixed-rate level-payment, fully amortized mortgage, consider a 30-year (360-month), $100,000 mortgage with a 8.125% mortgage rate. The monthly mortgage payment would be $742.50. Exhibit 1 shows for selected months how each monthly mortgage payment is divided between interest and repayment of principal. At the beginning of month 1, the mortgage balance is $100,000, the amount of the original loan. The mortgage payment for month 1 includes interest on the $100,000 borrowed for the month. Since the interest rate is 8.125%, the monthly interest rate is 0.0067708 (0.08125 divided by 12). Interest for month 1 is therefore $677.08 ($100,000 times 0.0067708). The $65.41 difference between the monthly mortgage payment of $742.50 and the interest of $677.08 is the portion of the monthly mortgage payment that represents repayment of principal. This $65.41 in month 1 reduces the mortgage balance.

The mortgage balance at the end of month 1 (beginning of month 2) is then $99,934.59 ($100,000 minus $65.41). The interest for the second monthly mortgage payment is $676.64, the monthly interest rate (0.0066708) times the mortgage balance at the beginning of month 2 ($99,934.59). The difference between the $742.50 monthly mortgage payment and the $676.64 interest is $65.86, representing the amount of the mortgage balance paid off with that monthly mortgage payment. Notice that the last mortgage payment in month 360 is sufficient to pay off the remaining mortgage balance.

Exhibit 1: Amortization Schedule for a Fixed-Rate Level-Payment, Fully Amortized Mortgage

Mortgage loan: $100,000
Mortgage rate: 8.125%
Monthly payment: $742.50
Term of loan: 30 years (360 months)

	Beginning of month mortgage balance	Monthly payment	Monthly Interest	Scheduled principal repayment	Ending mortgage balance
1	$100,000.00	$742.50	$677.08	$65.41	$99,934.59
2	99,934.59	742.50	676.64	65.86	99,868.73
3	99,868.73	742.50	676.19	66.30	99,802.43
4	99,802.43	742.50	675.75	66.75	99,735.68
25	98,301.53	742.50	665.58	76.91	98,224.62
26	98,224.62	742.50	665.06	77.43	98,147.19
27	98,147.19	742.50	664.54	77.96	98,069.23
74	93,849.98	742.50	635.44	107.05	93,742.93
75	93,742.93	742.50	634.72	107.78	93,635.15
76	93,635.15	742.50	633.99	108.51	93,526.64
141	84,811.77	742.50	574.25	168.25	84,643.52
142	84,643.52	742.50	573.11	169.39	84,474.13
143	84,474.13	742.50	571.96	170.54	84,303.59
184	76,446.29	742.50	517.61	224.89	76,221.40
185	76,221.40	742.50	516.08	226.41	75,994.99
186	75,994.99	742.50	514.55	227.95	75,767.04
233	63,430.19	742.50	429.48	313.02	63,117.17
234	63,117.17	742.50	427.36	315.14	62,802.03
235	62,802.03	742.50	425.22	317.28	62,484.75
289	42,200.92	742.50	285.74	456.76	41,744.15
290	41,744.15	742.50	282.64	459.85	41,284.30
291	41,284.30	742.50	279.53	462.97	40,821.33
321	25,941.42	742.50	175.65	566.85	25,374.57
322	25,374.57	742.50	171.81	570.69	24,803.88
323	24,803.88	742.50	167.94	574.55	24,229.32
358	2,197.66	742.50	14.88	727.62	1,470.05
359	1,470.05	742.50	9.95	732.54	737.50
360	737.50	742.50	4.99	737.50	0.00

As Exhibit 1 clearly shows, *the portion of the monthly mortgage payment applied to interest declines each month and the portion applied to reducing the mortgage balance increases.* The reason for this is that as the mortgage balance is reduced with each monthly mortgage payment, the interest on the mortgage balance declines. Since the monthly mortgage payment is fixed, an increasingly larger portion of the monthly payment is applied to reduce the principal in each subsequent month.

Our illustration assumes that the homeowner does not pay off any portion of the mortgage balance prior to the scheduled due date. But homeowners do pay off all or part of their mortgage balance prior to the maturity date. Payments made in excess of the scheduled principal repayments are called *prepayments*.

Prepayments occur for one of several reasons. First, homeowners prepay the entire mortgage when they sell their home because of a change of employment that necessitates moving or the purchase of a more expensive home. Second, the borrower may be moved to pay off part of the mortgage balance as market rates fall below the mortgage rate. This is referred to as refinancing a mortgage. Third, in the case of homeowners who cannot meet their mortgage obligations, the property is repossessed and sold. The proceeds of such a sale are used to pay off the mortgage in the case of a conventional mortgage. For an insured mortgage, the insurer will pay off the mortgage balance. Finally, if property is destroyed by fire or if another insured catastrophe occurs, the insurance proceeds are used to pay off the mortgage.

The effect of prepayments is that the amount and timing of the cash flow from a mortgage is not known with certainty. This risk is referred to as *prepayment risk*. For example, all that the investor in a $100,000, 8.125% 30-year FHA-insured mortgage knows is that as long as the loan is outstanding, interest will be received and the principal will be repaid at the scheduled date each month; then at the end of the 30 years, the investor would have received $100,000 in principal payments. What the investor does not know — the uncertainty — is for how long the loan will be outstanding, and therefore what the timing of the principal payments will be. This is true for all mortgage loans, not just fixed-rate level-payment, fully amortized mortgages.

Mortgage Passthrough Securities

A mortgage passthrough security is created when one or more holders of mortgages form a collection (pool) of mortgages and sell shares or participation certificates in the pool. A pool may consist of several thousand or only a few mortgages.

Cash Flow The cash flow of a mortgage passthrough security depends on the cash flow of the underlying mortgages. As we explained for mortgages, the cash flow consists of monthly mortgage payments representing interest, the scheduled repayment of principal, and any prepayments.

Payments are made to securityholders each month. However, neither the amount nor the timing of the cash flow from the pool of mortgages is identical to that of the cash flow passed through to investors. The monthly cash flow for a passthrough is less than the monthly cash flow of the underlying mortgages by an amount equal to servicing and other fees. The other fees are those charged by the issuer or guarantor of the passthrough for guaranteeing the issue (discussed later). The coupon rate on a passthrough, called the *passthrough coupon rate*, is less than the mortgage rate on the underlying pool of mortgage loans by an amount equal to the servicing and guaranteeing fees.

The timing of the cash flow is also different. The monthly mortgage payment is due from each mortgagor on the first day of each month, but there is a delay in passing through the corresponding monthly cash flow to the securityholders. The length of the delay varies by the type of passthrough security.

WAC and WAM Not all of the mortgages that are included in a pool of mortgages that are securitized have the same mortgage rate and the same maturity. Consequently, when describing a passthrough security, a weighted average coupon rate and a weighted average maturity are determined. A *weighted average coupon rate*, or WAC, is found by weighting the mortgage rate of each mortgage loan in the pool by the amount of the mortgage outstanding. A *weighted average maturity*, or WAM, is found by weighting the remaining number of months to maturity for each mortgage loan in the pool by the amount of the mortgage outstanding.

Types of Mortgage Passthrough Securities In the United

States, the three major types of passthrough securities are guaranteed by agencies created by the U.S. Congress to increase the supply of capital to the residential mortgage market and to provide support for an active secondary market: Government National Mortgage Association ("Ginnie Mae"), Federal National Mortgage Association ("Fannie Mae"), and Federal Home Loan Mortgage Corporation ("Freddie Mac").

While Fannie Mae and Freddie Mac are commonly referred to as "agencies" of the U.S. government, both are corporate instrumentalities of the U.S. government. That is, they are government sponsored enterprises. Their guarantee does not carry the full faith and credit of the U.S. government. In contrast, Ginnie Mae is a federally related institution because it is part of the Department of Housing and Urban Development. As such, its guarantee carries the full faith and credit of the U.S. government.

The securities associated with these three entities are known as *agency passthrough securities*. About 98% of all passthrough securities are agency passthrough securities. The balance of mortgage passthrough securities are privately issued. These securities are called *private-label mortgage passthrough securities* or *nonagency passthrough securities*.

Ginnie Mae mortgage-backed securities are guaranteed by the full faith and credit of the United States government with respect to timely payment of both interest and principal. That is, the interest and principal will be paid when due even if the borrowers fail to make their monthly mortgage payment. The security guaranteed by Ginnie Mae is called a *mortgage-backed security* (MBS). Only mortgages insured or guaranteed by either the Federal Housing Administration, the Veterans Administration, or the Farmers Home Administration can be included in a mortgage pool guaranteed by Ginnie Mae.

The mortgage passthrough security issued by Freddie Mac is called a *participation certificate* (PC). Freddie Mac offers passthroughs with one of two types of guarantees. All PCs issued under Freddie Mac's *Gold PC* program are guaranteed with respect to the timely payment of interest and principal. The Gold PC was first issued in the fall of 1990 and is the only type of PC that will be issued by Freddie Mac in the future. The other PCs are guaranteed with respect to the timely payment of interest but the scheduled principal is passed through as it is collected, with Freddie Mac guaranteeing only that the scheduled payment will be made no later than one year after it is due.

The mortgage passthrough securities issued by Fannie Mae are called *mortgage-backed securities* (MBS). These passthroughs are guaranteed with respect to the timely payment of both interest and principal.

There are many seasoned issues of the same agency with the same coupon rate outstanding at any given time. Each issue is backed by a different pool of mortgages. For example, there are many seasoned pools of GNMA 8s. One issue may be backed by a pool of mortgages all for California properties, while another may be backed by a pool of mortgages for primarily New York homes. Others may be backed by a pool of mortgages on homes in several regions of the country. Which pool is a dealer referring to when it refers to, say, GNMA 8s? They are not referring to any specific pool but they mean a "generic" 8% coupon Ginnie Mae security.

Non-agency or private-label passthrough securities are issued by commercial banks, thrifts, and private conduits. Unlike agency passthrough securities, non-agency passthrough securities are rated by the commercial rating companies. Often they are supported by credit enhancements so that they can obtain an investment grade credit rating. The development of private credit enhancement is the key to the success of this market and, indeed, the key to the development of all asset securitization. We shall describe credit enhancements later in this chapter when we discuss asset-backed securities.

Prepayment Conventions and Cash Flow In order to value a passthrough security, it is necessary to project its cash flow. The difficulty is that the cash flow is unknown because of prepayments. The only way to project a cash flow is to make some assumption about the prepayment rate over the life of the underlying mortgage pool.

Estimating the cash flow from a passthrough requires making an assumption about future prepayments. Two conventions have been used as a benchmark for prepayment rates — conditional prepayment rate and Public Securities Association prepayment benchmark.

The *conditional prepayment rate* (CPR) assumes that some fraction of the remaining principal in the pool is prepaid each month for the remaining term of the mortgage. The CPR assumed for a pool is based on the characteristics of the pool (including its historical prepayment experience) and the current and expected future economic environment.

The CPR is an annual prepayment rate. To estimate monthly prepayments, the CPR must be converted into a monthly prepayment rate, commonly referred to as the *single-monthly mortality rate* (SMM). A formula can be used to determine the SMM for a given CPR:

$$SMM = 1 - (1 - CPR)^{1/12}$$

Suppose that the CPR used to estimate prepayments is 6%. The corresponding SMM is:

$$SMM = 1 - (1 - 0.06)^{1/12}$$
$$= 1 - (0.94)^{0.08333} = 0.005143$$

An SMM of $w\%$ means that approximately $w\%$ of the remaining mortgage balance at the beginning of the month less the scheduled principal payment will prepay that month. That is,

Prepayment for month t = SMM
$$\times \text{(Beginning mortgage balance for month t}$$
$$- \text{Scheduled principal payment for month t)}$$

For example, suppose that an investor owns a passthrough in which the remaining mortgage balance at the beginning of some month is $290 million. Assuming that the SMM is 0.5143% and the scheduled principal payment is $3 million, the estimated prepayment for the month is:

$$0.005143 \times (\$290,000,000 - \$3,000,000) = \$1,476,041$$

The *Public Securities Association (PSA) prepayment benchmark* is expressed as a monthly series of annual prepayment rates.[1] The

---

[1] This benchmark is commonly referred to as a prepayment model, suggesting that it can be used to estimate prepayments. Characterization of this benchmark as a prepayment model is inappropriate.

PSA benchmark assumes that prepayment rates are low for newly originated mortgages and then will speed up as the mortgages become seasoned. Specifically, the PSA benchmark assumes the following prepayment rates for 30-year mortgages: (1) a CPR of 0.2% for the first month, increased by 0.2% per year per month for the next 29 months when it reaches 6% per year, and (2) a 6% CPR for the remaining years. This benchmark is referred to as "100% PSA" or simply "100 PSA."

Slower or faster speeds are then referred to as some multiple of PSA. For example, 50 PSA means one-half the CPR of the PSA benchmark prepayment rate; 165 PSA means 1.65 times the CPR of the PSA benchmark prepayment rate; 300 PSA means three times the CPR of the benchmark prepayment rate. A prepayment rate of 0 PSA means that no prepayments are assumed. The CPR is converted to an SMM using the equation above.

Exhibit 2 shows the monthly cash flow for a hypothetical passthrough security assuming (1) the underlying mortgages are fixed-rate level-payment, fully amortizing mortgages with a WAC of 8.125% and a WAM of 357 months, (2) a passthrough rate of 7.5%, and (3) a prepayment rate of 165 PSA. The cash flow is broken down into three components: (1) interest (based on the coupon passthrough rate), (2) the regularly scheduled principal repayment, and (3) prepayments based on 165 PSA. The notes to the exhibit explain how the value in the exhibit are obtained.

Extension Risk and Contraction Risk An investor who owns passthrough securities does not know what the cash flow will be because that depends on prepayments. As we noted earlier, this risk is called prepayment risk.

To understand the significance of prepayment risk, suppose an investor buys a 10% coupon Ginnie Mae at a time when mortgage rates are 10%. Let's consider what will happen to prepayments if mortgage rates decline to, say, 6%. There will be two adverse consequences. First, a basic property of fixed income securities is that the price of an option-free bond will rise. But in the case of a passthrough security, the rise in price will not be as large as that of an option-free bond because a fall in interest rates will give the borrower an incentive to prepay the loan and refinance the debt at a lower rate. This results in the same adverse consequence faced by holders of callable corporate and agency bonds. As in the case of those bonds, the upside price potential of a passthrough security is truncated because of prepayments. The second adverse consequence is that the cash flow must be reinvested at a lower rate. These two adverse consequences when mortgage rates decline is referred to as *contraction risk*.

Exhibit 2: Monthly Cash Flow for a $400 Million Passthrough with a 7.5% Passthrough Rate, a WAC of 8.125%, and a WAM of 357 Months Assuming 165 PSA

th	Outstanding Balance	SMM	Mortgage Payment	Net Interest	Scheduled Principal	Prepayment	Total Principal	Cash Flow
1	$400,000,000	0.00111	$2,975,868	$2,500,000	$267,535	$442,389	$709,923	$3,209,923
2	399,290,077	0.00139	2,972,575	2,495,563	269,048	552,847	821,896	3,317,459
3	398,468,181	0.00167	2,968,456	2,490,426	270,495	663,065	933,560	3,423,986
4	397,534,621	0.00195	2,963,513	2,484,591	271,873	772,949	1,044,822	3,529,413
5	396,489,799	0.00223	2,957,747	2,478,061	273,181	882,405	1,155,586	3,633,647
6	395,334,213	0.00251	2,951,160	2,470,839	274,418	991,341	1,265,759	3,736,598
7	394,068,454	0.00279	2,943,755	2,462,928	275,583	1,099,664	1,375,246	3,838,174
8	392,693,208	0.00308	2,935,534	2,454,333	276,674	1,207,280	1,483,954	3,938,287
9	391,209,254	0.00336	2,926,503	2,445,058	277,690	1,314,099	1,591,789	4,036,847
10	389,617,464	0.00365	2,916,666	2,435,109	278,631	1,420,029	1,698,659	4,133,769
11	387,918,805	0.00393	2,906,028	2,424,493	279,494	1,524,979	1,804,473	4,228,965
12	386,114,332	0.00422	2,894,595	2,413,215	280,280	1,628,859	1,909,139	4,322,353
13	384,205,194	0.00451	2,882,375	2,401,282	280,986	1,731,581	2,012,567	4,413,850
14	382,192,626	0.00480	2,869,375	2,388,704	281,613	1,833,058	2,114,670	4,503,374
15	380,077,956	0.00509	2,855,603	2,375,487	282,159	1,933,203	2,215,361	4,590,848
16	377,862,595	0.00538	2,841,068	2,361,641	282,623	2,031,931	2,314,554	4,676,195
17	375,548,041	0.00567	2,825,779	2,347,175	283,006	2,129,159	2,412,164	4,759,339
18	373,135,877	0.00597	2,809,746	2,332,099	283,305	2,224,805	2,508,110	4,840,210
19	370,627,766	0.00626	2,792,980	2,316,424	283,521	2,318,790	2,602,312	4,918,735
20	368,025,455	0.00656	2,775,493	2,300,159	283,654	2,411,036	2,694,690	4,994,849
21	365,330,765	0.00685	2,757,296	2,283,317	283,702	2,501,466	2,785,169	5,068,486
22	362,545,596	0.00715	2,738,402	2,265,910	283,666	2,590,008	2,873,674	5,139,584
23	359,671,922	0.00745	2,718,823	2,247,950	283,545	2,676,588	2,960,133	5,208,083
24	356,711,789	0.00775	2,698,575	2,229,449	283,338	2,761,139	3,044,477	5,273,926
25	353,667,312	0.00805	2,677,670	2,210,421	283,047	2,843,593	3,126,640	5,337,061
26	350,540,672	0.00835	2,656,123	2,190,879	282,671	2,923,885	3,206,556	5,397,435
27	347,334,116	0.00865	2,633,950	2,170,838	282,209	3,001,955	3,284,164	5,455,002
28	344,049,952	0.00865	2,611,167	2,150,312	281,662	2,973,553	3,255,215	5,405,527
29	340,794,737	0.00865	2,588,581	2,129,967	281,116	2,945,400	3,226,516	5,356,483
30	337,568,221	0.00865	2,566,190	2,109,801	280,572	2,917,496	3,198,067	5,307,869

Exhibit 2 (Continued)

Month	Outstanding Balance	SMM	Mortgage Payment	Net Interest	Scheduled Principal	Prepayment	Total Principal	Cash Flow
100	$170,142,350	0.00865	$1,396,958	$1,063,390	$244,953	$1,469,591	$1,714,544	$2,777,93
101	168,427,806	0.00865	1,384,875	1,052,674	244,478	1,454,765	1,699,243	2,751,91
102	166,728,563	0.00865	1,372,896	1,042,054	244,004	1,440,071	1,684,075	2,726,12
103	165,044,489	0.00865	1,361,020	1,031,528	243,531	1,425,508	1,669,039	2,700,56
104	163,375,450	0.00865	1,349,248	1,021,097	243,060	1,411,075	1,654,134	2,675,23
105	161,721,315	0.00865	1,337,577	1,010,758	242,589	1,396,771	1,639,359	2,650,11
200	56,746,664	0.00865	585,990	354,667	201,767	489,106	690,874	1,045,54
201	56,055,790	0.00865	580,921	350,349	201,377	483,134	684,510	1,034,85
202	55,371,280	0.00865	575,896	346,070	200,986	477,216	678,202	1,024,27
203	54,693,077	0.00865	570,915	341,832	200,597	471,353	671,950	1,013,78
204	54,021,127	0.00865	565,976	337,632	200,208	465,544	665,752	1,003,38
205	53,355,375	0.00865	561,081	333,471	199,820	459,789	659,609	993,08
300	11,758,141	0.00865	245,808	73,488	166,196	100,269	266,465	339,9
301	11,491,677	0.00865	243,682	71,823	165,874	97,967	263,841	335,6
302	11,227,836	0.00865	241,574	70,174	165,552	95,687	261,240	331,4
303	10,966,596	0.00865	239,485	68,541	165,232	93,430	258,662	327,2
304	10,707,934	0.00865	237,413	66,925	164,912	91,196	256,107	323,0
305	10,451,827	0.00865	235,360	65,324	164,592	88,983	253,575	318,8
350	1,235,674	0.00865	159,202	7,723	150,836	9,384	160,220	167,9
351	1,075,454	0.00865	157,825	6,722	150,544	8,000	158,544	165,2
352	916,910	0.00865	156,460	5,731	150,252	6,631	156,883	162,6
353	760,027	0.00865	155,107	4,750	149,961	5,277	155,238	159,9
354	604,789	0.00865	153,765	3,780	149,670	3,937	153,607	157,3
355	451,182	0.00865	152,435	2,820	149,380	2,611	151,991	154,8
356	299,191	0.00865	151,117	1,870	149,091	1,298	150,389	152,2
357	148,802	0.00865	149,809	930	148,802	0	148,802	149,7

Notes:

Column 2: This column gives the outstanding mortgage balance at the beginning of the month. It is equal to the outstanding balance at the beginning of the previous month reduced by the total principal payment in the previous month.

Column 3: This column shows the SMM for 165 PSA. Two things should be noted in this column. First, for month 1, the SMM is for a passthrough that has been seasoned three months. That is, the CPR is 0.8% times 1.65 or 1.32%. This is because the WAM is 357. Second, from month 27 on, the SMM is 0.0865 which corresponds to a CPR of 9.9% (6% times 1.65).

Column 4: The total monthly mortgage payment is shown in this column. Notice that the total monthly mortgage payment declines over time as prepayments reduce the mortgage balance outstanding. There is a formula to determine what the monthly mortgage balance will be for each month given prepayments.

Exhibit 2 (Concluded)

Notes:

Column 5: The monthly interest paid to the passthrough investor is found in this column. This value is determined by multiplying the outstanding mortgage balance at the beginning of the month by the passthrough rate of 7.5% and dividing by 12.

Column 6: This column gives the regularly scheduled principal repayment. This is the difference between the total monthly mortgage payment [the amount shown in column (4)] and the gross coupon interest for the month. The gross coupon interest is 8.125% multiplied by the outstanding mortgage balance at the beginning of the month, then divided by 12.

Column 7: The prepayment for the month is reported in this column. The prepayment is found as follows:

SMM × (Beginning mortgage balance for month t
– Scheduled principal payment for month t)

Column 8: The total principal payment, which is the sum of columns (6) and (7), is shown in this column.

Column 9: The projected monthly cash flow for this passthrough is shown in this last column. The monthly cash flow is the sum of the interest paid to the passthrough investor [column (5)] and the total principal payments for the month [column (8)].

Now let's look at what happens if mortgage rates rise to, say, 15%. The price of the passthrough, like the price of any bond, will decline. But again it will decline more because the higher rates will tend to slow down the rate of prepayment, in effect increasing the amount invested at the coupon rate, which is lower than the market rate. Prepayments will slow down, because homeowners will not refinance or partially prepay their mortgages when mortgage rates are higher than the contract rate of 10%. Of course, this is just the time when investors want prepayments to speed up so that they can reinvest the prepayments at the higher market interest rate. This adverse consequence of rising mortgage rates is called *extension risk.*

Therefore, prepayment risk encompasses contraction risk and extension risk. Prepayment risk makes passthrough securities unattractive for certain financial institutions to hold from an asset/liability perspective. Some institutional investors such as depository institutions are concerned with extension risk and others such as pension funds with contraction risk when they purchase a passthrough security. Is it possible to alter the cash flow of a passthrough so as to reduce the contraction risk and extension risk for institutional investors? This can be done, as we shall see later in this chapter.

Average Life The yield on mortgage passthrough securities are often compared to Treasury securities. When we speak of comparing a mortgage passthrough security to a comparable Treasury, what does "comparable" mean? The stated maturity of a mortgage passthrough security is an inappropriate measure because of prepayments. Instead, market participants have used two measures: Macaulay duration and average life. We discuss Macaulay duration in Chapter **YY**. The more commonly used measure is the average life.

The *average life* of a mortgage-backed security is the average time to receipt of principal payments (scheduled principal payments and projected prepayments), weighted by the amount of principal expected. Mathematically, the average life is expressed as follows:

$$\text{Average life} = \sum_{t=1}^{T} \frac{\text{Projected principal received at time t}}{12(\text{Total principal})}$$

where T is the number of months.

The average life of a passthrough depends on the PSA prepayment assumption. To see this, the average life is shown below for different prepayment speeds for the passthrough we used to illustrate the cash flow for 165 PSA in Exhibit 2:

PSA speed	50	100	165	200	300	400	500	600	700
Average life	15.11	11.66	8.76	7.68	5.63	4.44	3.68	3.16	2.78

Collateralized Mortgage Obligations

As we noted, there is prepayment risk associated with investing in a mortgage passthrough security. Some institutional investors are concerned with extension risk and others with contraction risk when they invest in a passthrough. This problem can be mitigated by redirecting the cash flows of mortgage-related products (passthrough securities or a pool of loans) to different bond classes, called *tranches*, so as to create securities that have different exposure to prepayment risk and therefore different risk/return patterns than the mortgage-related product from which they were created.

When the cash flows of mortgage-related products are redistributed to different bond classes, the resulting securities are called *collateralized mortgage obligations* (CMO). The creation of a CMO cannot eliminate prepayment risk; it can only distribute the various forms of this risk among different classes of bondholders.

Rather than list the different types of tranches that can be created in a CMO structure, we will show how two common types of tranches can be created. This will provide an excellent illustration of financial engineering. We will look at a plain vanilla sequential-pay CMO structure and a structure with planned amortization class bonds.

Sequential-Pay Tranches The first CMO was created in 1983 and was structured so that each class of bond would be retired sequentially. Such structures are referred to as *sequential-pay* CMOs. To illustrate a sequential-pay CMO, we discuss CMO-1, a hypothetical deal made up to illustrate the basic features of the structure. The collateral for this hypothetical CMO is a hypothetical passthrough with a total par value of $400 million and the following characteristics: (1) the passthrough coupon rate is 7.5%, (2) the weighted average coupon (WAC) is 8.125%, and (3) the weighted average maturity (WAM) is 357 months. This is the same passthrough that we used earlier in this chapter to describe the cash flow of a passthrough based on a 165 PSA assumption.

From this $400 million of collateral, four bond classes or tranches are created. Their characteristics are summarized in Exhibit 3. The total par value of the four tranches is equal to the par value of the collateral (i.e., the passthrough security). In this simple structure, the coupon rate is the same for each tranche and also the same as the coupon rate on the collateral. There is no reason why this must be so, and, in fact, typically the coupon rate varies by tranche.

Now remember that a CMO is created by redistributing the cash flow — interest and principal — to the different tranches based on a set of payment rules. The payment rules at the bottom of Exhibit 3 describe how the cash flow from the passthrough (i.e., collateral) is to be distributed to the four tranches. There are separate rules for the payment of the coupon interest and the payment of principal, the principal being the total of the regularly scheduled principal payment and any prepayments.

Exhibit 3: CMO-1: A Hypothetical Four-Tranche Sequential-Pay Structure

Tranche	Par Amount ($)	Coupon Rate (%)
A	194,500,000	7.5
B	36,000,000	7.5
C	96,500,000	7.5
D	73,000,000	7.5
Total	400,000,000	

Payment rules:

1. *For payment of periodic coupon interest:* Disburse periodic coupon interest to each tranche on the basis of the amount of principal outstanding at the beginning of the month.

2. *For disbursement of principal payments:* Disburse principal payments to tranche A until it is completely paid off. After tranche A is completely paid off, disburse principal payments to tranche B until it is completely paid off. After tranche B is completely paid off, disburse principal payments to tranche C until it is completely paid off. After tranche C is completely paid off, disburse principal payments to tranche D until it is completely paid off.

In CMO-1, each tranche receives periodic coupon interest payments based on the amount of the outstanding balance at the beginning of the month. The disbursement of the principal, however, is made in a special way. A tranche is not entitled to receive principal until the entire principal of the tranche before it has been paid off. More specifically, tranche A receives all the principal payments until the entire principal amount owed to that tranche, $194,500,000, is paid off; then tranche B begins to receive principal and continues to do so until it is paid the entire $36,000,000. Tranche C then receives principal, and when it is paid off, tranche D starts receiving principal payments.

While the priority rules for the disbursement of the principal payments are known, the precise amount of the principal in each period is not. This will depend on the cash flow, and therefore principal payments, of the collateral, which depends on the actual prepayment rate of the collateral. An assumed PSA speed allows the cash flow to be projected. Exhibit 2 shows the cash flow (interest, regularly scheduled principal repayment, and prepayments) assuming 165 PSA. Assuming that the collateral does prepay at 165 PSA, the cash flow available to all four tranches of CMO-1 will be precisely the cash flow shown in Exhibit 2.

To demonstrate how the priority rules for CMO-1 work, Exhibit 4 shows the cash flow for selected months assuming the collateral prepays at 165 PSA. For each tranche, the exhibit shows: (1) the balance at the end of the month, (2) the principal paid down (regularly scheduled principal repayment plus prepayments), and (3) interest. In month 1, the cash flow for the collateral consists of principal payment of $709,923 and interest of $2.5 million (0.075 times $400 million divided by 12). The interest payment is distributed to the four tranches based on the amount of the par value outstanding. So, for example, tranche A receives $1,215,625 (0.075 times $194,500,000 divided by 12) of the $2.5 million. The principal, however, is all distributed to tranche A. Therefore, the cash flow for tranche A in month 1 is $1,925,548. The principal balance at the end of month 1 for tranche A is $193,790,076 (the original principal balance of $194,500,000 less the principal payment of $709,923). No principal payment is distributed to the three other tranches because there is still a principal balance outstanding for tranche A. This will be true for months 2 through 80.

After month 81, the principal balance will be zero for tranche A. For the collateral, the cash flow in month 81 is $3,318,521, consisting of a principal payment of $2,032,196 and interest of $1,286,325. At the beginning of month 81 (end of month 80), the principal balance for tranche A is $311,926. Therefore, $311,926 of the $2,032,196 of the principal payment from the collateral will be disbursed to tranche A. After this payment is made, no additional principal payments are made to this tranche as the principal balance is zero. The remaining principal payment from the collateral, $1,720,271, is disbursed to tranche B. According to the assumed prepayment speed of 165 PSA, tranche B then begins receiving principal payments in month 81.

Exhibit 4 shows that tranche B is fully paid off by month 100, when tranche C now begins to receive principal payments. Tranche C is not fully paid off until month 178, at which time tranche D begins receiving the remaining principal payments. The maturity (i.e., the time until the principal is fully paid off) for these four tranches assuming 165 PSA would be 81 months for tranche A, 100 months for tranche B, 178 months for tranche C, and 357 months for tranche D.

Exhibit 4: Monthly Cash Flow for Selected Months for CMO-1 Assuming 165 PSA

Month	Tranche A			Tranche B		
	Balance	Principal	Interest	Balance	Principal	Interest
1	$ 194,500,000	$ 709,923	$1,215,625	$ 36,000,000	$0	$225,000
2	193,790,077	821,896	1,211,188	36,000,000	0	225,000
3	192,968,181	933,560	1,206,051	36,000,000	0	225,000
4	192,034,621	1,044,822	1,200,216	36,000,000	0	225,000
5	190,989,799	1,155,586	1,193,686	36,000,000	0	225,000
6	189,834,213	1,265,759	1,186,464	36,000,000	0	225,000
7	188,568,454	1,375,246	1,178,553	36,000,000	0	225,000
8	187,193,208	1,483,954	1,169,958	36,000,000	0	225,000
9	185,709,254	1,591,789	1,160,683	36,000,000	0	225,000
10	184,117,464	1,698,659	1,150,734	36,000,000	0	225,000
11	182,418,805	1,804,473	1,140,118	36,000,000	0	225,000
12	180,614,332	1,909,139	1,128,840	36,000,000	0	225,000
75	12,893,479	2,143,974	80,584	36,000,000	0	225,000
76	10,749,504	2,124,935	67,184	36,000,000	0	225,000
77	8,624,569	2,106,062	53,904	36,000,000	0	225,000
78	6,518,507	2,087,353	40,741	36,000,000	0	225,000
79	4,431,154	2,068,807	27,695	36,000,000	0	225,000
80	2,362,347	2,050,422	14,765	36,000,000	0	225,000
81	311,926	311,926	1,950	36,000,000	1,720,271	225,000
82	0	0	0	34,279,729	2,014,130	214,248
83	0	0	0	32,265,599	1,996,221	201,660
84	0	0	0	30,269,378	1,978,468	189,184
85	0	0	0	28,290,911	1,960,869	176,818
95	0	0	0	9,449,331	1,793,089	59,058
96	0	0	0	7,656,242	1,777,104	47,852
97	0	0	0	5,879,138	1,761,258	36,745
98	0	0	0	4,117,880	1,745,550	25,737
99	0	0	0	2,372,329	1,729,979	14,827
100	0	0	0	642,350	642,350	4,015
101	0	0	0	0	0	0
102	0	0	0	0	0	0
103	0	0	0	0	0	0
104	0	0	0	0	0	0
105	0	0	0	0	0	0

Exhibit 4 (Concluded)

Month	Tranche C Balance	Tranche C Principal	Tranche C Interest	Tranche D Balance	Tranche D Principal	Tranche D Interest
1	$96,500,000	$ 0	$603,125	$ 73,000,000	$0	$456,250
2	96,500,000	0	603,125	73,000,000	0	456,250
3	96,500,000	0	603,125	73,000,000	0	456,250
4	96,500,000	0	603,125	73,000,000	0	456,250
5	96,500,000	0	603,125	73,000,000	0	456,250
6	96,500,000	0	603,125	73,000,000	0	456,250
7	96,500,000	0	603,125	73,000,000	0	456,250
8	96,500,000	0	603,125	73,000,000	0	456,250
9	96,500,000	0	603,125	73,000,000	0	456,250
10	96,500,000	0	603,125	73,000,000	0	456,250
11	96,500,000	0	603,125	73,000,000	0	456,250
12	96,500,000	0	603,125	73,000,000	0	456,250
95	96,500,000	0	603,125	73,000,000	0	456,250
96	96,500,000	0	603,125	73,000,000	0	456,250
97	96,500,000	0	603,125	73,000,000	0	456,250
98	96,500,000	0	603,125	73,000,000	0	456,250
99	96,500,000	0	603,125	73,000,000	0	456,250
100	96,500,000	1,072,194	603,125	73,000,000	0	456,250
101	95,427,806	1,699,243	596,424	73,000,000	0	456,250
102	93,728,563	1,684,075	585,804	73,000,000	0	456,250
103	92,044,489	1,669,039	575,278	73,000,000	0	456,250
104	90,375,450	1,654,134	564,847	73,000,000	0	456,250
105	88,721,315	1,639,359	554,508	73,000,000	0	456,250
175	3,260,287	869,602	20,377	73,000,000	0	456,250
176	2,390,685	861,673	14,942	73,000,000	0	456,250
177	1,529,013	853,813	9,556	73,000,000	0	456,250
178	675,199	675,199	4,220	73,000,000	170,824	456,250
179	0	0	0	72,829,176	838,300	455,182
180	0	0	0	71,990,876	830,646	449,943
181	0	0	0	71,160,230	823,058	444,751
182	0	0	0	70,337,173	815,536	439,607
183	0	0	0	69,521,637	808,081	434,510
184	0	0	0	68,713,556	800,690	429,460
185	0	0	0	67,912,866	793,365	424,455
350	0	0	0	1,235,674	160,220	7,723
351	0	0	0	1,075,454	158,544	6,722
352	0	0	0	916,910	156,883	5,731
353	0	0	0	760,027	155,238	4,750
354	0	0	0	604,789	153,607	3,780
355	0	0	0	451,182	151,991	2,820
356	0	0	0	299,191	150,389	1,870
357	0	0	0	148,802	148,802	930

Exhibit 5: Average Life for the Collateral and the Four Tranches of CMO-1

Prepayment speed (PSA)	Average life for				
	Collateral	Tranche A	Tranche B	Tranche C	Tranche D
50	15.11	7.48	15.98	21.02	27.24
100	11.66	4.90	10.86	15.78	24.58
165	8.76	3.48	7.49	11.19	20.27
200	7.68	3.05	6.42	9.60	18.11
300	5.63	2.32	4.64	6.81	13.36
400	4.44	1.94	3.70	5.31	10.34
500	3.68	1.69	3.12	4.38	8.35
600	3.16	1.51	2.74	3.75	6.96
700	2.78	1.38	2.47	3.30	5.95

Let's look at what has been accomplished by creating the CMO. First, as shown earlier in this chapter the average life for the passthrough is 8.76 years, assuming a prepayment speed of 165 PSA. Exhibit 5 reports the average life of the collateral and the four tranches assuming different prepayment speeds. Notice that the four tranches have average lives that are both shorter and longer than the collateral thereby attracting investors who have a preference for an average life different from that of the collateral.

There is still a major problem: there is considerable variability of the average life for the tranches. However, there is some protection provided for each tranche against prepayment risk. This is because prioritizing the distribution of principal (i.e., establishing the payment rules for principal) effectively protects the shorter-term tranche A in this structure against extension risk. This protection must come from somewhere. In fact, it comes from the three other tranches. Similarly, tranches C and D provide protection against extension risk for tranches A and B. At the same time, tranches C and D benefit because they are provided protection against contraction risk, the protection coming from tranches A and B.

Planned Amortization Class Tranches Many investors were still concerned about investing in an instrument that they continued to perceive as posing significant prepayment risk because of the substantial average life variability despite the innovations designed to reduce prepayment risk. Traditional corporate bond buyers sought a structure with both the characteristics of a corporate bond (either a bullet maturity or a sinking-fund type schedule of principal repayment) and high credit quality. While CMOs satisfied the second condition, they did not satisfy the first.

In 1987, CMO issuers began issuing bonds with the characteristic that if prepayments are within a specified range, the cash flow pattern is known. The greater predictability of the cash flow for these tranches, referred to as *planned amortization class* (PAC) bonds, occurs because there is a principal repayment schedule that must be satisfied. PAC bondholders have priority over all other tranches in the CMO structure in receiving principal payments from the underlying collateral. The greater certainty of the cash flow for the PAC bonds comes at the expense of the non-PAC classes, called the *support* or *companion* bonds. It is these bonds that absorb the prepayment risk. Because PAC bonds have protection against both extension risk and contraction risk, they are said to provide *two-sided prepayment protection.*

To illustrate how to create a PAC bond, we will use as collateral the $400 million passthrough with a coupon rate of 7.5%, an 8.125% WAC, and a WAM of 357 months. The second column of Exhibit 6 shows the principal payment (regularly scheduled principal repayment plus prepayments) for selected months assuming a prepayment speed of 90 PSA, and the next column shows the principal payments for selected months assuming that the passthrough prepays at 300 PSA.

The last column of Exhibit 6 gives the *minimum* principal payment if the collateral speed is 90 PSA or 300 PSA for months 1 to 349. (After month 349, the outstanding principal balance will be paid off if the prepayment speed is between 90 PSA and 300 PSA.) For example, in the first month, the principal payment would be $508,169.52 if the collateral prepays at 90 PSA and $1,075,931.20 if the collateral prepays at 300 PSA. Thus, the minimum principal payment is $508,169.52, as reported in the last column of Exhibit 6. In month 103, the minimum principal payment is also the amount if the prepayment speed is 90 PSA, $1,446,761, compared to $1,458,618.04 for 300 PSA. In month 104, however, a prepayment speed of 300 PSA would produce a principal payment of $1,433,539.23, which is less than the principal payment of $1,440,825.55 assuming 90 PSA. So, $1,433,539.23 is reported in the last column of Exhibit 6. In fact, from month 104 on the minimum principal payment is the one that would result assuming a prepayment speed of 300 PSA.

Exhibit 6: Monthly Principal Payment for $400 Million 7.5% Coupon Passthrough with an 8.125% WAC and a 357 WAM Assuming Prepayment Rates of 90 PSA and 300 PSA

Month	At 90% PSA	At 300% PSA	Minimum principal payment — the PAC schedule
1	$508,169.52	$1,075,931.20	$508,169.52
2	569,843.43	1,279,412.11	569,843.43
3	631,377.11	1,482,194.45	631,377.11
4	692,741.89	1,683,966.17	692,741.89
5	753,909.12	1,884,414.62	753,909.12
6	814,850.22	2,083,227.31	814,850.22
7	875,536.68	2,280,092.68	875,536.68
8	935,940.10	2,474,700.92	935,940.10
9	996,032.19	2,666,744.77	996,032.19
10	1,055,784.82	2,855,920.32	1,055,784.82
11	1,115,170.01	3,041,927.81	1,115,170.01
12	1,174,160.00	3,224,472.44	1,174,160.00
13	1,232,727.22	3,403,265.17	1,232,727.22
14	1,290,844.32	3,578,023.49	1,290,844.32
101	1,458,719.34	1,510,072.17	1,458,719.34
102	1,452,725.55	1,484,126.59	1,452,725.55
103	1,446,761.00	1,458,618.04	1,446,761.00
104	1,440,825.55	1,433,539.23	1,433,539.23
105	1,434,919.07	1,408,883.01	1,408,883.01
211	949,482.58	213,309.00	213,309.00
212	946,033.34	209,409.09	209,409.09
213	942,601.99	205,577.05	205,577.05
346	618,684.59	13,269.17	13,269.17
347	617,071.58	12,944.51	12,944.51
348	615,468.65	12,626.21	12,626.21
349	613,875.77	12,314.16	3,432.32
350	612,292.88	12,008.25	0
351	610,719.96	11,708.38	0
356	603,003.38	10,295.70	0
357	601,489.39	10,029.78	0

In fact, if the collateral prepays at *any* speed between 90 PSA and 300 PSA, the minimum principal payment would be the amount reported in the last column of Exhibit 6. For example, if we had included principal payment figures assuming a prepayment speed of 200 PSA, the minimum principal payment would not change: from month 1 through month 103, the minimum principal payment is that generated from 90 PSA, but from month 104 on, the minimum principal payment is that generated from 300 PSA.

This characteristic of the collateral allows for the creation of a PAC bond, assuming that the collateral prepays over its life at a constant speed between 90 PSA to 300 PSA. A schedule of principal repayments that the PAC bondholders are entitled to receive before any other bond class in the CMO is specified. The monthly schedule of principal repayments is as specified in the last column of Exhibit 6, which shows the minimum principal payment. While there is no assurance that the collateral will prepay between these two speeds, a PAC bond can be structured to assume that it will.

Exhibit 7 shows a CMO structure, CMO-2, created from the $400 million, 7.5% coupon passthrough with a WAC of 8.125% and a WAM of 357 months. There are just two tranches in this structure: a 7.5% coupon PAC bond created assuming 90 to 300 PSA with a par value of $243.8 million and a support bond with a par value of $156.2 million.

Exhibit 8 reports the average life for the PAC bond and the support bond in CMO-2 assuming various *actual* prepayment speeds. Notice that between 90 PSA and 300 PSA, the average life for the PAC bond is stable at 7.26 years. However, at slower or faster PSA speeds, the schedule is broken, and the average life changes, lengthening when the prepayment speed is less than 90 PSA and shortening when it is greater than 300 PSA. Even so, there is much greater variability for the average life of the support bond.

In practice, CMO structures that include a PAC tranche typically do not have just one PAC tranche. Rather, there are several PAC tranches created from the same tranche. For example, several PAC tranches that pay off in sequence can be created with a total par value equal to $243.8 million, which is the amount of the single PAC bond in CMO-2. This allows for the creation of PACs with a wide-range of average lives.

Exhibit 7: CMO-2: CMO Structure with One PAC Bond and One Support Bond

Tranche	Par amount ($)	Coupon rate (%)
P (PAC)	243,800,000	7.5
S (Support)	156,200,000	7.5
Total	400,000,000	

Payment rules:

1. *For payment of periodic coupon interest:* Disburse periodic coupon interest to each tranche on the basis of the amount of principal outstanding at the beginning of the month.

2. *For disbursement of principal payments:* Disburse principal payments to tranche P based on its schedule of principal repayments as given in column (4) of Exhibit 6. Tranche P has priority with respect to current and future principal payments to satisfy the schedule. Any excess principal payments in a month over the amount necessary to satisfy the schedule for tranche P are paid to tranche S. When tranche S is completely paid off, all principal payments are to be made to tranche P regardless of the schedule.

Exhibit 8: Average Life for PAC Bond and Support Bond in CMO-2 Assuming Various Prepayment Speeds

Prepayment rate (PSA)	PAC Bond (P)	Support Bond (S)
0	15.97	27.26
50	9.44	24.00
90	7.26	18.56
100	7.26	18.56
150	7.26	12.57
165	7.26	11.16
200	7.26	8.38
250	7.26	5.37
300	7.26	3.13
350	6.56	2.51
400	5.92	2.17
450	5.38	1.94
500	4.93	1.77
700	3.70	1.37

Credit Risk A CMO can be viewed as a business entity. The assets of this business are the collateral; that is, the passthrough securities or pool of mortgage loans backing the deal. The collateral for a CMO is held in trust for the exclusive benefit of all the bondholders. The liabilities are the payments due to the CMO tranches. The liability obligation consists of the par value and monthly interest payment that is owed to each tranche. The CMO or, equivalently, the business, is structured so that, even under the worst possible consequences concerning prepayments, all the liabilities will be satisfied.

Credit risk exposure depends on who the issuer of the CMO is. An issuer is either (1) a government-sponsored enterprise (such as Freddie Mac or Fannie Mae) or (2) a private entity. CMOs issued by government-sponsored enterprises are referred to as *agency CMOs.* Those issued by a private entity can be divided into two types. A private entity that issues a CMO but whose underlying collateral is a pool of passthroughs guaranteed by an agency is called a *private-label CMO.* If the collateral for a CMO is a pool of whole loans the structure is referred to as a *whole loan CMO.*

The guarantee of a government-sponsored enterprise depends on the financial capacity of the agency. CMOs issued by private entities are rated by commercial rating agencies. There are various ways that such issues can be credit enhanced as described later when we discuss asset-backed securities.

Stripped Mortgage-Backed Securities

A mortgage passthrough security divides the cash flow from the underlying pool of mortgages on a pro rata basis to the securityholders. A stripped mortgage-backed security is created by altering that distribution of principal and interest from a pro rata distribution to an unequal distribution. The result is that the securities created will have a price/yield relationship that is different from the price/yield relationship of the underlying passthrough security.

In the most common type of stripped mortgage-backed securities all the interest is allocated to one class (called the *interest only* or *IO class*) and all the principal to the other class (called the *principal only* or *PO class*). The IO class receives no principal payments.

The PO security is purchased at a substantial discount from par value. The return an investor realizes depends on the speed at which prepayments are made. The faster the prepayments, the higher the investor's return. For example, suppose there is a mortgage pool consisting of only 30-year mortgages, with $400 million in principal, and that investors can purchase POs backed by this mortgage pool for $175 million. The dollar return on this investment will be $225 million. How quickly that dollar return is recovered by PO investors determines the actual return that will be realized. In the extreme case, if all homeowners in the underlying mortgage pool decide to prepay their mortgage loans immediately, PO investors will realize the $225 million immediately. At the other extreme, if all homeowners decide to remain in their homes for 30 years and make no prepayments, the $225 million will be spread out over 30 years, which would result in a lower return for PO investors.

Let's look at how the price of the PO would be expected to change as mortgage rates in the market change. When mortgage rates decline below the coupon rate, prepayments are expected to speed up, accelerating payments to the PO holder. Thus, the cash flow of a PO improves (in the sense that principal repayments are received earlier). The cash flow will be discounted at a lower interest rate because the mortgage rate in the market has declined. The result is that the PO price will increase when mortgage rates decline. When mortgage rates rise above the coupon rate, prepayments are expected to slow down. The cash flow deteriorates (in the sense that it takes longer to recover principal repayments). Couple this with a higher discount rate, and the price of a PO will fall when mortgage rates rise.

An IO has no par value. In contrast to the PO investor, the IO investor wants prepayments to be slow. The reason is that the IO investor receives interest only on the amount of the principal outstanding. When prepayments are made, less dollar interest will be received as the outstanding principal declines. *In fact, if prepayments are too fast, the IO investor may not recover the amount paid for the IO.*

Let's look at the expected price response of an IO to changes in mortgage rates. If mortgage rates decline below the coupon rate, the prepayments are expected to accelerate. This would result in a deterioration of the expected cash flow for an IO. While the cash flow will be discounted at a lower rate, the net effect typically is a decline in the price of an IO. If mortgage rates rise above the coupon rate, the expected cash flow improves, but the cash flow is discounted at a higher interest rate. The net effect may be either a rise or fall for the IO. Thus, we see an interesting characteristic of an IO: its price tends to move in the same direction as the change in mortgage rates: (1) when mortgage rates fall below the coupon rate and (2) for some range of mortgage rates above the coupon rate.

Both POs and IOs exhibit substantial price volatility when mortgage rates change. The greater price volatility of the IO and PO compared to the passthrough is due to the fact that the combined price volatility of the IO and PO must be equal to the price volatility of the passthrough.

ASSET-BACKED SECURITIES

While the securitization of residential mortgage loans is by far the largest type of asset that has been securitized, securities backed by other assets have been securitized. Total issuance of asset-backed securities in 1994 and 1995 was $79.4 billion and $109.2 billion, respectively. As of mid-1995, issuance in Europe has been more than $50 billion.[2] The majority of this volume, however, represents the securitization of mortgage loans and is thus not comparable to the issuance figures cited for ABS issuance in the United States. By far, the largest issuance is in the United Kingdom. Securitization of residential mortgages was 81% of total issuance.

In this section we will discuss the basic features of asset-backed securities and look at the characteristics of some of the major types of asset-backed securities.

Major Types of Asset-Backed Securities

The four largest sectors of the asset-backed securities (ABS) market in the United States are credit card-backed receivable securities, auto-loan backed securities, home-equity loan backed securities, and manufactured-housing loan backed securities.

---

[2] Paul Taylor, "Securitization in Europe," in Anand K. Bhattacharya and Frank J. Fabozzi (eds.), *Asset-Backed Securities* (New Hope, PA: Frank J. Fabozzi Associates, 1996).

Credit card ABS are backed by credit card receivables. Credit cards are originated by banks (e.g., Visa and MasterCard), retailers (e.g., JC Penney and Sears), and travel and entertainment companies (e.g., American Express). The major issuers of auto-loan backed securities are General Motors Acceptance Corporation, Chrysler Financial, and Ford Credit.

Home-equity loan securities (HELS) are backed by home-equity loans. A home-equity loan (HEL) is a loan backed by residential property. Typically, the loan is a second lien on property that has already been pledged to secure a first lien. In some cases, the lien may be a third lien. In recent years, some loans have been first liens. That is, the borrower only has a HEL. Loans with similar credit quality are included in the same pool of loans that back HELS. The credit quality of the borrower generally falls into one of the following four categories: A (highest credit quality), B, C, and D (lowest credit quality). Unfortunately, there is no industry standard for defining A, B, C, and D ratings.

Manufactured-housing backed securities are backed by loans on manufactured homes. In contrast to site-built homes, manufactured homes are built at a factory and then transported to a manufactured home community or private land. These homes are more popularly referred to as mobile homes. The loan may be either a mortgage loan (for both the land and the mobile home) or a consumer retail installment loan. Manufactured-housing backed securities are issued by Ginnie Mae and private entities. As explained earlier, Ginnie Mae is a federally-related agency whose securities are guaranteed by the full faith and credit of the U.S. government. The underlying manufactured-housing loans that are collateral for the securities issued and guaranteed by Ginnie Mae are loans guaranteed by the Federal Housing Administration or Veterans Administration. Loans not backed by these two entities are called conventional loans. Manufactured-housing backed securities that are backed by such loans are called *conventional manufactured-housng backed securities*. These are the securities issued by private entities.

Cash Flow of Asset-Backed Securities

In creating an asset-backed security, issuers have drawn from the structures used in the mortgage-backed securities market described earlier in this chapter. Asset-backed securities have been structured as passthroughs and as structures with multiple bond classes or tranches just like collateralized mortgage obligations.

Modeling defaults for the collateral is critical in estimating the cash flow of an asset-backed security. Proceeds that are recovered in the event of a default result in a prepayment of the loan prior to the scheduled principal repayment date. Prepayments also occur as a result of refinancing. In projecting prepayments it is critical to determine whether borrowers typically take advantage of a decline in interest rates below the loan rate to refinance.

Auto-Loan Backed Securities For asset-backed securities backed by auto loans, borrowers pay regularly scheduled monthly loan payments (interest and scheduled principal repayments) and may make prepayments. For securities backed by auto loans, prepayments result from (1) sales and trade-ins requiring full payoff of the loan, (2) repossession and subsequent sale of the vehicle, (3) loss or destruction of the vehicle, (4) payoff of the loan with cash to save interest cost, and (5) refinancing of the loan at a lower interest cost.

While refinancings may be a major reason for prepayments of mortgage loans, they are of minor importance for auto loans. Moreover, the interest rates for the auto loans underlying several issues are substantially below market rates if they are offered by manufacturers as part of a sales promotion.

There is good historical information on the other causes of prepayments. Therefore, the cash flow of securities backed by auto loans do not have a great deal of uncertainty despite prepayments.

Credit Card Receivable Backed Securities For credit card receivable asset-backed securities, interest to holders of credit card-backed issues is paid periodically (e.g, monthly or semiannually). In contrast to auto loan asset-backed securities, the principal is not amortized. Instead, for a specified period of time, referred to as the *lockout period* or *revolving period*, the principal payments made by credit card borrowers are retained by the trustee and reinvested in additional receivables. The lockout period can vary from 18 months to 10 years.

After the lockout period, the principal is no longer reinvested but distributed to investors. This period is referred to as the *principal-amor-*

tization period. There are three different amortization structures that have been used in credit card receivable structures: (1) passthrough structure, (2) controlled-amortization structure, and (3) bullet-payment structure.

In a *passthrough structure*, the principal cash flows from the credit card accounts are paid to the security holders on a pro rata basis.[3] In a *controlled amortization structure*, a scheduled principal amount is established. The scheduled principal amount is sufficiently low so that the obligation can be satisfied even under certain stress scenarios. The investor is paid the lesser of the scheduled principal amount and the pro rata amount. In a *bullet-payment structure*, the investor receives the entire amount in one distribution. Since there is no assurance that the entire amount can be paid in one lump sum, the procedure is for the trustee to place principal monthly into an account that generates sufficient interest to make periodic interest payments and accumulate the principal to be repaid.

There are provisions in credit card receivable-backed securities that requires earlier amortization of the principal if certain events occur. Such provisions, which are referred to as either *early amortization* or *rapid amortization provisions*, are included to safeguard the credit quality of the issue. The only way that the cash flow can be altered is by the triggering of the early amortization provision.

Early amortization is invoked if the trust is not able to generate sufficient income to cover the investor coupon and the servicing fee. Other events that may trigger early amortization are the default of the servicer, credit support decline below a specified amount, or the issuer violating agreements regarding pooling and servicing.

Home-Equity Loan Backed Securities Home-equity loans can be either closed end or open end. A *closed-end HEL* is structured the same way as a fixed-rate, fully amortizing residential mortgage loan. That is, it has a fixed maturity, a fixed interest rate, and the payments are structured to fully amortizing the loan by the maturity date. The cash flow of a pool of closed-end HELs is then comprised of interest, regularly scheduled principal repayments, and prepayments, just as

---

[3] For a more detailed discussion of these amortization structures, see Robert Karr, Greg Richter, R.J. Shook, and Lirenn Tsai, "Credit-Card Receivables," in *Asset-Backed Securities*.

with mortgage-backed securities. Thus, it is necessary to have a prepayment model and a default model to forecast cash flows. The prepayment speed is measured in terms of a conditional prepayment rate which we discussed earlier.

With an *open-end HEL* the homeowner is given a credit line and can write checks or use a credit card for up to the amount of the credit line. The amount of the credit line depends on the amount of the equity the borrower has in the property. There is a revolving period over which the homeowner can borrow funds against the line of credit. At the end of the term of the loan, the homeowner either pays off the amount borrowed in one payment or the outstanding balance is amortized.

There are differences in the prepayment behavior for home-equity loans and standard mortgage loans. Wall Street firms involved in making markets in home-equity loan backed securities have developed prepayment models for these loans. The Prudential Securities prepayment model, for example, finds that the key difference between the prepayment behavior of home-equity loans and standard mortgage loans is the important role played by the credit characteristics of the borrower.[4]

Manufactured-Housing Backed Securities The typical loan for a manufactured home is 15 to 20 years. The loan repayment is structured to fully amortize the amount borrowed. Therefore, as with residential mortgage loans and HELs, the cash flow consists of interest, regularly scheduled principal, and prepayments. However, prepayments are more stable for manufactured-housing backed securities because they are not sensitive to refinancing.

There are several reasons for this.[5] First, the loan balances are typically small so that there is no significant dollar savings from refinancing. Second, the rate of depreciation of mobile homes may be such that in the earlier years the depreciation is greater than the amount of the loan paid off. This makes it difficult to refinance the loan. Finally, typically borrowers who have purchased mobile homes are individuals who have lower credit quality and therefore find it difficult to obtain funds to refinance.

---

[4] Lakhbir Hayre, Charles Huang, and Tom Zimmerman, *Analysis of Home-Equity Loan Securities* (Prudential Securities, August 1993).

[5] Zimmerman and Koren, "Manufactured Housing Securities," in *Asset-Backed Securities.*

As with residential mortgage loans and HELs, prepayments on manufactured-housing backed securities are measured in terms of the conditional prepayment rate.

Credit Risk

Asset-backed securities expose investors to credit risk. The nationally recognized rating organizations that rate corporate debt issues also rate asset-backed securities.[6] In analyzing the credit quality of the pool of loans, the rating companies look at whether the loans were properly originated, comply with consumer lending laws, the characteristics of the loans, and the underwriting standards used by the originator.

All asset-backed securities are credit enhanced. Credit enhancement is used to provide greater protection to investors against losses (i.e., defaults by the borrowers of the underlying loans). The amount of credit enhancement necessary depends on two factors. The first factor is the historical loss experience on similar loans made by the lender. The second factor is the rating sought by the issuer. For a given historical loss experience, more credit enhancement is needed to obtain a triple A rating than to obtain a single A rating.

Credit enhancement can take one or more of the following forms: third-party guarantees, reserve funds or cash collateral, recourse to the issuer, overcollateralization, and senior/subordinated structures. A third-party guarantee can be either a letter of credit from a bank or a policy from an insurance company. The rating of the third-party guarantor must be at least as high as the rating sought. Thus, if the third-party guarantor has a single A rating, a triple A rating for the asset-backed security cannot be obtained by using only this guarantee.

A reserve fund or cash collateral is a fund established by the issuer of the asset-backed security that may be used to make principal and interest payments when there are losses. Recourse to the issuer specifies that if there are losses, security holders can look to the investor to make up all or part of the losses.

---

[6] For a discussion of how one rating company, Fitch Investors Service, assesses the credit risk of an asset-backed security, see Mary Griffin Metz and Suzanne Mistretta, "Evaluating Credit Risk of Asset-Backed Securities," Chapter 27 in Frank J. Fabozzi (ed.), *The Handbook of Fixed Income Securities* (Burr Ridge, IL: Irwin Professional Publishing).

Overcollateralization involves establishing a pool of assets with a greater principal amount than the principal amount of the asset-backed securities. For example, the principal amount of an issue may be $100 million but the principal amount of the pool of assets is $102 million.

In a senior/subordinated structure two classes of asset-backed securities are issued. The senior class has priority over the subordinated class with respect to the payment of principal and interest from the pool of assets. Thus, it is the subordinated piece that accepts the greater credit risk and provides protection for the senior class. The protection is greater, the larger the amount of the principal of the subordinated class relative to the senior class. Thus, for a $100 million issue, greater protection against losses is afforded the senior class if the principal for that class is $70 million and the subordinated class is $30 than if it is $80 million for the senior class and $20 million for the subordinated class.

Today, the most common type of credit enhancement is the cash collateral and the senior/subordinated structure. In auto-loan backed securities, credit enhancement typically consists of a combination of subordination, partially funded reserve account, and a mechanism to build in some overcollateralization.[7] The amount of credit enhancement necessary to obtain a particular credit rating is based on a cash flow analysis of the security structure undertaken by a commercial rating company from whom a rating is sought.

SUMMARY

This chapter has provided a bird's eye view of the various types of mortgage-backed securities and asset-backed securities. The structure and cash flow characteristics of these products are reviewed.

---

[7] Metz and Mistretta, "Evaluating Credit Risks of Asset-Backed Securities," p. 602.

Chapter 12

Collateralized Borrowing via Dollar Rolls

Steven J. Carlson
Managing Director
Lehman Brothers

John F. Tierney C.F.A.
Senior Vice President
Fixed Income Division
Lehman Brothers

The mortgage securities market offers investors a specialized form of reverse repurchase agreement known as a *dollar roll*. A dollar roll is a collateralized short-term financing, where the collateral is mortgage securities. These transactions provide security dealers with a liquid and flexible tool for managing temporary supply/demand imbalances in the market. An investor initiates a dollar roll by delivering securities to a dealer and agreeing to repurchase similar securities on a future date at a predetermined price. The investor assumes some delivery risk at the end of the roll period, for unlike a normal reverse repurchase agreement, the dealer is not obligated to return the identical securities to the investor. In return for this privilege, the dealer extends a favorable borrowing rate to the investor that may be anywhere from a few basis points to several points below current repo market rates.

This chapter is adapted from Steven J. Carlson and John F. Tierney, "Collateralized Borrowing via Dollar Rolls," Chapter 6 in Frank J. Fabozzi (ed.) *The Handbook of Mortgage-Backed Securities* (Chicago, IL: Probus Publishing, 1995).

This chapter first introduces collateralized borrowing via the dollar roll transaction. Second, it describes a methodology for calculating the cost of funds using an example of a typical transaction. Third, it describes the risks to the calculated cost of funds due to prepayments, the delivery option, and adverse selection. Fourth, it takes a snapshot view of the dollar roll market for 30-year agency securities using breakeven analysis. Finally, it displays dollar roll prices (drops) and their associated borrowing costs for GNMA securities for the 12-month period from January 1993 to December 1993, offering some insights into TBA (to be announced) GNMA trading.

DOLLAR ROLL DEFINED

A dollar roll can be thought of as a collateralized borrowing, where an institution pledges mortgage passthroughs to a dealer to obtain cash. The dealer is said to "roll in" the securities. In contrast to standard reverse repurchase agreements, the dealer is not obliged to return securities that are identical to the originally pledged collateral. Instead the dealer is required to return collateral which is "substantially identical." In the case of mortgage passthroughs, this means that the coupon and security type, i.e., issuing agency and mortgage collateral, must match. As long as certain criteria are met, dollar rolls may be accounted for as financing transactions (rather than sales/purchases) for financial accounting purposes. According to the American Institute of Certified Public Accountants, the securities used in a dollar roll must meet the following conditions to satisfy the substantially identical standard.[1] The securities must:

1. Be collateralized by similar mortgages, e.g., 1- to 4-family residential mortgages;

2. Be issued by the same agency and be a part of the same program;

---

[1] For a detailed discussion of "substantially identical," see "Definition of the Term Substantially the Same for Holders of Debt Instruments, as Used in Certain Audit Guides and a Statement of Position," The American Institute of Certified Public Accountants, Statement of Position 90-3, February 13, 1990. Investors considering dollar rolls should discuss these issues with an accountant to ensure the transaction receives the desired accounting treatment.

3. Have the same original stated maturity;

4. Have identical coupon rates;

5. Be priced to have similar market yields; and,

6. Satisfy "good delivery" requirements, i.e., the aggregate principal amounts of the securities delivered and received back must be within 2.5% of the initial amount delivered.

The flexibility in returning collateral has value for a dealer because it provides a convenient avenue for covering a short position. That is, a trader may require a particular security for delivery this month, and by entering into a dollar roll agreement can effectively extend a delivery obligation to next month. If a dealer were required to return the identical security sold, as in the case of a standard repurchase agreement, the dealer would be unable to cover a short position. Dollar rolls offer dealers a convenient way to obtain promised mortgage securities, avoiding much of the cost of failing to make timely delivery. In theory, the dealer (the short coverer) will be willing to pay up to the cost of failure to deliver for the short-term opportunity to borrow or purchase securities required to meet a delivery commitment. For this reason most dollar rolls are transacted close to the monthly settlement date for mortgage-backed securities. Dollar rolls also allow dealers to even out the supply and demand for mortgage securities in the current settlement month and "back" months. Primary market mortgage originators frequently sell anticipated new mortgage security production in the forward market, for delivery 1 to 3 months (or more) in the future. This expected supply provides liquidity to the dollar roll market, by ensuring that dealers will have the securities required to close out dollar roll transactions.

In return for this service, dealers often offer dollar roll financing at extremely cheap rates and on flexible terms. Unlike most collateralized borrowings, there is no haircut, or requirement for over-collateralization. The investor gets 100% of the full market price, not a two to four point haircut as in a 1- to 3-month reverse repo. Dollar roll transactions are generally opened or closed as of the settlement date of each month, with the terms set some time prior to settlement. They typically cover the 1-month period between consecutive settlement dates, but they may also extend over multiple months, for up to 11 months. The dollar roll market also allows investors to negotiate more flexible borrowing windows. For example, terms can be arranged for 34, 44, or 89 days (reverse repos tend to centralize around 30-, 60-, or 90-day intervals) thus enabling the investor to exploit short-term investment opportunities, such as certificates of deposit or banker's acceptances.

DOLLAR ROLL: COST OF FUNDS EVALUATION

In calculating the actual cost of funds obtained through a dollar roll there are several key considerations:

1. Price of securities sold versus price of securities repurchased. In a positive carry (or a positively sloped yield curve) environment, the repurchase price will be lower than the original purchase price. The drop (dollar roll price) is the difference between the initial and ending prices plus the difference between the dealer's bid/ask prices.

2. Size of coupon payments.

3. Size of principal payments, both prepayments and scheduled amortization.

4. Collateral attributes of securities rolled in and securities rolled out.

5. Delivery tolerances. Both parties can over- or under-deliver. Most dollar roll agreements allow for the delivery of plus or minus 2.5% of the face amount.

6. Timing. The position of settlement dates within the months of the transaction impacts the accrued interest (paid to the seller at each end of the transaction). The days between settlements is the length of the borrowing period.

Each of these factors can influence the effective cost of funds implied by the dollar roll. For illustrative purposes, the calculations for a typical roll are described in the following section.

Dollar Roll Transaction Example

On January 7, 1994, a dealer and a mortgage security investor enter into a 1-month dollar roll agreement as described in Exhibit 1. The dealer agrees to purchase $1,000,000 of recent production GNMA 7s at 102 and ^{22}/32nds on January 19, 1994, and the investor agrees to repurchase $1,000,000 of face value GNMA 7s at 102 and ^{12}/32nds on February 16, 1994. (The value of the drop is therefore ^{10}/32nds of a point in price.) Good delivery is the delivery of anywhere from $975,000 to $1,025,000 of unpaid principal amount, since the investor and the dealer have the option of delivering plus or minus 2.5% of the original amount agreed upon. For the moment, let us assume that both parties deliver the notional quantity of securities, $1,000,000 of face value. On the first settlement date, January 19, the investor delivers the GNMA 7s and receives $1,030,375 in cash. Twenty-eight days later, on February 16, the investor will purchase GNMA 7s from the dealer and pay $1,026,667. This amounts to a bonus to the investor of $3,708 resulting from the drop.

During the 28 days of the agreement, the dealer receives both coupon payments and principal payments from the security sold by the investor. As a result, the investor forgoes the coupon income due in February, equal to $5,833 (7%/12 × $1,000,000). The principal payments from the security will also be paid to the dealer. Because all payments of principal are made at par value, whoever owns a premium security loses the premium on the principal paid down (through normal amortization and prepayments). This month, it will be the dealer. The payment of principal to the dealer represents an opportunity gain to the investor equal to the premium times the February principal payment. Had this transaction been done with a passthrough security selling at a discount to its par value, principal payments to the dealer would be viewed as an opportunity loss from the investor's perspective.

The exact size of the investor's opportunity gain in this example depends on prepayments for January. Since these figures are not available until early February, a projection must be made. A good indicator of the next month's prepayments is the prior month's prepayment rate for comparable maturity securities. The last 1-month annualized constant prepayment rate (CPR) for new production GNMA 7s with a weighted average maturity of 350 months is 2%. If we assume this annual constant prepayment rate, the investor's opportunity gain is $66 ($45 for prepayments + $21 for scheduled amortization). In this scenario, the investor effectively borrows $1,030,375 for 28 days at a cost of $2,058, giving an effective annual cost of 2.57%. This figure compares favorably with other cost of funds as of January 7, 1994, particularly the 1-month GNMA repo rate of 3.15%.

Exhibit 1: Sample Cost of Funds Calculation for Dollar Roll

Dollar Roll	
Transaction Amount:	$1,000,000
GNMA:	7.00%
Servicing	0.50%
Remaining Months to Maturity	350
Prepayment Assumption (CPR)	2.00%
Trade Date:	1/7/94
Days of Accrual to 1st Settlement (1/19/94)	18
Days of Accrual to 2nd Settlement (2116194)	15
Days Between Settlement Dates	28
Roll in Price	102-22
Drop:	10/32
Roll Out Price	102/12
Principal Payments	
Scheduled Amortization	$796
Prepayments	$1,681
Cash Rolled in (Borrowed)	$1,030,375 (7%/12 × 18/30 × $1,000,000) + ($1,000,000 × $102 22/32/100)
Cash Rolled Out	$1,026,667 (7%/12 × 15/30 × $1,000,000) + ($1,000,000 × $102 12/32/100)
Price Spread (Dollar Roll)	$3,708 ($1,030,375 - $1,026,667)
Interest Payment Foregone	($5,833) (7%/12 × $1,000,000)
Principal Paydown Premium Gain:	
Due to Prepayment	$45 ($1,681 × $2 22/32/100)
Due to Scheduled Amortization	$21 ($796 × $2 22/32/100)
Total Financing Cost	($2,058) ($3,713 - $5,833 + $45 + $21)
Effective Annual Financing	2.57% ($2,053/$1,030,380 × 360/28)

RISKS

The cost calculation presented above is subject to risk arising from three sources. The first is prepayment uncertainty. If GNMAs trade close to par, then this risk is minimal; dollar rolls of coupons that trade away from par involve increased risk of prepayment. The second type of risk arises because the effective cost of funds can be influenced by the quantity of loans actually delivered. Since both parties have delivery tolerances, each has an option that is implicitly written by the other party. The third source of risk is the problem of adverse selection; investors are likely to be returned pools that exhibit less desirable characteristics. The impact of each of these risks is described below.

Prepayment Risk

In the cost of funds example, we assumed a CPR of 2.0%, but a faster prepayment rate reduces the effective borrowing cost. The investor gains because he avoids receiving the principal payments at par. If the security actually pays down at a 16% CPR, the effective cost of borrowing is reduced to 2.15%, a savings of 42 basis points over the expected borrowing cost of 2.57% (see Exhibit 2).

Exhibit 2: Dollar Roll Sensitivity Analysis
(Breakeven Financing Rates for Security Used in Exhibit 1)

Drop	Annual Prepayment Rates (% CPR)								
	0	2	4	6	8	10	12	14	16
0-14	1.07	1.01	0.96	0.90	0.85	0.79	0.73	0.67	0.61
0-13	1.46	1.40	1.35	1.29	1.24	1.12	1.12	1.06	0.99
0-12	1.85	1.79	1.74	1.68	1.62	1.56	1.50	1.44	1.38
0-11	2.24	2.18	2.13	2.07	2.01	1.95	1.89	1.83	1.75
0-10	2.63	2.57	2.51	2.46	2.40	2.34	2.27	2.21	2.15
0-09	3.02	2.96	2.90	2.84	2.78	2.72	2.66	2.60	2.53
0-08	3.41	3.35	3.29	3.23	3.17	3.11	3.05	2.98	2.92
0-07	3.80	3.74	3.68	3.62	3.56	3.50	3.43	3.37	3.30
0-06	4.19	4.13	4.07	4.01	3.94	3.88	3.82	3.75	3.68

Exhibit 2 extends the example by presenting a sensitivity analysis of the effective cost of borrowing under various prepayment rate assumptions. Different prepayment rates can significantly change the effective cost of funds for GNMA 7s. This fact makes the dollar roll a useful tool for institutions that anticipate faster prepayments over a given period than the rest of the market participants do (the reverse is true for discounts). For dollar roll transactions with securities priced at or near par, prepayments become less important. Exhibit 2 also shows the effective cost of borrowing at various dollar roll prices. As the drop increases, the cost of funds decreases because the borrower repurchases the securities at a lower price.

Delivery Risk

The preceding example was based on the assumption that both parties to the dollar roll return exactly the notional amount of the transaction and deliver a substantially identical security that will bring the same price. In reality, both parties have delivery tolerances because they can under- or over-deliver by 2.5%. The delivery tolerance theoretically gives both parties put options: that is, the option but not the obligation to sell securities to each other. If the market price of the security to be rolled rises/falls between the contract date of the roll and the initial settlement, the investor will have an incentive to under/over deliver securities. For example, if the market price has risen before the roll is executed, the investor would deliver less securities at the lower roll price (i.e., would not exercise the put option on the balance of the acceptable amount of securities). Likewise, if at the end of the roll transaction, the market price of the underlying security is higher/lower than the repurchase price of the roll agreement, the dealer will have an incentive to under/over deliver securities. The effective cost of funds will be lower/higher than projected if the dealer under/over delivers relative to what the investor initially delivered. The investor's option has an exercise date as of the first settlement date and an "at-the-money" strike price equal to the roll in price. The dealer's exercise date is the final settlement date, and the strike price is lower by the amount of the drop, or slightly "out-of-the-money."

In practice, neither party can fine tune deliveries to exploit fully the ex-post value to their delivery options. Fine tuning the delivery for either the dealer or investor becomes difficult when the delivery tolerance is only plus or minus 2.5%. These options exist in a notional sense, in most cases.[2]

Adverse Selection Risk

Because the dealer is not obliged to return the identical collateral, the dealer and the investor both have a clear incentive not to deliver eligible collateral with attractive specified attributes, i.e., short WAM and fast prepay pools in the case of discounts or long WAM and slow prepay pools in the case of premiums. As a consequence, the parties would be ill-advised to deliver pools with above average attributes that could command a higher price. As a result, both parties usually transact the dollar roll with pools that are average or less attractive than the universe of deliverable securities. As long as both parties recognize this, there is little chance that one party or the other will be affected negatively.

Investors who wish to use high quality, specified securities for dollar rolls can stipulate that the securities returned must be of similar quality and/or that the drop be increased in recognition of the securities' more attractive attributes. As long as the lender and the borrower recognize that dollar rolls, like all TBA transactions, trade to the lowest common denominator, both parties will benefit from the transaction.

BREAKEVEN ANALYSIS

As has been demonstrated above, an assessment of the relative value of dollar rolls should include the alternative financing costs (that is, the 1-month repo rate), the size of the drop, and the expected prepay-

---

[2] This has been the case since April 11, 1987, when the PSA reduced delivery tolerance from [plus/minus] 5% to [plus/minus] 2.5%. The value of the delivery option is determined by the maturity of the roll agreement (the longer the roll maturity, the greater the dealer's delivery option) and by the price volatility of the coupon rolled (the greater the volatility, the greater the value of the dealer's option).

ment rate of the passthrough. These three factors are interrelated. For example, the size of the drop and the expected prepayment rate determines an implied repo rate for the dollar roll transactions. If the market rate is above this level, dollar rolls make sense, barring any outside considerations. Or combining a target short-term financing rate with the expected prepayment rate can help the borrower find a breakeven level for the drop. If the offered drop is larger than the breakeven level, again a dollar roll makes sense. Since the characteristics of the passthroughs involved in a dollar roll are not fixed, breakeven analysis must be used judiciously. Prepayment sensitivity plays an important roll in the analysis. Dollar rolls on current coupons have little sensitivity to prepayments, while rolls on discounts and premiums are quite sensitive. A small increase in CPR on a premium security will drive the implied financing rate down, while the opposite will occur for a discount security. Because prepayment opportunity gain/loss is an important factor in dollar roll valuation, investors must keep prepayment sensitivity in mind when doing a breakeven analysis. An example of a breakeven/sensitivity analysis for actually traded passthroughs appears in Exhibit 3.

To illustrate the use of the breakeven analysis, we offer the following example. Suppose an investor is evaluating a dollar roll on a GNMA 7. He receives a quote of $10/32$nds for a 1-month roll. Using the previous month's CPR, he calculates the implied financing rate to be 2.58%, 57 basis points below the current GNMA repo rate of 3.15%. On review of his breakeven levels, he sees that prepayments could slow to near 0% CPR and the implied financing rate would remain below 3.15%, and that the breakeven drop is $8+/32$nds. From this analysis, the investor knows that, financially, the trade is priced in his favor. He then considers the risk factors discussed earlier and makes his decision.

As mentioned, dollar roll deliveries are made on a TBA basis. As a general rule, a borrower will not use a security for a dollar roll that investors are willing to pay a premium for in the "specified pool" market. This is true because the borrower is likely to end the dollar roll with a security that trades in the TBA market (with a lower price). Against this background, the breakeven analysis should be based only on those securities likely to be traded in the TBA market.

Exhibit 3: Dollar Roll Breakeven and Sensitivity Market Analysis for Selected 30-Year Coupons (January 7, 1994)
(Target Financing Rate Is the GNMA Repo Rate: 3.15%)

Type	Coupon	Age	Price	Drop (32nds)	1 month CPR	Implied Fin.Rate	Breakeven Values (Target Fin. Rate: 3.15%) CPR	Drop (32nds)	Sensitivity Analysis Change in Fin. Rate Drop falls of 1/32 (bp)	Change of 1% CPR (bp)
GNMA	6.00%	1	97-09	9	0.5	2.27	2.6	7	+41	3.0
GNMA	6.50%	1	100-05	9	0.5	2.64	NA	8+	+40	0.0
GNMA	7.00%	2	102-22	10	1.6	2.58	NA	8+	+40	3.0
GNMA	7.50%	3	104-18	9	8.0	3.02	5.3	8+	+38	5.0
GNMA	8.00%	10	105-24	4	19.5	4.42	35.2	7+	+37	8.0
GNMA	8.50%	10	106-06	-2	43.2	4.74	55.9	2+	+36	11.2
FNMA	6.00%	2	92-12	9	1.2	2.28	27.7	7	+41	3.0
FNMA	6.50%	2	100-05	10	1.4	2.23	NA	7+	+40	0.2
FNMA	7.00%	2	102-15	11	2.5	2.18	NA	8+	+39	2.6
FNMA	7.50%	2	104-03	10	8.6	2.66	NA	8+	+38	4.6
FNMA	8.00%	15	105-08	7	30.0	2.66	23.2	5+	+37	7.6
FNMA	8.50%	35	105-22	0	52.0	3.27	53.0	0+	+35	11.9
FHLMC	6.00%	1	97-16	9	0.8	2.27	28.0	6+	+41	NA
FHLMC	6.50%	1	100-08	10	1.5	2.23	NA	7+	+40	0.2
FHLMC	7.00%	3	102-17	10	2.8	2.56	NA	8+	+39	2.7
FHLMC	7.50%	3	104-01	8	10.8	3.34	14.8	8+	+38	4.7
FHLMC	8.00%	15	104-28	5	32.5	3.40	35.8	5+	+37	7.4
FHLMC	8.50%	30	105-11	1	62.5	1.93	52.9	3+	+35	14.1

To offer a longer term perspective, Exhibit 4 shows the one-month dollar roll prices (drops) along with the computed effective annual financing rates (using actual prepayments for TBA type loans), the one-month GNMA repo rate, and the benchmark GNMA coupon. This analysis of the bids on GNMA dollar rolls shows some interesting aspects of TBA trading activity, as well as highlighting some attractive financing opportunities that were available in 1993. The savings in finance costs can be seen by observing the difference between the dollar roll implied repo rate and the actual GNMA repo rate. Dollar rolls with coupons near current production tend to offer the lowest financing opportunities. This is mostly due to large forward sales of these coupons by mortgage originators wishing to hedge their origination pipelines. Heavy activity of this type tends to depress forward prices, thus increasing the drop. This translates into attractive financing opportunities for borrowers who hold pools with these coupons.

Dollar roll drops on premiums varied widely throughout 1993, largely due to changing prepayment expectations. Early in the year, drops for GNMA 9s and 9.5s were 9/32nds to 12/32nds and implied financing rates were roughly in the 3-4% range. During June and July, drops on GNMA 9s and 9.5s collapsed to 4/32nds and 2/32nds, respectively, but the implied financing rates were only 25 bp and 35 bp. These implied financing rates were calculated based on prepayment rates for the prior month, which were far more rapid than market expectations, and projections by prepayment models. Later in the year, roll drops fell to or below zero as the market revised its prepayment expectations upward and in line with reality, and implied financing rates rose to near 3%.

During 1994 and 1995, dollar roll financing levels have been far less volatile. For securities near the current coupon, financing rates have been fairly consistently about 30 to 50 bp below GNMA repo rates. This change was due to a sharp slowdown in refinancing activity and new MBS originations, and much lower demand for CMO collateral. If mortgage rates fall sufficiently to set off another major wave of refinancings, dollar roll levels are likely to become very attractive again.[3]

SUMMARY

Dollar rolls often offer an attractive means of borrowing at low cost primarily because they allow dealers to cover their short positions. We have focused our discussion of dollar rolls on GNMA fixed rate passthroughs but it should be noted that there are also very active markets for dollar rolls in conventional fixed-rate and ARM passthroughs, and that similar cost of funds savings can be found in these transactions. This chapter has demonstrated a methodology for calculating the effective cost of funds obtained through dollar rolls, and outlined the primary risks associated with the cost of funds calculation.

---

[3] Beginning in 1997, dollar rolls become subject to Financial Accounting Standard 125, Accounting for Transfers and Servicing of Financial Assets and Extinguishments of Liabilities. Under this standard dollar rolls are defined as financing transactions, continuing previous practice. But the accounting changes in that the party receiving collateral at the beginning of the transaction (typically the dealer) is required to recognize those assets on the balance sheet, causing a ballooning of the balance sheet.

This development does not change the underlying structure or economics of the dollar roll transaction. However, some dealers sensitive to the size of their reported balance sheet may become more selective in their willingness to offer dollar roll financing, especially at quarter-end when dealers typically seek to reduce their balance sheets. This could cause dollar roll pricing to become marginally less attractive than historically. But this problem may be mitigated by the trend among dealers to change their reporting period from the traditional calendar quarter to a non-calendar quarter.

For more information about FAS 125, **see Chapter ??.**

Exhibit 4: GNMA Dollar Roll Prices, Dollar Roll Implied Repo Rates, and GNMA Repo Rates for 12-Month Period
{January-93 through December-93}

Date	Jan-93	Feb-93	Mar-93	Apr-93	May-93	Jun-93	Jul-93	Aug-93	Sep-93	Oct-93	Nov-93	Dec-93
1 mo. GNMA Repo Rate	3.20%	3.20%	3.25%	3.15%	3.15%	3.25%	3.18%	3.18%	3.25%	3.18%	3.10%	3.35%
Benchmark GNMA	7.00%	7.00%	7.00%	7.00%	7.00%	6.50%	6.50%	6.50%	6.00%	6.00%	6.00%	6.50%
GNMA Coupon	Roll Drops											
6.0	NA	NA	NA	NA	NA	NA	NA	NA	11	11	11	11
6.5	NA	NA	15	15	13	13	13	10	10	9	8	9
7.0	11	14	11	12	12	10	10	11	9	9	10	10
7.5	13	13	12	10	12	10	10	12	9	9	8	8
8.0	13	14	12	12	13	10	9	12	8	10	4	4
8.5	12	13	9	8	5	6	6	5	3	-2	-2	-2
9.0	11	12	9	3	1	4	4	10	0	0	-2	-2
9.5	5	9	4	4	2	2	2	1	0	0	0	-3
10.0	7	7	7	4	4	4	2	2	2	9	0	0
GNMA Coupon	Implied Repo Rates (%)											
6.0	NA	NA	NA	NA	NA	NA	NA	NA	1.55	1.77	2.57	1.47
6.5	NA	NA	0.72	0.49	2.15	1.23	1.42	3.02	2.35	2.96	3.21	2.68
7.0	2.96	2.13	2.71	2.09	2.90	2.79	2.92	3.09	3.12	3.34	3.41	2.65
7.5	2.55	2.85	2.72	3.22	3.27	3.14	3.26	3.15	3.47	3.64	4.29	3.59
8.0	2.87	2.87	3.03	2.68	3.06	3.13	3.53	3.11	3.58	2.71	4.76	3.78
8.5	3.48	3.47	4.33	3.97	5.16	3.88	3.87	5.01	5.10	6.92	6.69	6.15
9.0	3.44	3.48	3.68	4.37	3.16	0.12	0.25	0.37	2.77	2.99	4.47	2.12
9 5	2.90	2.73	4.40	3.19	1.75	1.54	0.35	3.26	2.48	2.90	3.43	2.78
10.0	2.08	3.24	3.49	3.58	2.30	2.34	1.41	3.71	2.19	2.90	4.11	2.43

Chapter 13

Understanding Cash Collateral Reinvestment Risks

Frank J. Fabozzi
Adjunct Professor of Finance
School of Management
Yale University

Eliot Jacobowitz
Vice President
Information Management Network

The lender of securities that accepts cash as collateral will either invest the cash itself or use the services of a professional money manager. There is a wide range of investment strategies that can be used with a corresponding range of risk/return profiles. Typically the investment vehicles selected by the recipient of cash collateral or the money manager engaged are fixed income securities. In Chapter 10 we discussed the risks associated with investing in these securities.

A reassessment of these risks in light of recent market developments has led to a renewed interest in the sleepy backwaters of securities lending generally and in cash collateral reinvestment risk particularly. While historically the securities lending business has avoided the scrutiny of the financial press, events of the last several years have altered many common perceptions, particularly on the cash collateral reinvestment and internal risk control sides.

Specifically, as interest rates steadily rose in 1994, the yield curve flattened in 1995 and market volatility increased in 1996, there has been a resulting appreciation of some of the basic risks that were previously either taken for granted or overlooked in earlier rising interest rate environments. As performance results began to suffer, beneficial owners discovered that some lenders were using relatively illiquid instruments with heightened interest rate change sensitivity (e.g. structured notes, range notes, inverse floaters) in cash collateral reinvestment programs. As the financial press began focusing on the number of unpleasant investment surprises which were rocking the normally staid beneficial owner community, many market participants began to reexamine their programs. One outcome of this reevaluation was the recognition that cash collateral reinvestment management should be properly seen as a leveraged portfolio management function of a (significant portion of a) fund's short-term investment management allocation and not as an isolated activity requiring minimal oversight.

Our purpose in this chapter is to review the various strategies that money managers can and have employed to invest cash collateral. Our perspective in this chapter is not how to manage a cash collateral fund. Rather, it is to explain the risks associated with these strategies so that a lender of securities who turns cash over to a money manager can understand how that manager will attempt to generate a return. By understanding the risks associated with a strategy, the lender of securities can assess if the potential risks suit its profile before funds are given to a manager. In addition, an understanding of how returns can be generated can be used to assess the performance of a money manager.

MEASURING RETURN

A lender of securities who receives cash collateral seeks to invest those funds for a short time period. That is, the investment horizon is short. The money manager's actual performance is measured in terms of total return. The total return considers the total dollars received from the following three sources: (1) the total coupon interest received over the investment horizon, (2) any capital gain (or capital loss — negative dollar return) at the end of the investment horizon, and (3) reinvestment income generated from reinvesting interim cash flows.

Calculation of a portfolio's total return is not always simple. Several important issues must be addressed in developing a methodology for calculating a portfolio's return. While we will not discuss these issues here, we will note that because different methodologies are available and these methodologies can lead to quite disparate results, it is sometimes quite difficult to compare the performance of managers. Consequently, there is a great deal of confusion concerning the meaning of the data provided by money managers to their clients and their prospective clients. This has led to abuses by some managers in reporting performance results. To mitigate this problem the Committee for Performance Standards of the Association of Investment Management and Research has established standards for calculating performance results and for presenting those results.

Regrettably, overall securities lending program efficiency is often judged as a strict function of cash collateral reinvestment performance. However, security lending collateral reinvested revenues are supplemented by security rental fee income, largely driven by a security's degree of "specialness." An evaluation of program revenue that did not overemphasize reinvestment income over security rental fee income might reduce some of the pressure on lenders to significantly outperform short-term indexes by assuming additional risks. Furthermore, the absence of industry cash collateral reinvestment benchmarks makes comparison shopping an inexact and exploitable exercise. The "chicken or the egg" paradox has thus far precluded the establishment of an industry-accepted benchmark that might otherwise be subjected to derision or worse, nonacceptance.

As a result of competitive pressures, fierce competition among lenders has at times resulted in the pursuit of yield grab, a trend which is further exacerbated by the growth in the unbundling of custody and lending services as well as the outsourcing of cash collateral management to specialty firms. Another complicating element that encourages additional risk taking by lenders arises out of the fact that securities lending program revenues have historically been packaged as a custody fee offsetting mechanism. As third-party lenders and others have demonstrated, the businesses actually have little to do with each other economically, as securities lending returns are largely ability-driven whereas custody is an increasingly commoditized business that is primarily efficient and volume-driven by economies of scale. As a result, a number of managers may have taken on additional risks in collateral reinvestment in order to attract clients with consistently competitive returns which already factor in a custody fee offset.

BENCHMARKS TO GAUGE PERFORMANCE

In Chapter 10, we discussed the various risks associated with investing in fixed income securities. A money manager who actively manages a portfolio is essentially making a bet that the risk or risks accepted will generate an enhanced return that is sufficient to compensate for the risk incurred.

To assess whether a money manager has in fact added value by incurring the risks inherent in the portfolio, it is necessary to have a benchmark by which to measure performance. The benchmark depends on the investment objectives and investment horizon of the beneficial owner. If the investment objective is safety of principal and the investment horizon is short term, then the median performance of money market funds would be a suitable benchmark. In contrast, for a beneficial owner who has a more aggressive posture and has a longer term investment horizon, one of the bond market indexes produced by Lehman Brothers, Salomon Brothers, or Merrill Lynch might be more suitable. Alternatively, a customized index that is designed by the investor working with an advisor may merit consideration.

Inherent in the selection of any benchmark is a set of risks. If the money manager's performance deviates from that of the selected benchmark, the beneficial owner must be able to identify why this occurred. There are vendor services that can identify the factors that generated the deviation from the benchmark's return. The models that perform this task are called *return attribution models*. While such models are far from perfect in explaining the manager's performance, they are extremely insightful in getting a handle as to where a manager was placing bets.

Typically, a manager who significantly underperforms the benchmark will be dismissed. Unfortunately, a manager who significantly outperforms the benchmark will be maintained and, if additional funds are available, will be given more funds to manage without assessing the reasons for the significant outperformance. It is in just such instances that it is imperative that a beneficial owner should undertake return attribution analysis. Significant outperformance means that the risks that the manager accepted were significantly different from that of the benchmark. Outperformance means that the manager's bets paid off in this instance. However, in a subsequent period, the bets may backfire causing a substantial portfolio loss.

To illustrate this point, suppose the selected benchmark is the median return on a money market fund and that a manager outperformed this benchmark by 500 basis points in a declining interest rate environment. Furthermore, suppose that the reason for this performance was due to the fact that the duration of the portfolio was large. As explained in Chapter 10, duration is a measure of a portfolio's interest rate risk. More specifically, it measures the approximate percentage change in a portfolio's value for a 100 basis point change in interest rates. Then it is clear that this manager made an interest rate bet that paid off in a declining interest rate environment. Thus, the beneficial owner is basically buying the interest rate forecasting skills of the manager. Since no manager can perfectly forecast interest rates, there will be a time where there will be a significant underperformance due to a greater interest rate risk than that is inherent in the benchmark.

This situation is not uncommon. There are newspaper accounts of investors who were "shocked" that a manager produced a disastrous return when in previous periods that manager far outperformed the benchmark. Post mortem analysis of the portfolio shows that the manager took on certain risks that the investor may not have been willing to accept if such risks were identified a priori.

While not involving securities lending, the Orange County Investment Pool (OCIP) provides an excellent example of why one should closely monitor a manager who appears to be doing a great job. During a declining interest rate environment, OCIP continuously produced extremely high returns. The manager for this fund, Robert Citron the county treasurer, was viewed as star/savior by the county's supervisory board. The board was not concerned and made no effort to determine the reason for the high returns. In fact, a basic analysis would have uncovered that Mr. Citron was taking on significant interest rate risk.

When interest rates increased in 1994, the portfolio realized a $1.7 *billion* loss. The only surprise to the citizens of Orange County should have been that the board of supervisors was surprised that this could happen!

The net result of events of 1994 and beyond has been that the ranks of owners who will take securities lending returns for granted as a "guaranteed" means of generating a "risk-free return" have declined to nearly zero. Beneficial owners now understand that regardless of any particular lender's investment expertise and/or familiarity with weathering adverse market conditions, all investment decision-making ultimately must be determined by the party that will be held responsible for any potential gains (losses), the owner of the securities. This is especially important, for as mentioned earlier, a beneficial owner's securities lending cash collateral portfolio often times represents one of the single largest allocations in the overall investment management portfolio. Notwithstanding any informal understandings reached with lenders, the owner will ultimately be judged as the hero or the villain. Finally, since balance sheet constraints preclude most lenders from indemnifying adverse cash collateral reinvestment performance, the general industry practice is not to indemnify investment returns. While some clients may have been made whole in the past, there is no guarantee that this will be the trend going forward.

ACTIVE PORTFOLIO STRATEGIES

A beneficial owner must impose constraints on a money manager so that there will not be exposure to unacceptable risks. The constraints are typically expressed in terms of maximum maturity or duration, credit quality of issues, currency denomination, use of derivative instruments, use of leverage, and maximum exposure to particular issues. Subject to these constraints, there are a variety of active portfolio strategies that a money manager can employ. In this section we provide an overview of each.

Interest Rate Expectations Strategies

A portfolio manager who believes that he or she can accurately forecast the future level of interest rates will alter the portfolio's sensitivity to interest rate changes. This involves increasing a portfolio's duration if interest rates are expected to fall and reducing duration if interest rates are expected to rise. The degree to which the duration is permitted to deviate from the benchmark's duration should be controlled by the client.

The duration of a portfolio can be altered in one or more of the following ways: (1) changing the composition of the cash market instruments in the portfolio; (2) borrowing funds via reverse repos; or (3) using futures or options. The second and third methods allow the manager to create leverage which can be used to quickly increase or decrease duration. In fact, the use of futures and options (commonly referred to as derivatives) is a quick and cost effective means for altering a portfolio's duration.

The key to an interest rate expectations strategy is, of course, an ability to forecast the direction of future interest rates. The academic literature does not support the view that interest rates can be forecasted so that risk-adjusted excess returns can be consistently realized. It is doubtful whether betting on future interest rates will provide a consistently superior return. A manager who can predict the movement of interest rates consistently is foolish to work for anyone. Given the instruments in the marketplace available for leveraging, a person with the gift of perfectly predicting interest rate movements could in a short period become the wealthiest individual in the world.

Yield Curve Strategies

The yield curve for U.S. Treasury securities shows the relationship between maturity and yield. The shape of the yield curve changes over time. *Yield curve strategies* involve positioning a portfolio to capitalize on expected changes in the shape of the Treasury yield curve. Here we will describe the different ways in which the Treasury yield curve has shifted and the different types of yield curve strategies.

A shift in the yield curve refers to the relative change in the yield for each Treasury maturity. A *parallel shift in the yield curve* refers to a shift in which the change in the yield for all maturities is the same. A *nonparallel shift in the yield curve* means that the yield for all maturities does not change by the same number of basis points.

A nonparallel yield curve shift involves a twist in the slope of the yield curve. This refers to a flattening or steepening of the yield curve. In practice, the slope of the yield curve is measured by the spread between some long-term Treasury yield and some short-term

Treasury yield. For example, some practitioners refer to the slope as the difference between the 30-year Treasury yield and the 1-year Treasury yield. Others refer to it as the spread between the 30-year Treasury yield and the 6-month Treasury yield. Regardless of how it is defined, a *flattening of the yield curve* means that the yield spread between the yield on a long-term and short-term Treasury has decreased; a *steepening of the yield curve* means that the yield spread between a long-term and short-term Treasury has increased.

In portfolio strategies that seek to capitalize on expectations based on short-term movements in yields, the dominant source of return is the impact on the price of the bonds in the portfolio. This means that the maturity of the bonds in the portfolio will have an important impact on the portfolio's return. For example, a total return over a 1-year investment horizon for a portfolio consisting of bonds all maturing in one year will not be sensitive to changes in how the yield curve shifts one year from now. In contrast, the total return over a 1-year investment horizon for a portfolio consisting of bonds all maturing in 30 years will be sensitive to how the yield curve shifts because one year from now the value of the portfolio will depend on the yield offered on 29-year bonds. As we know from Chapter 10, long maturity bonds have substantial price volatility when yields change.

A portfolio consisting of equal proportions of bonds maturing in one year and bonds maturing in 30 years will have quite a different total return over a 1-year investment horizon than the two portfolios we previously described when the yield curve shifts. The price of the 1-year bonds in the portfolio will not be sensitive to how the 1-year yield has changed but the price of the 30-year bonds will be highly sensitive to how long-term yields have changed.

The key point is that for short-term investment horizons, the spacing of the maturity of bonds in the portfolio will have a significant impact on the total return. Consequently, yield curve strategies involve positioning a portfolio with respect to the maturities of the bonds across the maturity spectrum. There are three yield curve strategies: (1) bullet strategies, (2) barbell strategies, and (3) ladder strategies.

In a *bullet strategy*, the portfolio is constructed so that the maturity of the bonds in the portfolio are highly concentrated at one point on the yield curve. In a *barbell strategy*, the maturity of the bonds included in the portfolio are concentrated at two extreme maturities. Actually, in practice when managers refer to a barbell strategy it is relative to a bullet strategy. For example, a bullet strategy might be to create a portfolio with maturities concentrated around 10 years while a corresponding barbell strategy might be a portfolio with 5-year and 20-year maturities. In a *ladder strategy* the portfolio is constructed to have approximately equal amounts of each maturity. So, for example, a portfolio might have equal amounts of bonds with 1 year to maturity, 2 years to maturity, etc.

Each of these strategies will result in different performance when the yield curve shifts. The actual performance will depend on both the type of shift and the magnitude of the shift. Consequently, yield curve strategies require a forecast of the direction of the shift and a forecast of the type of twist.

Yield Spread Strategies

The bond market is classified into sectors in several ways: by type of issuer (Treasury, agencies, corporates, and mortgage-backeds), quality or credit (risk-free Treasuries, triple-A, double-A, etc.), coupon (high-coupon/premium bonds, current-coupon/par bonds, and low-coupon/discount bonds), and maturity (short-, intermediate- and long-term). Yield spreads between maturity sectors involve changes in the yield curve as we have discussed in the previous section.

Yield spread strategies involve positioning a portfolio to capitalize on expected changes in yield spreads between sectors of the bond market in which the money manager is permitted to invest.

Arbitrage Strategies

Often money managers refer to "arbitrage" strategies. There are two types of arbitrage strategies, riskless arbitrage strategies and risk arbitrage strategies.

Riskless Arbitrage In a riskless arbitrage transaction, a money manager may be able to find a security trading at different prices in two different markets. If there are price discrepancies in various markets, it may be possible to lock in a profit after transaction costs by selling the security in the market where it is priced higher and buying it in the market where it is priced lower.

Money managers don't hold their breath waiting for such situations to occur, because such occurrences are rare. However, there are situations where packages of securities and derivative contracts, combined with borrowing, can produce a payoff identical to another security or package of securities, but the two are priced differently. The key point is that an arbitrage transaction is not exposed to any adverse movement in the market price of the securities in the transaction or any credit risk.

Risk Arbitrage Risk arbitrage does involve risk despite the fact that the term arbitrage suggests the absence of risk. The type of risk involved depends on the strategy. The most popular types of risk arbitrage strategies have involved mortgage-backed securities, particularly floating-rate securities.

One such common strategy involves the use of leverage via a reverse repurchase agreement to purchase a floating-rate tranche of a collateralized mortgage obligation (CMO)[1]. Typically, an agency CMO is purchased so that the maximum leverage can be obtained and there is no credit risk. The funding cost is LIBOR plus some spread. The objective is to earn a spread over LIBOR on a leveraged basis. Thus, if a manager pays 1-month LIBOR flat to fund the purchase of a CMO floater with a coupon of 1-month LIBOR plus 80 basis points, then on an unleveraged basis, the manager earns 80 basis points. If only an 8% haircut is required and the security is purchased at par, $8 has to be invested per $100 of the security purchased. The spread income realized is then $0.80 per $100 par value of the security purchased. The simple annual return is 10% ($0.80 divided by the $8 equity investment). In a low yield environment, this is quite an attractive return.

While there is no credit risk with this strategy, there are three types of risk. First, floating-rate CMO tranches have a cap (i.e., maximum coupon rate). Thus, there is the possibility interest rates will rise to the point where the maximum coupon rate will be less than the funding cost, resulting in a negative spread. This risk is referred to as "cap risk." Second, there is price risk. While the price risk of a floating-rate CMO is less than that of a fixed-rate security, its price will still decline if the cap is reached (at which time the security will act

---

[1] CMOs are described in Chapter 11.

just like a fixed-rate security) or if the market demands a wider spread to LIBOR. Thus, there is interest rate risk. Finally, the more complex the floating-rate CMO and the higher its spread to LIBOR, the less the liquidity. In fact, a large spread to LIBOR should be a clear indication of the liquidity risk.

CONCLUSION

All portfolio strategies involve some type of risk. A beneficial owner who allows a money manager to reinvest cash collateral should be aware of the risks associated with a strategy. A major risk faced by investors is *risk risk*, which we define as the risk associated with not understanding the risks accepted by a manager. Owners must therefore assess whether cash strategies suit both their general portfolio guidelines as well as their securities lending collateral reinvestment risk profiles, as these respective risk tolerances and performance objectives may in fact be independent of each other. At the very least, an effective cash collateral reinvestment program should explicitly state the range of acceptable investments given a beneficial owner's risk tolerance. All instructions and guidelines should be clearly written, explicit and mutually-understood. Daily reports should be available and reviewed carefully to ensure adherence to program guidelines.

It is particularly important to analyze the performance of a money manager who considerably outperforms a benchmark. While that money manager may be the top performer last period, in some future period the bets can backfire resulting in a disastrous outcome for the portfolio.

Always remember that there are no free lunches in financial markets — some lunches are just more palatable than others. While financial markets are not perfect, they do make managers pay for bets that turn out to be wrong and payoff when those bets turn out to be correct.

Chapter 14

Tax Issues Associated with Securities Lending

Richard J. Shapiro
Partner
Ernst & Young LLP

INTRODUCTION

The typical securities lending transaction involves the owner of securities lending the securities to a broker and the broker using these borrowed securities to cover short sales or fail sales where a third party seller has failed to deliver securities to the broker on the settlement date. Additionally, securities lending is utilized in connection with certain arbitrage or derivative trading strategies. This chapter focuses on the Federal income tax consequences of securities lending transactions.

GENERAL TERMS AND PRINCIPLES

Before delving into the technical and sometimes arcane world of the Internal Revenue Code (the "Code"), Treasury Regulations ("Regulations"), case law and the like, it may be helpful to review some of the terms and general principles that will be repeated throughout the chapter.

The author gratefully acknowledges the assistance of Alyse Ferraro Skidmore and Sidney Schwartz in the preparation of this chapter.

Securities Loan

A securities loan is a transaction in which the beneficial owner of securities (the securities lender) loans the securities to another party (the securities borrower). The securities borrower is obligated to return identical securities to the securities lender at some time in the future. Typically, the securities borrower will dispose of the securities (e.g., in connection with a short sale) and then purchase the identical securities in the market to replace the lender's securities.

Generally, the securities borrower provides collateral for the loan in the form of cash, a letter of credit, Treasury obligations, or other securities at least equal in value to the securities loaned. The collateral is generally marked to market on a daily basis and is increased or decreased as necessary. During the term of the loan, cash collateral is typically invested for the benefit (and the risk) of the securities lender. The income generated from the invested cash is returned to the securities borrower; however, a percentage of the income is paid as consideration to the lender for the securities loan. If the collateral is a letter of credit, or government or other securities, then the securities borrower will pay a predetermined fee to the securities lender. If an intermediary is involved (e.g., a broker or a bank) then the fee is split between the intermediary and the securities lender. These fees paid by the borrower to the lender for the use of the securities are known as "borrow fees" when the fee is based on the value of the securities, whereas when the borrower posts cash collateral, the lender's fee ("embedded fee") is the income earned from investing the cash less an agreed upon percentage of the income which is rebated to the borrower ("rebate").

Dividends or interest on the loaned securities are paid to the registered owner of the securities during the period of the loan. However, an equal amount, known as a "substitute payment" or an "in lieu of payment," is required to be paid by the securities borrower to the securities lender.

At the end of the term of the loan, the securities are returned to the securities lender and the collateral is returned to the securities borrower. The lender may terminate the loan upon notice, typically of not more than five business days.

Short Sales

Securities are sold that are not owned by the seller. The short seller is required to return the borrowed securities as well as pay to the lender all dividends/interest and other distributions made with respect to the loaned securities. A corporate lender of stock is not entitled to the dividends received deduction.[1]

Fail Sales

Securities are loaned to a broker in order to cover sales of stock by sellers who own the shares they are selling but whose certificates are either lost or have yet to be delivered to the broker. Under the lender's agreement with the broker, the borrowed securities as well as dividends and other distributions made with respect to the loaned securities are the lender's property. A fail sale is taxed in the same manner as a short sale, so that a corporate lender of stock in connection with a fail sale is not entitled to the dividends received deduction.[2]

Repurchase Agreement

A repurchase agreement ("repo") is a secured financing agreement. The vast similarities between repos and securities lending transactions necessitate a detailed description of a repo transaction and a comparison of the transactions. A repo is a financing transaction in which an owner of securities (the "seller")[3] sells the securities (typically, U.S. government obligations) to another party (the "purchaser")[4] and simultaneously agrees to repurchase the securities from the purchaser at a fixed future date (the "repurchase date") at the original sales price plus a specified interest rate ("repo margin"). In effect, money is temporarily exchanged for a security which, upon its subsequent return, will require repayment of the funds plus interest. By contrast, a securities loan involves the exchange of a security for a contract right to repurchase the same security.

A repo transaction when viewed from the perspective of the purchaser is commonly referred to as a "reverse repo." The duration of a repo may vary from one day to the maturity date of the underlying

---

[1] Rev. Rul. 60-177, 1960-1 C.B. 9. *See*, note 26, *infra.*
[2] *Id.*
[3] The seller can also be called the "debtor" or the "repoing party."
[4] The purchaser is also known as the "creditor" or the "reverse repoing party."

security ("repo to maturity"). At the repurchase date, repos are often "rolled over" or renewed until the maturity date of the security. In fact, it is this flexibility of term which has made repurchase agreements a favorite among many financial officers for investing corporate funds on a temporary basis. Additionally, tax-exempt organizations and regulated investment companies ("RICs") have been frequent lenders of securities as a means of obtaining additional income.

In many respects, repos and securities loans are substantially alike. In both transactions the recipient of the securities forwards funds to the counterparty until both positions are reversed at the date stipulated in the agreement. In each transaction the economic benefits and risks of ownership are retained by the securities owner. Further, collateral is posted by the borrower in a securities loan as well as the seller in a repo. Also, the securities borrower and the repo purchaser (under common industry practice) may freely dispose the subject securities.

The following example illustrates the substantial similarities between the repo and the securities loan. Corporation S ("S") needs to cover a short sale with certain governmental securities. To obtain the needed securities, S enters into an agreement with an owner ("O") of the required securities. Under the agreement, O will transfer the securities to S in return for cash. At a specified date in the future, S will return the securities to O and the cash will be returned to S.

Economically, the transaction described has the effect of a secured loan, in that O obtains cash and transfers securities as collateral. However, the same result could be achieved by structuring the transaction as either a repo or a securities loan.

If the transaction is in the form of a securities loan, then O would be referred to as a securities lender and S would be the securities borrower. Pursuant to the securities loan agreement, O would loan the securities to S and S would provide O with cash collateral. During the term of the loan, O would receive income from the investment of the collateral and S would be required to pay O an amount equivalent to the interest coupon on the securities. At the end of the term of the loan, S would return the same (or identical) securities to O. Effectively, O would be compensated for allowing S to use the securities, to the extent the income earned from the invested collateral exceeds the rebate to S.

On the other hand, if the transaction were structured as a repo, then O, as the repoing party (or seller-debtor), would purport to sell the securities to S, the reverse repoing party (or buyer-creditor), thus giving S the use of the securities and O the use of the cash. During the period of the agreement S would be required to pay an amount equivalent to the coupon interest on the securities to O. At the end of the term S would purport to resell the securities to O at an enhanced price. Effectively, S would be compensated for allowing O to use the cash, to the extent that the "resale" price exceeded the "sale" price.

In light of these similarities, it is often difficult to rationalize the differing tax treatments that apply to these two transactions.

CURRENT TAX TREATMENT (DOMESTIC)

Securities Lending Transactions

The current tax treatment governing securities lending is based, in part, on Section 1058 of the Code and the proposed regulations issued under that provision of the Code. Although Section 1058 of the Code is a relatively recent development, enacted in 1978[5], the analysis behind its general principles and thus the basic foundation for the current tax treatment of securities lending transactions can be traced back to 1926 with the U.S. Supreme Court's decision in *Provost v. U.S.*[6] In that case, the Supreme Court described a stock loan in the following manner:

> When the transaction is thus completed, neither the lender nor the borrower retains any interest in the stock that is the subject matter of the transaction and that has passed to and become the property of the purchaser.

[5] *See*, Senate Finance Committee Report on P.L. 95-345 (1978) (the "Committee Report"); S. Rep. No. 762, 95th Cong., 2d Sess. 3, *reprinted in* 1978 U.S. Code Cong. & Admin. News 1286, which made Code Section 1058 applicable to amounts received after December 31, 1976 regardless of the taxpayer's year-end.

[6] 269 US 443 (1926). In *Provost v. U.S.*, the Supreme Court examined the appropriateness of imposing a stamp tax on a "loan" and "return" transaction as a taxable exchange. *Id. Also, see* GCM 36948 (1976), which, citing *Provost,* held that the transfer of securities in a securities "loan" was a disposition and not a loan for Federal income tax purposes. However, if securities not differing materially in kind or extent were delivered, the disposition might be non-taxable under then existing law. GCM 36948 (1976).

Neither the borrower nor the lender has the status of a stockholder of the corporation whose stock was dealt in, nor any legal relationship to it. Unlike the pledgee of stock, who must have specific stock available for the obligor on payment of his loan, the borrower of stock has no interest in the stock nor the right to demand it from any other. For that reason he can be neither a pledgee, trustee nor bailee for the lender, and he is not the one "with whom stock has been deposited as collateral security for money loaned." For the incidents of ownership, the lender has substituted the personal obligation, wholly contractual, of the borrower to restore him, on demand, to the economic position in which he would have been, as the owner of the stock, had the loan transaction had not been entered into.[7]

Section 1058 and Proposed Treasury Regulations

Section 1058 of the Code and the proposed regulations issued with respect to that section provide for an exception to the general recognition principles of Section 1001 of the Code[8] where certain requirements are satisfied. Taxpayers who enter into a "qualifying" lending agreement pursuant to the provisions of Section 1058 of the Code can receive non-recognition treatment with respect to the gain or loss realized on the transfer of the securities. The lender will not recognize gain or loss on the exchange of the securities for the obligation of the borrower, nor will the lender recognize gain or loss on the exchange of the rights under the loan agreement in return for securities identical to the securities transferred.[9]

Qualified Loans To qualify for non-recognition treatment, a lending agreement must satisfy the three requirements specifically enumerated in Section 1058(b) of the Code and any requirements as

---

[7] 269 US 443 (1926).

[8] Generally, the gain or loss realized on an exchange of property is recognized unless specifically exempted from the recognition provisions of Section 1001 of the Code and the Regulations issued thereunder. IRC §1001(c).

[9] IRC §1058(a); Prop. Treas. Reg. §1.1058-1(a).

prescribed by regulations. First, the agreement must provide that the borrower is required to return to the lender securities identical to those lent to the borrower.[10] For purposes of Section 1058, the term "securities" is defined in Section 1236(c) of the Code, and includes shares of stock in any corporation, certificates of stock or interest in any corporation, notes, bonds, debentures, other evidences of indebtedness, or any evidences of an interest in or right to subscribe to or purchase any of the foregoing.[11] "Identical securities" are securities of the same class and issue as the securities lent to the borrower.[12] However, if the agreement permits the borrower to return equivalent securities in the event of a reorganization, recapitalization or merger of the issuer of the securities during the term of the loan, this requirement will be deemed satisfied.[13]

The second requirement mandates that the agreement must require the borrower to make payments to the lender equivalent to all interest, dividends, and other distributions which the owner of the securities is entitled to for the period during which the securities are borrowed.[14]

The third requirement specifically enumerated in the Code is that the agreement can not reduce the risk of loss or opportunity for gain of the transferor of the securities in the securities transferred.[15]

Section 1058(b)(4) of the Code grants the Internal Revenue Service ("Service") the authority to prescribe additional requirements through regulations. The proposed regulations require the agreement to be in writing and require that the lender be allowed to terminate the loan upon notice of not more than 5 business days.[16]

---

[10] IRC §1058(b)(1); Prop. Treas. Reg. §1.1058-1(b)(1). The significance of the return of "identical" securities is rooted in general recognition provisions of Section §1001 of the Code and Treasury Regulation §1.1001-1 which indicate that where there is material difference in the property exchanged the taxpayer must recognize the gain or loss on the exchange. Similarly, in Revenue Ruling 57-451, the Service utilized Sections 421 and 1036 of the Code to provide for non-recognition treatment where the stock of the same corporation is exchanged. Rev. Rul. 57-451, 1957-2 C.B. 295. *See* GCM 36948, *supra*, note 6.

[11] Prop. Treas. Reg. §1.1058-1(b)(1).

[12] *Id.*

[13] *Id. See, Special Rule for Mergers, Recapitalizations and Reorganizations, infra.*

[14] IRC §1058(b)(2); Prop. Treas. Reg. §1.1058-1(b)(2).

[15] IRC §1058(b)(3); Prop. Treas. Reg. §1.1058-1(b)(3).

[16] Prop. Treas. Reg. §1.1058-1(b).

If these requirements are met the lending transaction "qualifies" for Section 1058 non-recognition treatment. The proposed regulations provide the following illustration of these rules.[17]

> *Example*: A owns 1,000 shares of XYZ stock. A instructs A's broker, B, to sell the XYZ stock. B sells to C. After the sale, B learns that A will not be able to deliver to B certificates representing the 1,000 shares in time for B to deliver them to C on the settlement date. B effects the delivery by borrowing stock from a third party, D. D is a non-exempt organization having a large position in XYZ stock. This borrowing is evidenced by a written agreement with the following terms:
>
> 1. D will transfer to B certificates representing 1,000 shares of XYZ common stock.
> 2. B will pay D an amount equivalent to any dividends or other distributions paid on the XYZ stock during the period of the loan.
> 3. Regardless of any increases or decreases in the market value of XYZ common stock, B will transfer to D 1,000 shares of the XYZ common stock of the same issue as that of the XYZ common stock transferred from D to B.
> 4. B agrees that upon notice of 5 business days, B will return identical securities to D.[18]

The example concludes that the agreement between B and D satisfies the requirements of Proposed Treasury Regulation Section 1.1058-1. The agreement is in writing. It requires the borrower, B, to return to the lender, D, identical securities and to pay to D amounts equivalent to any dividends or other distributions paid on the stock during the period of the loan. It does not reduce D's risk of loss or opportunity for gain because, regardless of the fluctuations in the market value of XYZ common stock, B is obligated to return 1,000 shares of XYZ common stock.[19]

---

[17] Prop. Treas. Reg. §1.1058-2, Ex.(1).
[18] *Id.*
[19] *Id.*

Collateral Consequences Where the taxpayers enter into a qualifying loan agreement pursuant to Section 1058 of the Code, the parties receive non-recognition treatment on the qualifying transaction. In addition, the lender's basis and holding period in the lent stock are impacted.

Basis Consistent with other non-recognition provisions of the Code, the lender's basis in the identical securities returned by the borrower will be the same as the lender's basis in the securities lent to the borrower.[20] In other words, the lender will have a substituted basis in the exchanged securities to preserve the gain or loss inherent in the securities. Similarly, the lender's basis in the contractual obligation received from the borrower in exchange for the lender's securities will be equal to the lender's basis in the securities exchanged.[21]

Although the proposed regulations are silent as to the treatment of original issue discount ("OID"), it appears that in transactions where the loaned security is an OID obligation, any OID accruing during the time that the bonds are lent out under a loan arrangement are not included in the lender's basis when the bonds are returned.[22] The treatment of the in lieu of payment in connection with OID obligations is unclear.

Holding Period The lender's holding period is determined under Treasury Regulation Section 1.1223-2.[23] Accordingly, the holding period in the hands of the lender of the securities received by the lender from the borrower at the termination of the agreement includes both the period for which the lender held the securities which were transferred to the borrower *and* the period between the transfer of the securities from the lender to the borrower and the return of the securities to the lender.[24]

---

[20] Prop. Treas. Reg. §1.1058-1(c)(1).

[21] Prop. Treas. Reg. §1.1058-1(c)(2).

[22] *See* American Bar Association Section of Taxation, Committee on Financial Transactions, Securities Loans Task Force, Report on Securities Lending Transactions Governed by Section 1058 (April 22, 1991); Rev. Rul. 74-482, 1974-2 C.B. 267.

[23] Prop. Treas. Reg. §1.1058-1(g). The Committee Report indicates that where the lender does not recognize gain or loss under Section 1058 of the Code, then upon the borrower's transfer of the securities in satisfaction of the contractual obligation, the lender will have a tacked holding period in the securities which are returned.

[24] Treas. Reg. §1.1223-2(a).

Treatment of Payments to Lender A payment made by the borrower in lieu of interest, dividends, or any other distribution is treated by the lender as a fee for the temporary use of property.[25] The payment does not retain the character of the income that is being replaced (i.e., interest or dividend), because the lender holds a contractual obligation, and not the security itself. Thus, for example, a payment received by a lender in lieu of a dividend is treated as ordinary income and not as a dividend for purposes of the corporate dividends received deduction.[26] Similarly, where the obligation lent is a tax-exempt security, the lender has ordinary income, not tax-exempt income.[27] Generally, the Service requires information reporting with respect to substitute dividend and interest payments.[28]

Special Rules for Regulated Investment Companies and Tax-Exempt Entities As a result of the special rules for regulated investment companies ("RICs") and tax-exempt entities, these potential lenders are not discouraged from engaging in securities lending. Under the Committee Report, payments received on security loans which satisfy certain requirements can retain their interest or dividend character for certain purposes.[29] With regard to RICs,

---

[25] Prop. Treas. Reg. §1.1058-1(d).

[26] *Id. See* Rev. Rul. 60-177, 1961-1 C.B. 9, in which the Service held that an amount equal to a cash dividend paid to a lender in a short sale transaction is not a dividend for purposes of the corporate dividends received deduction because the lender is no longer considered the shareholder for purposes of IRC §316. *See also,* PLR 8828003 which applies the disallowance of the dividends received deduction of Revenue Ruling 60-177 to both the lender and borrower in the "fail sale" context. The Service reasoned that the purchaser was not entitled to the dividends received deduction on the loaned stock because the purchaser was not the owner of the stock on the ex-dividend date. Additionally, the seller was not entitled to the dividends received deduction, either, because the seller was required to make an in lieu, or substitute, payment to the buyer. *Id. See also,* note 92, *infra.*

[27] Rev. Rul. 80-135, 1980-1 C.B. 402. *See,* note 57, *infra,* which discusses the elimination of the tax-exempt status on payments received in a repo transaction where the underlying security is a U.S. government security. *See,* Rev. Rul. 79-108, 1979-1 C.B. 466, which disallowed an exclusion from gross income under Section 103 of the Code where municipal obligations are issued solely to derive an arbitrage profit. *See also,* note 93, *infra.*

[28] Treas. Reg. §1.6045-2. Information reporting is generally not required in the case of substitute dividend payments made to individuals. Treas. Reg. §1.6045-2(a). Additionally, such reporting requirements are not imposed upon substitute payments made to tax-exempt organizations, individual retirement plans and certain U.S. and foreign governmental organizations. Treas. Reg. §1.6045-2(b).

[29] S. Rep. No. 762, 95th Cong., 2d Sess. 1978, 1978-2 C.B. 357.

the income received from substitute payments is characterized the same as the income from the underlying securities for purposes of the RIC diversification requirements.[30] For example, RICs are able to satisfy the gross income test of Section 851(b)(2)[31] of the Code because the substitute payments are considered interest or dividend income depending on the underlying security. However, where such payments are passed through to the shareholders of these lending RICs, the payments would not be treated as dividends for purposes of the dividends received deduction.[32]

Special rules also apply in the case of amounts received by tax-exempt organizations.[33] Income from substitute payments ("payments made with respect to securities loans") will not be taken into account in computing unrelated business taxable income ("UBTI")[34]

---

[30] *Id.* See, PLR 9030048 for illustration of the RICs ability to use its securities loans to satisfy its asset diversification requirements, which is one of the prerequisites to the special tax treatment of RICs.

[31] The gross income test is another requirement for RIC tax treatment. If a RIC fails either the asset diversification or gross income test, the entity may lose the pass through nature of a RIC and become a taxable entity. Thus, the ability for the securities loan assets and income to qualify under these tests is essential to the ability of the RIC to be able to utilize secured loan transactions as a means of generating additional income.

[32] Committee Report, 1978-2 C.B. 357. This limitation on the characterization of the payments as dividends for purposes of the dividends received deduction is consistent with the general treatment of securities loan transactions, as seen in note 26, *supra*. As such, the special rules regarding the retention of the character of the underlying payment provides RICs with the ability to engage in securities lending transactions without violating the requirements for RIC status under the Code, but does not provide RIC shareholders with a benefit not afforded to other securities lenders.

[33] The proposed regulations provide that "*except as otherwise provided in section 512(a)(5), a payment of amounts required to be paid by the borrower ... shall be treated by the lender as a fee for the temporary use of property.*" Prop. Treas. Reg. §1.1058-1(d) (Emphasis Added). The legislative history of Section 512 of the Code indicates that "Congress did not intend for ordinary or routine investment activities of a section 501(a) organization in connection with its securities portfolio to be treated as the conduct of a trade or business for purpose of section 513." Rev. Rul. 78-88, 1978-1 C.B. 163. "Taxing such income is inconsistent with the generally tax-free treatment accorded to exempt organizations' income from investment activities." S. Rep. No. 94-1172, 94th Cong., 2d Sess. 3,4 (1976). However, this exclusion from taxation does not extend to organizations which hold the securities in the ordinary course of their trade or business or hold such securities as inventory. *Id.*

[34] "Unrelated business taxable income" is defined pursuant to Sections 512 and 513 of the Code as income derived by any organization through any trade or business the conduct of which is not substantially related to the exercise or performance of its tax exempt functions. Section 511 of the Code imposes income tax on a tax-exempt entity's UBTI. IRC §511(a).

in the hands of a tax-exempt lender,[35] provided that the agreement with regard to the loaned securities satisfies certain requirements.[36] Further, income received by a tax-exempt lender in connection with a qualified loan agreement is not taxable to the lender as debt financed property[37] nor as acquisition indebtedness.[38] Payments made with respect to securities loans are deemed to be derived from the securities loaned and not from collateral security or the investment of collateral security from the loans.[39]

Transactions Collateralized by Cash In transactions where the loan is collateralized by cash, the cash is usually invested for the account and at the risk of the securities lender. The income from the invested capital is returned to the securities borrower, a rebate, except that a percentage of the income or return on the invested col-

---

[35] Section 512(a) of the Code through its reference to the modifications in subsection (b) excludes "payments with respect to securities loans" from the definition of UBTI. IRC §512(a). Section 512(a)(5) of the Code defines payment with respect of securities as all amount received in respect of a security ... including, (i) amounts in respect of dividends, interest or other distributions; (ii) fees computed by reference to the period beginning with the transfer of securities by the owner and ending with transfer of identical securities back to the transferor ...; (iii) income from collateral security for such a loan; and (iv) income from the investment of collateral security. IRC §512(a)(5).

[36] Section 512 of the Code requires provisions similar to Section 1058 of the Code to establish a "qualified loan" for purposes of receiving non-recognition treatment. IRC §512. For example, Section 512 of the Code requires that the transferor be able to terminate the loan upon notice of not more than five days. IRC §512(a)(5)(B). This is the same requirement as under the Proposed Regulations under Section 1058 of the Code.

[37] S. Rep. No. 762 at 1294, in which the Committee agreed with Service's position in Revenue Ruling 78-88 that the income earned by an exempt organization which lends securities ... pursuant to a typical securities lending transaction is not taxable as debt financed income. P.L. 95-345. However, if an exempt organization incurs indebtedness to purchase loaned securities, any income from the securities would be considered debt financed income and subject to taxation as UBTI under Sections 512 and 514 of the Code. *Id.*

[38] IRC §514(c)(8)(C). As discussed in note 34, *supra*, tax-exempt organizations are taxed on their UBTI. The significance of debt financed property and acquisition indebtedness, for our purposes, is simply that the Code subjects the tax-exempt entities to tax on these purchases or investments if the transactions meet the technical definition set forth in the Code. As such, the exemption from tax on these transactions, when entered into pursuant to a qualified loan arrangement, does not discourage tax-exempt entities from becoming lenders in such transactions.

[39] IRC §514(c)(8)(A). Additionally, any deductions which are directly connected with collateral security for such loan, or with the investment of collateral security, are deemed to be deductions which are directly connected with the securities loaned. IRC §514(c)(8)(B).

lateral is paid to the securities lender as a fee. If the loan is collateralized by other securities, the borrow fee is a predetermined amount for the use of the securities paid to the securities lender. Although not specifically addressed in Section 1058 of the Code or in the proposed regulations, the borrow fee should also be characterized as a "fee" for the temporary use of property and, as such, should constitute ordinary income to the lender.

Special Rule for Mergers, Recapitalizations and Reorganizations In the case of a merger, recapitalization, or reorganization of the issuer of securities lent pursuant to Section 1058, the loan transaction is deemed terminated immediately prior to the merger, recapitalization, or reorganization and a second Section 1058 transaction is deemed entered into immediately following the merger, recapitalization, or reorganization on terms identical to the original Section 1058 transaction.[40] Thus, the borrower of the securities is deemed to have returned the securities to the lender immediately prior to the merger, recapitalization, or reorganization and immediately thereafter the lender and borrower are deemed to have entered into a second Section 1058 loan transaction, on terms identical to the original Section 1058 loan transaction.[41] However, this special rule does not apply in the case where the lender ultimately is repaid with securities identical to the securities originally transferred.[42]

The proposed regulations illustrate these rules with the same facts from the example noted above,[43] with the following additions:

> *Example:* 1. Upon D's transfer to B of the certificates representing the 1,000 shares of XYZ common stock, B will transfer to D, cash equal to the market value of the XYZ common

---

[40] Prop. Treas. Reg. §1.1058-1(f)

[41] *Id.* This rule permits the parties in securities lending transactions to continue to engage in their transactions without amending, or closing and re-entering into, agreements due to internal changes in the corporation of the stock or securities of which are underlying the lending arrangement. Additionally, the rule is consistent with the treatment accorded to such tax-free reorganizations.

[42] *Id.*

[43] *See,* note 17, *supra.*

stock on the business day preceding the transfer, as collateral for the stock. The collateral will be increased or decreased daily to reflect increases or decreases in the market value of the XYZ stock during the period of the loan.

2. B agrees that upon notice of five (5) business days, B will return to D 1,000 shares of XYZ common stock, or the equivalent thereof in the event of reorganization, recapitalization or merger of XYZ during the term of the loan. Upon delivery of the stock to D, D will return the cash collateral to B. [44]

According to the proposed regulation, the agreement between B and D satisfies the requirements for a qualified loan agreement. If XYZ merged into another corporation and B returns an equivalent amount of stock in the resulting corporation, the qualified loan agreement is deemed terminated immediately before the merger. Thus, D is deemed to be the owner of the XYZ common stock at the time of the merger. D does not recognize gain or loss upon the transfer of the XYZ common stock to B or upon the return of the stock of the resulting corporation to D.[45]

Failure to Comply with Requirements If a transfer of securities is intended to comply with these rules but the contractual obligation does not satisfy the requirements of a qualified loan agreement, gain or loss is recognized upon the initial transfer of the securities in accordance with the rules of Section 1001 of the Code.[46] For example, if the agreement provided that the lender must give notice in excess of five business days to terminate the agreement, the agreement would not satisfy the contractual requirements of Proposed Treasury Regulation Section 1.1058-1(b)(3), and gain or loss would be recognized upon the initial transfer. The holding

---

[44] Prop. Treas. Reg. §1.1058-2, Ex. (2).

[45] *Id.*

[46] Prop. Treas. Reg. §1.1058-1(e)(1). Whether a secured loan transaction which fails to qualify under Section 1058 of the Code will produce a taxable gain or loss is uncertain. Although Section 1001 of the Code is a general recognition provision, there are several exceptions which could give a secured loan which failed to satisfy Section 1058 of the Code non-recognition treatment. *See,* notes 6 and 10, *supra.*

period in the hands of the lender of the securities transferred to the borrower terminates on the day the securities are transferred to the borrower, and the holding period in the hands of the borrower of the property transferred to it begins on the date that the securities are delivered pursuant to the transfer loan agreement.[47]

Whereas, if the agreement satisfies the requirements of Section 1058 of the Code but the borrower fails to return to the lender the requisite identical securities or otherwise defaults under the agreement, gain or loss is recognized on the day the borrower fails to return identical securities as required by the agreement, or otherwise defaults.[48] In this case, the holding period in the hands of the lender, of the securities transferred to the borrower, terminates on the day the borrower fails to return the identical securities, and, similarly, the holding period in the hands of the borrower begins on the day the borrower fails to deliver or otherwise defaults.[49]

Application of the Wash Sale Rules Finally, it is important to note that Section 1091 of the Code and the related regulations thereunder apply the wash sale rules[50] to losses recognized as the result of the failure to comply with Section 1058. In other words, the application of the wash sale rules may prevent the recognition of a loss that would otherwise be recognized under Section 1058.[51] A similar nonrecognition provision is applicable to short sales, which can prevent a taxpayer from recognizing a loss on its short position.[52]

---

[47] Prop. Treas. Reg. §1.1223-2(b)(1).

[48] Prop. Treas. Reg. §1.1058-1(e)(2).

[49] Prop. Treas. Reg. §1.1223-2(b)(2).

[50] In general, the wash sale rules disallow losses which lack economic substance because the taxpayer has not truly "disposed" of the interest in the security. Under Section 1091 of the Code, a loss is disallowed if 30 days before or after the sale or disposition of the stock or security, the taxpayer has acquired by purchase or exchange or has entered into a contract or option to acquire substantially identical stock or securities. IRC §1091(a).

[51] Prop. Treas. Reg. §1.1223-2(b)(2).

[52] The wash sale rule, described in note 50, *supra*, applies to short sales. A closing of a short sale or entering into a short sale, depending on the facts, can be deemed a sale date for purposes of applying the wash sale rule. Also, a realized loss on a short sale is deferred if, during the period beginning 30 days before and ending 30 days after the date of the closing, the taxpayer either sold substantially identical stock or securities or entered to another short sale transaction on substantially identical stock or securities. IRC §1091(e).

Repurchase Agreements

The key element in determining the tax treatment of a repo transaction is whether a sale or a secured loan has occurred. If, based upon the particular facts and circumstances, a sale of securities has indeed taken place, gain or loss will be recognized by both the seller and the purchaser.[53] Alternatively, if the transaction is deemed a securities loan, gain or loss may not be recognized on either the transfer or the return of the securities.[54] The factors to which the courts and the Service have looked in characterizing the transaction as either a loan or a sale include the intent of the parties, which party exercised control over the securities, which party bore the risk of loss, whether the seller was contractually obligated to pay interest to the buyer, and whether the seller had the right to repurchase the securities.[55]

The typical repo transacted in today's capital markets is treated by the Service and the courts as a loan collateralized by the underlying securities. If the repo is treated as a loan the seller is considered to have retained the benefits and burdens of ownership, and, as such, the seller will recognize gain or loss only upon the ultimate disposition (or "sale") of the securities underlying the repurchase agreement.[56] No gain or loss is recognized by either the seller upon the initial transfer of the securities to the purchaser, nor by the purchaser upon returning the securities to the seller. Although not formally ruled upon by the Service, loan characterization should

---

[53] IRC § 1001. However, there are several provisions which disallow losses, including but not limited to the wash sale rules under Section 1091 of the Code and the straddle rules under Section 1092 of the Code. The purpose of these provisions is to defer tax losses until taxpayers are truly out of the position, or have reduced the investment in the loss position, and to prevent creation of tax losses which have not economically occurred.

[54] IRC § 1058. *See, Section 1058* discussion, *supra.*

[55] *See, Citizen's National Bank of Waco v. U.S.,* 551 F.2d 832 (Ct. Cl. 1977), 1977-1 U.S.T.C. 9298; Rev. Rul. 74-2, 1974-1 C.B. 24. *See also,* Rev. Rul. 77-59, 1977-1 C.B. 196, in which, a REIT's purchase agreement involving U.S. Treasuries were treated as a loan; Rev. Rul. 60-177, 1960-1 C.B. 9, in which the Service held that substitute payments received by the lender were not dividends for certain federal tax purposes because the lender did not retain ownership of the stock; and Rev. Rul. 57-451, 1957-2 C.B. 295, where the Service ruled that a shareholder who loaned securities to satisfy a broker's short sale obligation had transferred all incidents of ownership.

[56] *See,* Rev. Rul. 79-108, 1979-1 C.B. 75; Rev. Rul. 77-59, 1977-1 C.B. 196; Rev. Rul. 74-27, 1974-1 C.B. 24.

be equally appropriate where different certificates (although identical securities) are returned upon repurchase. With the purchaser being insulated from the risk of market fluctuation of the repoed securities, the phrase "sale and repurchase" is not to be construed literally, as a true sale does not occur.

With respect to the contractual interest payments or "repo margin," the purchaser includes this amount in gross income (sourced based upon the seller's residence)[57] and is taxed at the ordinary rates, while the seller incurs otherwise deductible interest expense.[58] If the repoed securities are tax-exempt, however, the seller's interest expense is lost under the federal tax provision which disallows such expenses when incurred to purchase or carry tax-exempt securities.[59] Also, if interest payments are payable on the underlying securities, the purchaser is liable to pay the seller any substitute payments during the life of the repo.

One type of repo where a logical argument can be made for sale (rather than loan) treatment under certain circumstances is the "repo to maturity." Since the term of the repo coincides with the maturity date of the collateral and the repurchase price equals the proceeds of the collateral, the seller is not in a position to profit from or lose on the market fluctuation of the security.[60] Indeed, several recent court cases have denied the seller's interest deduction relating to Treasury bill repos to maturity.[61]

---

[57] *See*, IRC §861. The sourcing of gross income has significant tax consequences in cross-border (or international) transactions, discussed later in the chapter.

[58] In *Nebraska Dept. of Revenue v. Loewenstein*, the Supreme Court held that the "interest income earned from repurchase agreements involving federal securities is not interest on 'obligations of the U.S. Government,'" but rather interest on loans to a private party. 115 S.Ct. 557 (1994). As such, the state of Nebraska was able to tax the interest income. *Id.*

[59] IRC §163(j).

[60] Commentators were concerned that Treasury Regulation 1.1058-1(e) could be used to treat a repo to maturity as a failed Section 1058 transaction and, thus, a sale. *See, e.g.*, Lee Sheppard, "On the Border: IRS Contemplates Narrow Mission of Section 1058," 49 *Tax Notes* (August 27, 1990), p.1083. Indeed, the Service held the positions that such repos should be treated as sales because the beneficial ownership shift to the borrower. *Id.*

[61] *See, U.S. v. Wexler,* 31 F.3d 117, 94-2 U.S.T.C. 50,361 (3d Cir. 1994); *U.S. v. Charles Agee Atkins and William S. Hack,* 869 F.2d 135, 89-1 U.S.T.C. 9195 (2d Cir. 1989); *Steven R. Sheldon and Ellen G. Sheldon v. Comm'r,* 94 T.C. 738 (1990), *citing, Goldstein v. Comm'r,* 44 T.C. 284 (1965), *affd.,* 364 F.2d 734 (2d Cir. 1966).

CROSS BORDER SECURITIES LENDING

Background

Cross border securities lending transactions involve a broader set of issues not significant or relevant in a purely domestic setting. For example, in a cross border transaction the characterization of payments made or received is significant because of the interrelationship of the withholding at source, characterization, and sourcing rules. The United States ("U.S."), as a taxing authority, is particularly concerned with the "inbound stock loan" transaction and the potential ability of foreign investors to avoid foreign withholding tax through such exchanges.[62] The example below illustrates one of the U.S.'s revenue concerns.

Securities Loans

Inbound Stock Loan Example A foreign investor (L) owns shares in XYZ Corporation, a publicly traded U.S. company. L lends the XYZ stock to a U.S. broker-dealer (B), with the right to terminate the loan upon five days notice to B. B sells the XYZ stock to a U.S. investor (P). P pays B cash for the XYZ stock and B uses the cash as collateral. The collateral is marked to market daily to ensure that the cash collateral equals the fair market value of the stock on that day. If the XYZ corporation pays a dividend, B is required to make a payment to L equal to the dividends that L would have received if L still owned the XYZ stock (substitute dividend payments). L makes payments to B of $X as a rebate reflecting a percentage of the interest earned on the cash collateral. Upon termination, B gives L identical, but not the actual original, shares of the XYZ stock and L returns the cash collateral to B. If L merely held the stock of XYZ corporation, the U.S. government would collect a 30% withholding tax (assuming no lower treaty rate is applicable)

---

[62] As discussed later in this chapter, "the Service is concerned that foreign lenders of U.S. securities are attempting to convert U.S. source dividend and interest income into substitute payments to avoid U.S. withholding tax" by claiming that substitute payments are exempt from withholding tax as "industrial or commercial profits" or "other income" under income tax treaties. "ABA Members Say Cross-Border Regs Exceed Legislative Authority," 92 *Tax Analysts, Tax Notes Today* (April 23, 1992), *available in* Lexis as 92 TNT 87-38, Fedtax, TNT.

on the dividends received by L, the foreign investor. In contrast, under the loan transaction, unless the substitute dividend payments are subject to the 30% withholding tax (assuming no lower treaty rate is applicable), the U.S. government may not collect any tax on the transaction. [63]

Out-Bound Concern Additionally, the Service is concerned that U.S. lenders of U.S. securities could use the substitute payments paid by foreign borrowers to increase the U.S. lender's foreign tax credit by claiming that the substitute payments are foreign source income.[64]

Withholding at Source Nonresident alien individuals, foreign corporations, foreign partnerships and foreign fiduciaries are subject to U.S. withholding at source.[65] The U.S. government requires withholding at source at a 30 percent rate (or lower treaty rate)[66] on "fixed or determinable annual or periodical" ("FDAP") income from sources within the United States that is not effectively connected with the conduct of a U. S. trade or business.[67] Where the U.S. has a treaty with a foreign country, the withholding rate under the treaty varies according to the type of income and from treaty to treaty.

FDAP income includes, in part, interest, dividends, rent, compensation and remunerations.[68] Capital gains (other than certain pension distributions and certain gains from the sale or exchange of patents, trademarks, copyrights)[69] and "portfolio interest"[70] are exempt from withholding. Portfolio interest is interest (including OID) paid on portfolio debt investment obligations issued after July 18, 1984 meeting

---

[63] Adapted from David P. Hariton, "Withholding on Cross-Border Stock Loans and Other Equity Derivatives," *Taxes* (December 1994), pp. 1050-1051.

[64] 92 *Tax Analysts, Tax Notes Today* (April 23, 1992), *available in* Lexis as 92 TNT 87-38, Fedtax, TNT. Commentators have noted that this strategy is generally limited to financial institutions due to the limitations placed on foreign tax credits under the Code. *Id.*

[65] Foreign taxpayers are required to file a Form W-8 or substitute form indicating their non-resident or foreign status.

[66] To reduce the applicable withholding tax rate to reflect the lower treaty rate, the foreign investor must file IRS Form 1001 with the U.S. withholding agent.

[67] IRC §871(a)(1).

[68] IRC §871(a)(1)(A).

[69] IRC §871(a)(1).

[70] IRC §871(h)(2).

certain requirements intended to ensure that U.S. persons are not avoiding U.S. taxation with respect to those instruments. For example, interest on bearer instruments "targeted at foreign markets"[71] is considered portfolio interest and, thus, is exempt from withholding. Interest on registered obligations can be exempt from withholding, provided that the withholding agent is in receipt of a statement documenting that the beneficial owner is not a U.S. person.[72] Additionally, no withholding is required on interest from deposits[73] which are not effectively connected with the conduct of a trade or business.

The question of withholding is important for borrowers and lenders alike. For U.S. tax purposes, every person having the control, receipt, custody, disposal, or payment of any item of income subject to withholding at source of any nonresident alien, foreign partnership, or foreign corporation has the obligation to withhold.[74] Any person required to deduct and withhold tax is liable for such tax.[75]

As noted above, treaties often provide for reduced rate of tax withholding on various types of payments, such as dividends and interest. Treaties generally do not explicitly provide for a reduced rate of withholding for substitute payments in lieu of dividends or interest or for related securities lending payments. However, other provisions of treaties, such as "industrial or commercial profit," "business profit," or "other income" provisions may serve to eliminate or reduce withholding.[76] This is the case both as to U.S. withholding tax and withholding on the part of other countries at source under their income tax treaties with the U. S. and with other countries.

---

[71] "Targeted at foreign markets" for purposes of the portfolio interest exemption means that there are arrangements to ensure that the obligation will be sold or resold only to non-resident aliens, the interest on the obligation is payable outside of the U.S. and the face of the obligation states that a U.S. person holding such obligation will be subject to the requirements of the U.S. law. IRC §871(h)(2)(A).

[72] IRC §871(h)(2)(B).

[73] IRC §871(i). For purposes of this section, deposits mean the amounts deposited with U.S. banks, savings and loan associations, or similar institutions, and certain deposits with insurance companies.

[74] IRC §1441(a).

[75] IRC §1461.

[76] For an example of an "industrial or commercial profit" (sometimes called a "business profit") treaty provision, *see,* note 107, *infra.* For an example of an "other income" treaty provision, *see,* note 108, *infra.*

Income Sourcing Whether U.S. withholding is required on a payment depends on whether the payment is from U.S. sources. In the context of securities lending, there are potentially at least six alternative approaches available in determining the source of such income and payments: (i) the location or place of use of loaned securities; (ii) the place where the lending activity occurs; (iii) the source of the underlying securities' income; (iv) the residence of the borrower; (v) the residence of the lender; or (vi) some combination of the above.[77]

The Code and the Regulations provide sourcing rules which are dependent on the nature of an income item. However, securities lending transactions are not explicitly covered by these rules. For example, the source of interest income is generally determined by reference to the residence of the debtor.[78] Thus, interest on obligations of noncorporate residents and domestic corporations generally constitutes domestic U.S. source income, while interest paid by foreign residents is foreign source income. The source of dividend income generally depends on the nationality or place of incorporation of the corporate payer.[79] Thus, dividend distributions by U.S. corporations are domestic U.S. source income, while dividends of foreign corporations are foreign source income. Rents and royalty income are sourced at the location, or place of use, of the leased or licensed property.[80] Gain from the sale of personal property is generally determined by the seller's residence,[81] except in the case of inventory property which is sourced where title to the goods pass.[82]

---

[77] *See,* New York State Bar Association Tax Section, "Report on Proposed Regulations on Certain Payment Made Pursuant to Securities Lending Transactions" (July, 1992); ABA Section of Taxation Financial Transactions Committee Subcommittee on Securities Investors and Broker/Dealers, Securities Loans Task Force, "ABA Committee Reports on Securities Lending Transactions" (April, 1991).

[78] IRC §861(a)(1).

[79] IRC §861(a)(2).

[80] IRC §861(a)(4).

[81] IRC §865(a). As such, income from the sale of personal property by a U.S. "resident" is sourced to the U.S. A U.S. resident is defined as an individual who is a citizen or resident alien, who does not have a tax home outside the U.S., or non-resident alien with a U.S. tax home. IRC §865(g). Additionally, a domestic corporation, partnership or trust is a U.S. resident for purposes of these sourcing rules. IRC §7701(a)(30).

[82] IRC §861(a)(6); Treas. Reg. §1.861-7(a).

Income from "notional principal contracts" is generally residence based.[83]

Substitute Payments In January 1992, the Internal Revenue Service issued Cross Border Proposed Regulations[84] relating to the source, character, and income tax treaty treatment of substitute interest[85] and dividend[86] payments made pursuant to cross border securities lending transactions. If these regulations are finalized in substantially this form, these regulations would apply to transactions between a U.S. person and a foreign person qualifying under Section 1058 of the Code and transactions substantially similar to Section 1058 transactions (whether or not each of the requirements of Section 1058 of the Code is satisfied).[87]

---

[83] Treas. Reg. §1.863-7(b). A notional principal contract is a financial instrument that provides for the payment of amounts by one party to another at specified intervals calculated by reference to a specified index upon a notional principal amount in exchange for specified consideration or a promise to pay similar amounts. Treas. Reg. §1.863-7(a). To determine if a security loan could constitute a notional principal contract, commentators have applied Treasury Regulation Section 1.446-3 which defines a "notional principal amount" to include "any specified amount of property that, when multiplied by a specified index, measures a party's rights or obligations under the contract." Since the lent stock could be argued to constitute an amount of property which measures the lender's rights and the borrower's obligation under the loan agreement, a stock loan could be viewed as a notional principal contract, provided that the transaction is treated as "sale" of the stock, rather than a "loan." If the agreement is considered a loan then it would be excluded from the definition of notional principal amount which excludes any amount which is "borrowed or loaned between the parties as part of the contract." Hariton, "Withholding on Cross-Border Stock Loans and Other Equity Derivatives," p. 1055. Note that the notional principal contract provision does not apply to transactions relating to the treatment of certain non-functional currency transactions pursuant to Section 988 of the Code. Treas. Reg. §1.863-7(a).

[84] The Proposed Treasury Regulations issued under Sections 861, 871, 881, 894 and 1441 are referred to as the "Cross Border Regulations."

[85] Prop. Treas. Reg. §1.861-2.

[86] Prop. Treas. Reg. §1.861-3. The proposed regulations define a substitute interest or dividend payment as a payment, made to the transferor of a security in a securities lending transaction, of an amount equivalent to an interest or dividend payment which the owner of the transferred security is entitled to receive during the term of the transaction. Prop. Treas. Reg. §§1.861-2; 1.861-3.

[87] *Id.* Commentators believe the term "substantially similar transactions" is intended to extend these provisions to transactions that are similar to Section 1058 lending transactions but which fail to satisfy one or more of the technical requirements of Section 1058. *See* "New York State Bar Association Tax Section; Report on Proposed Regulations on Certain Payments Made Pursuant to Securities Lending Transactions" ("NYSBA"), reprinted in *Tax Analyst, Tax Notes Today* (July 24, 1992).

The Cross Border Proposed Regulations provide that, for purposes of determining the source and character of cross border substitute payments, a substitute payment will be treated as interest or dividend income received (as the case may be) with respect to the transferred security.[88] The purpose of this rule is, in part, to ensure that a non-U.S. owner of U.S. securities cannot create different U.S. withholding tax results by lending its securities to a U.S. borrower instead of holding the securities directly.[89]

Under this provision, substitute dividend payments in a cross border context with respect to stock of a U.S. corporation would be treated as U.S. source dividends for withholding, foreign tax credit limitation, and income tax treaty purposes.[90] Thus, payments made in lieu of a dividend on the stock of a U.S. corporation would be subject to U.S. withholding tax of 30 percent (or at a lower treaty rate, if applicable) of the gross payment. Similarly, substitute interest payments with respect to bonds, notes, or other debt obligations of U.S. residents, U.S. corporations, or the U.S. government transferred in such a lending transaction would be treated as U.S. source interest for withholding, foreign tax credit, and income tax treaty purposes. In addition, the Cross Border Proposed Regulations provide that where a foreign person transfers U.S. securities the interest of which qualifies as portfolio interest, the substitute interest payments would also qualify as portfolio interest, provided an executed Form W-8 or substantially similar form has been received by the withholding agent.[91]

Despite this "look-through" approach, such substitute dividend payments would *not* be eligible for the corporate dividends received deduction (substitute dividend payments are not dividends under general tax principles),[92] and substitute interest payments received on state and local bonds (otherwise exempt from federal

---

[88] Prop. Treas. Reg. §§1.861-2; 1.861-3.

[89] *See,* note 62, *supra.*

[90] *See* Prop. Treas. Reg. §§1.861-2; 1.861-3; 1.894-1.

[91] Prop. Treas. Reg. §1.871-7(b)(2).

[92] Rev. Rul. 60-177, 1960-1 C.B. 9. The Service denied the dividends received deduction to the recipient of the substitute dividend on the basis that there can only be one true owner of the shares and, as such, the shares should not be able to produce the benefit for more than one party. *Id. See* also, note 26, *supra.*

income tax) would *not* be excludable from income.[93] This would be consistent with the treatment of substitute dividend and interest payments in a purely domestic context.

These regulations have yet to be adopted; the source, character and income tax treaty treatment of substitute payments made prior to the effective date of these regulations are to be determined under "all the facts and circumstances of a particular transaction."[94] By their terms, the regulations will be effective with respect to transfers of securities made more than 30 days after the date the regulations are published in final form in the Federal Register.[95]

Thus, the question as to the appropriate treatment of both substitute payments subject to the regulations prior to finalization as well as substitute payments outside their scope remains unsettled. If it is assumed that substitute payments constitute FDAP income,[96]

---

[93] Rev. Rul. 80-135, 1980-1 C.B. 18. In Revenue Ruling 80-135, the Service denied lenders the tax-exempt nature underlying the substitute interest payment. The Service relied on the Supreme Court decision in *Provost*, 268 U.S. 443 (1926), which held that because title passes to the buyer of a security loaned in a short sale transaction, the result is that the lender is not in receipt of interest on the loaned tax-exempt bond. *Id. See* also, note 27, *supra*.

[94] Preamble to Cross Border Proposed Regulations (Proposed Sections 861, 871, 881, 894, and 1441 Regulations), 57 Fed. Reg. 860 (1992). The vague language of the Cross Border Proposed Regulations, as quoted above, has been seen as an attempt by the Service to prevent the abuses previously discussed in notes 62-64. 92 *Tax Analyst, Tax Notes Today*, available in Lexis as 92 TNT 87-38, Fedtax, TNT. As such, lenders, borrowers and withholding agents remain in an uncertain position since there are no assurances that taxpayers who take positions consistent with the Proposed Regulations might not subsequently discover that the final regulations have taken a differing approach. *Id.*

[95] Preamble to the Proposed Section 1058 Regulations.

[96] At first glance, it would appear that substitute payments should constitute FDAP income as such payments are made to the lender to replace the interest or dividend income forgone as a result of the securities loan. These amounts would be periodic and determinable, in that the payments under the lending transactions could be ascertained through calculations based on the amounts set forth in the loan agreement. Treas. Reg. §1.1441-2(a).

However, since substitute payments are payments derived from contractual obligations, such payments may not retain the character of the lent securities. *See,* Hariton, "Withholding on Cross-Border Stock Loans and Other Equity Derivatives," *Taxes,* (December 1994) p.1050. If such payment is no longer dividend income, defined as a payment made from a corporation's current or accumulated earnings and profits, nor interest income, defined as compensation for the use or forbearance of money, then the substitute payments might not be FDAP income.

The Supreme Court's holding in *Provost* and Section 1058 of the Code could be viewed to support this change in the character of the substitute because both the holding in *Provost* and Section 1058 of the Code are premised on the treatment of a securities loan as an exchange and transfer, rather than a loan. As such, it may not be appropriate to characterize the income received by the lender, in the form of a substitute payment, based on the property sold.

the issue remains what type of FDAP income are substitute payments. As previously noted, the proposed Section 1058 regulations provide that substitute payments are fees for the temporary use of property.[97] Thus, for domestic purposes at least, substitute payments would be treated as analogous to rent. Under that characterization, the source of the income would be the place where the relevant tangible or intangible property is used.

While it may not matter in a purely domestic context, that may not be an appropriate interpretation in a cross border setting. If one uses the rental analogy, arguably, it is the person who buys the "lent" securities from the borrower who is "using" the securities. A practical problem results in that the lender will, generally, not have nor have any means of determining the identity, no less the residence, of the short purchaser. An additional issue is the effect the rent characterization would have on the U.S. capital markets since the characterization as rent would have the effect of denying certain foreign investors in U.S. government securities the benefit of the portfolio interest exemption.[98]

Instead, notwithstanding the language of the proposed regulations under Section 1058, the *Provost* decision[99] suggests that a securities "loan" is more in the nature of an exchange and transfer than a "loan," in that a securities loan is an exchange of ownership rights for a bundle of contractual rights with respect to the securities. [100] Thus, where a lender holds a position derived from contractual rights, the lender maintains the right to have the position in the securities returned, and not an ownership position in the underlying securities.

Until the proposed regulations are finalized, there is no definitive or conclusive answer. Adopting the residence of the lender as the basis of the sourcing rules for substitute payments would be the better approach.[101] Policy considerations support the application of the lender's residence as the basis for sourcing income. A

---

[97] Prop. Reg. §1.1058-1(d). *See*, note 25, *supra.*

[98] *See*, notes 102-103, *infra.*

[99] 269 US 443 (1926). *See*, note 6, *supra.*

[100] *Id.*

[101] *See e.g.,* "Clearing House Says Lending Fee Income Should Be Sourced Based on Lender's Residence," 92 *Tax Analyst, Tax Notes Today* (August 13, 1992), available in Lexis as 92 TNT 165-78, Fedtax, TNT; "NYSBA," *Tax Analyst, Tax Notes Today* (July 13, 1992).

sourcing rule which imposes withholding taxes on fees paid to foreign lenders by U.S. borrowers in connection with cross border securities loans would place foreign borrowers at an advantage over U.S. borrowers because the U.S. borrower would have to pay a higher fee to the foreign lender to cover the lender's additional costs, specifically the withholding tax.[102] This would "diminish the liquidity and efficiency of the [U.S.] capital markets."[103] Under the lender's residence sourcing approach, substitute payments received by lenders who are not U.S. persons should be exempt from U.S. withholding tax.

As just noted, the proposed regulations would only apply to substitute payments made in cross border transactions (i.e., payments made by a U.S. borrower to a foreign person or a foreign borrower to a U.S. person). Thus, the regulations would not purport to control the tax consequences of payments made by a foreign borrower to a foreign lender of U.S. securities nor to payments made by a U.S. borrower to a U.S. lender with respect to foreign securities.

Where a transaction involves a U.S. borrower of foreign securities from a U.S. lender, any gain or loss would be sourced to the United States and, as such, would not have any withholding tax implications, although the income and gain, if any, would be subject to U.S. taxation. The recognition of gain or loss on the lending transaction would, in part, be dependent upon qualifying under Section 1058 of the Code. As previously discussed, a qualifying loan agreement would not create a taxable gain or loss under the non-recognition provisions of Section 1058 of the Code. Alternatively, a non-qualifying lending transaction between two U.S. taxpayers may or may not create taxable gain or loss.[104]

On the other hand, a foreign borrower of U.S. securities from a foreign lender may have withholding tax considerations depending on the character and source of the income. If the income is considered income from personal property, the foreign taxpayer would not be subject to U.S. taxation because the income would be sourced

---

[102] 92 *Tax Analyst, Tax Notes Today* (August 13, 1992), available in Lexis as 92 TNT 165-78, Fedtax, TNT.

[103] *Id.*

[104] *See,* note 46, *supra.*

based on the residence of the lender.[105] If the income is considered a fee, the lender will probably be exempt from U.S. taxation under a "commercial and industrial" or "other income" treaty provision.[106]

Many treaties exempt "commercial and industrial profits" or "business profits" derived in one contracting state by a resident of the other contracting state unless they are attributable to a permanent establishment of such resident in the other contracting state. An example of the business profits provision is Article 7 of the U.S.-United Kingdom ("U.K.") treaty.[107]

Even if the lender is not engaged in business, substitute payments under a limited number of treaties may be exempt under an "other income" provision, which specifically exempts income not dealt with elsewhere in a treaty that is part of the counterparty's trade or business, provided the income is not derived in the active conduct of a trade or business through a permanent establishment in the United States. An example of such an "other income" provision is Article 22 of the U.S. - U. K. income tax treaty.[108] However, since the proposed regulations fail to address the source, character and income tax treaty treatment of fees paid to a lender of securities, the above treatment is uncertain.[109]

Borrow Fees Neither the Proposed Section 1058 nor proposed cross border regulations address the source and characterization of fees paid to a lender of securities, though the Service has invited comments con-

---

[105] IRC §865(a). *See,* note 81, *supra.*

[106] *See,* notes 107-108, *infra.*

[107] The following is an excerpt from Article 7 of the U.S. - U.K. treaty indicating that the income is exempt unless conducted through a permanent establishment. "The business profits of an enterprise of a Contracting State shall be taxable only in that State unless the enterprise carries on business in the other Contracting State through a permanent establishment situated therein." U.S. - U.K. Treaty, signed on December 31, 1975, and brought into force on March 25, 1980.

[108] The following is an excerpt from Article 22 of the U.S. - U.K. treaty indicating that the income that is not otherwise addressed is exempt: "Items of income of a resident of a Contracting State, wherever arising, not dealt with in the foregoing Articles of this Convention shall be taxable only in that State." *Id.*

[109] Some commentators have recommended that the Treasury promulgate regulations to source securities lending fees by reference to the residence of the lender in a manner consistent with the treatment of notional principal contracts. For example, *see,* "NYSBA," *Tax Analyst, Tax Notes Today* (July 7, 1992). However, to date no action has been taken by the Treasury. For a discussion of the treatment of notional principal contracts, *see,* note 83, *supra.*

cerning such payments. This has led to many U.S. borrowers treating the fees paid to lenders as neither dividends nor interest but as some unspecified type of FDAP income, subject to 30 percent U.S. withholding tax unless an exception from withholding applies. As with substitute payments, many foreign lenders claim exemption from, or reduction of, the U. S. withholding tax on such fees based on "business profits," "industrial or commercial profits," or "other income" provisions of the U.S. income tax treaty with the jurisdiction where the lender resides. On the income side, the receipt of loan fees would be ordinary taxable income, not taxable to an exempt organization.

Arguably, borrow fees should be treated the same as substitute payments, as compensation for the temporary use of the securities with the residence of the lender providing the source of the income.[110] In one private letter ruling, the Service has held that borrow fees paid to a securities lender constituted income derived from the active conduct of an insurance business and therefore "industrial and commercial profits" under the terms of the applicable treaty.[111] The ruling specifically did not address the treatment of substitute payments, nor did it address the situation where the lender was not engaged in a financial services business.

Income on Collateral Rebates are generally treated as interest for tax purposes since the fees compensate the borrower for the lender's use of the borrower's cash collateral during the securities loan period. Interest is generally sourced to the U.S. if it is paid on interest bearing obligations of U.S. non-corporate residents or domestic U.S. corporations.[112] If the securities lending arrangement is treated as an interest

---

[110] It is important to note that the purpose of borrow fees is quite different from the purpose of substitute payments. 92 *Tax Analyst, Tax Notes Today* (April 23, 1992). Where substitute payments merely reimburse the lender for the income lost due to the lending arrangement, borrow fees are compensatory, a fee for permitting the borrower to use the lender's property. Additionally, the borrow fees do not bear the causal relationship to the underlying security as does the substitute payment. *Id.* As such, characterizing borrow fees as ordinary compensatory income does not raise the same concerns caused by the characterization of substitute payments as compensatory.

With regard to the sourcing of the income, borrow fees encompass the same concerns and practical problems previously discussed in the context of substitute payments.

[111] PLR 8822061.

[112] IRC §861.

bearing obligation, rebates might be viewed as U.S. source interest income to a foreign borrower. Under that theory, exemption from the 30 percent withholding tax would likely be available under an applicable treaty or the portfolio interest rules.[113] Alternatively, a rebate might be treated as a fee and, thus, taxed as some type of FDAP income, subject to 30 percent U.S. withholding tax unless a treaty exemption applies.

CFC Income The objective of Subpart F[114] of the Code is to minimize the tax-deferral benefits enjoyed by the shareholders of controlled foreign corporations ("CFCs")[115] on foreign sourced income that is not repatriated to the U.S. This provision taxes U.S. shareholders on certain income, generally passive in nature, earned by the foreign corporation.[116] Currently, Subpart F income includes all income with respect to debt securities subject to Section 1058 of the Code, although there is proposed legislation to expand the definition and include equity securities subject to Section 1058 of the Code in the calculation of Subpart F income.[117]

Repurchase Agreements

The primary issue regarding the treatment of repos in cross border transactions is the same as in the domestic setting: should the repo

---

[113] IRC §§871; 881. *See,* "Withholding at Source," *supra.*

[114] Subpart F (Sections 951-§964 of the Code) is the mechanism by which the U.S. government taxes income earned by foreign corporations which is attributable to investments made by "U.S. shareholders." For purposes of Subpart F, a U.S. shareholder is defined as a U.S. person who owns ten per cent or more of the total combined voting power of all classes of voting stock of the foreign corporation. IRC §951(b).

[115] Defined in Section 957 of the Code, a CFC is a foreign corporation in which U.S. shareholders own more than 50 per cent of the total combined voting power and value of all classes of stock. IRC §957(a).

[116] A CFC is subject to U.S. taxation on income which is effectively connected to the conduct of a U.S. trade or business. IRC §882. Additionally, a CFC is subject to tax on its FDAP income. IRC §881. Thus, a CFC with no income producing connections with the U.S. will not be subject to U.S. taxation. The U.S. shareholders of a CFC, on the other hand, are taxed on the shareholders' share of the CFC's Subpart F income. IRC §951.

[117] The outcome of budget talks in 1996 will govern whether Subpart F of the Code will include income with respect to the transfer of equities subject to IRC §1058. Presented in the Revenue Reconciliation Bill of 1995 and in the Revenue Reconciliation Bill of 1996 is a proposal to create a new category of subpart F income, income from notional principal contracts for taxable years beginning after 1995, which would include transfers of equity under qualified securities lending transactions.

be treated as a sale or loan? Generally, repos are characterized as loans for U.S. tax purposes and the seller in the repo remains the owner of the securities.[118] As such, the payments received by the true owner are characterized and source based on the underlying securities and the withholding tax, if any, will be impacted by applicable treaty provisions.[119]

Specifically, the treatment of the "repo margin"[120] is deemed to be interest income and, as such, the source of the income is the residence of the obligor. As previously discussed, where the obligor is a U.S. person, the interest income will be subject to FDAP withholding at 30 per cent (or lesser treaty rate).[121] An exemption from withholding will generally be available if the term of the loan is less than or equal to 183 days. Additionally for obligations with terms in excess of 183 days, the portfolio interest exception may apply.[122]

The proposed regulations do not cover cross border repos that are characterized as loans; however the extent to which these regulations in final form should and will apply is unclear.[123]

---

[118] See, note 55, supra.

[119] See, Committee Report No. 95-762, 95th Cong. 2d Sess., p. 8, n. 5, in which the committee states that the proposed regulations are "not intended to change the tax treatment of 'repurchase agreements' in which loans of money collateralized by securities are structured as sales and repurchase of securities."

[120] "Repo margin" is the amount of interest specified in the contract above the original sales price to compensate the purchaser for the use of the cash. The repo margin provides the same function as the borrow fee in the securities loan transactions.

[121] See, "Withholding at Source," supra.

[122] IRC §871(h)(2). See, PLR 8442047, in which the income from a repo agreement, which was treated as income from a discount loan with a maturity of less than six months, was exempt from foreign withholding tax under Section 881(a)(3)(B) of the Code. However, this result would be uncertain under the Proposed Regulations under Section 881 of the Code. Whereas, the Service in its ruling emphasized the fact that none of the repo agreements extended beyond six months, the proposed regulation indicates that the holding of the instrument in excess of 6 months is irrelevant. Prop. Treas. Reg. §1.881-2(b)(2).

[123] See, "NYSBA," Tax Analyst, Tax Notes Today (July 24, 1992), in which the New York State Bar Association Task Force stated that, in its opinion, the expansion of the proposed regulations to repos characterized as loans is unnecessary but the application of the look through approach to repos not characterized as loans would be appropriate. See also, 92 Tax Analyst, Tax Notes Today (April 23, 1992), in which the American Bar Association stated that the application of the proposed regulations is misfounded.

Chapter 15

The Accounting Treatment of Securities Lending Transactions

Susan C. Peters

Vice President and Product Development Manager

State Street Bank and Trust Company

Until very recently, the accounting treatment of securities lending transactions was unclear. Lenders were left to their own devices on the accounting and reporting of securities lending transactions. The accounting treatment of securities lending transactions has now been clarified for government entities by the Government Accounting Standards Board (GASB) and non-government entities by the Financial Accounting Standards Board (FASB). The SEC has also become interested in securities lending, although not in quite as comprehensive a fashion as FASB and GASB. The SEC recently issued rules that affect the accounting and disclosure treatment of fee offsetting arrangements entered into with respect to custody fees and securities lending income.

In May 1995, GASB issued Statement No. 28 entitled *Accounting and Financial Reporting for Securities Lending Transactions* (GASB Statement No. 28).[1] In July 1996, the Financial Accounting

---

[1] As will be discussed further in this chapter, several other statements also affect the accounting treatment of securities lending. See, e.g., GASB Statement No 3, *Deposits with Financial Institutions, Investments (including Reverse Repurchase Agreements)* (April 1986) (Statement No. 3) and GASB Interpretation No 3, *Financial Reporting for Reverse Repurchase Agreements; an interpretation of GASB Statement No. 3* (January 1996), GASB Statement No. 25, *Financial Reporting for Defined Benefit Pension Plans and Note Disclosures for Defined Contribution Plans* (GASB Statement No. 25).

The views expressed herein are the sole responsibility of the author and do not necessarily reflect the opinions of State Street Bank and Trust Company.

Standards Board issued Statement of Financial Accounting Standards No. 125 entitled *Accounting for Transfers and Servicing of Financial Assets and Extinguishment of Liabilities* (SFAS 125). Finally, the SEC recently adopted amendments to Rule 6-07 of Regulation S-X requiring that registered investment companies include as expenses the amount of any reduction in custody fees arising as a result of an agreement to make portfolio securities available for loan.

Each of FASB and GASB approached the concept of securities loans from very different perspectives. GASB applied a risk and reward analysis as the basis for the development of securities lending accounting rules for government organizations. Government entities tend to participate actively in securities lending programs and began making inquiries of GASB on the proper accounting treatment. GASB determined that accounting practices among government entities were inconsistent and that while many chose to report the loaned securities on the balance sheet as assets, the balance sheet typically did not address all assets and liabilities flowing from the transaction.[2]

FASB approached the topic from a very different perspective. One of the critical issues affecting the accounting treatment of loaned securities is whether the loaned securities should remain on the balance sheet, notwithstanding that title to the securities passes to the borrower. FASB began examining circumstances in general where an entity may transfer assets and yet maintain elements of control sufficient to justify continued maintenance of such assets on the balance sheet. This led FASB to examine securitized transactions, repurchase agreements, reverse repurchase agreements, and loans of securities. FASB sought to apply a financial components approach to the treatment of assets on the balance sheet that was consistent with previous FASB Statements on recognition and derecognition of assets.

Finally, the Securities Commission, in its statement, was attempting to deal with the very narrow issue of registered investment companies under-reporting custody costs.

GASB STATEMENT NO. 28

The accounting treatment required by GASB Statement No. 28 falls into three categories: (1) balance sheet item, (2) additional disclosure

---

[2] GASB Statement No. 28, p.1, paragraph 2.

of information regarding the securities lending program in which the government entity participates, and (3) classification of securities lending collateral and loaned securities in the categories of custodial credit risk required by GASB Statement No. 3. Exhibit 1 indicates the data that needs to be captured for balance sheet purposes.

Government Entities

The GASB accounting rules will apply to any state, municipal, or federal government organization. Typical examples will be state employee retirement systems, state operating funds, or funds specifically set up for the purpose of managing funds for state or local government purposes. It will also include commingled funds that contain the assets of several government entities. There will be gray areas, such as funds in which government funds invest which may include monies contributed by other investors. State university funds and hospitals may also be difficult to categorize, depending upon whether the source of their funds is derived principally from a government or from private sources.

Lenders Having Multiple Funds

GASB Statement No. 28 recognizes that the manner in which reporting is done will vary among lenders. The only guidance offered in the Statement is that if a component of a larger fund is significant compared to the whole fund, then separate accounting might be appropriate. As a consequence, whether a separate breakdown of accounting information is provided on a portfolio by portfolio basis or in the aggregate will depend upon the internal accounting practices of the lender.

Effective Date

GASB Statement No. 28 applies to financial statements for periods beginning after December 15, 1995. Many lenders may also require that, for comparison purposes, collection of data in the form required by GASB Statement No. 28 for the year immediately preceding the accounting change.

Exhibit 1: Summary of Data Collection Requirements GASB Statement No. 28

Entities and effective date:

Affected Entities	All Government entities
Time Periods	Financial Statement Periods commencing after December 15, 1995.

Accounting treatment:

Item	Treatment	Data capture
Loaned securities	Report as assets	Determine as of date of preparation of financial statements
Cash Collateral	Report as asset. If invested, report investment securities as asset in appropriate line item. Assets accounted for at fair market value. Obl-igation to return cash collateral is reported as liability.	Determine as of date of preparation of financial statements
Securities Collateral	Do not report as asset unless lender has right to pledge or dispose of securities. In circumstances where the lender takes direct title to the securities held as collateral, such securities should be reported as assets. Disclose loaned securities collateralized by securities not reported as assets in custodial risk statement.	Determine as of date of preparation of financial statements. Quantify value of loaned securities collateralized by securities not reported as assets.
Triparty collateral	Do not report as asset. Disclose loaned securities collateralized by cash held in a tri-party arrange-ment as part of the custodial risk statement.	Quantify value of loaned securities collateralized by cash (or securities) held in a tri-party arrangement.
Letters of Credit	Do not report as asset. Disclose loaned securities collateralized by letters of credit as part of custo-dial risk statement.	Quantify value of loaned securities collateralized by letters of credit.

Exhibit 1 (Continued)
Accounting treatment:

Item	Treatment	Data capture
Borrower rebates paid by lender	Report as expense	Aggregate rebates earned by borrower during the period covered by financial statements
Fees paid by lender to agent	Report as expense	Aggregate fees earned by agent during the period covered by the financial statements
Borrow fees paid by borrower	Report as income	Aggregate fees earned by lender during the period covered by the financial statements
Income from investment of cash collateral	Report as income	Aggregate income earned by lender from the investment of cash collateral (before deduction of rebates or fees)

Accounting Treatment

GASB notes in Statement No. 28 that the accounting treatment of securities loans and reverse repurchase transactions are substantially the same from an economic perspective. While a purist might argue that a reverse repurchase agreement is a sale of securities the purpose of which is to raise cash and a securities loan is a loan of securities collateralized by cash, the economic effect of each transaction is fundamentally identical to the other.[3] For this reason, GASB concluded that securities sold under reverse repurchase transactions and loaned securities should be treated identically for accounting purposes. The treatment of collateral varies with the rights of the lender to such collateral and, in the case of cash collateral, depends upon the manner in which the cash is invested.

Loaned Securities Government entities should report loaned securities as assets on both their balance sheets and on statements of plan net assets required for defined benefit pension plans.[4] There is no separate line item for loaned securities as opposed to securities not on loan.

---

[3] In a footnote to GASB Statement No.28, the Board notes that income distributions on reversed securities retain their original form for federal tax purposes. Readers of the Statement should be cautious about accepting this statement at face value without a thorough analysis of the IRS' position on the tax treatment of repurchase and reverse repurchase transactions. In the author's view, the IRS has permitted retention of the tax treatment of distributions on securities subject to repurchase transactions only in defined circumstances, such as cases where the recipient of the securities has no right to transfer such securities to a third party.

[4] See GASB Statement No. 25.

Cash Collateral Investments made with cash collateral should be reported as assets in the appropriate line item for the particular asset. As an example, if cash collateral is invested in U.S. Treasury bonds, repurchase transactions, and commercial paper, such investments should be added to the appropriate line item for each asset class. In the event that the lender's agent has agreed to indemnify the lender for any loss associated with the investment of cash collateral, such investments should nevertheless be reported on the balance sheet as assets. The securities in which cash is invested are reported at their fair market value. The obligation to return cash collateral (or securities held as collateral where the lender has a right of disposition) is reflected as a liability.

Triparty Custody of Collateral In certain cases, the lender and its agent may find that there is a benefit to holding collateral in a triparty custody arrangement. In such circumstances, the lender's agent receives cash collateral from the borrower and transfers such cash to the borrower's clearing bank. Under a typical tri-party arrangement, during the day, the collateral remains in the form of cash in an account in the lender or its agent's name, and overnight, the cash is substituted for an equal value of securities. Such cash (or securities, as applicable) are not reported as assets.

Securities as Collateral Securities received as collateral are not reported as assets, unless the lender has the right to further pledge or sell those securities. Lenders typically give up the right to pledge, sell, hypothecate, or otherwise engage in transactions with respect to securities held as collateral.

In certain jurisdictions, lenders of securities are advised that when lending securities to borrowers resident in such countries, it is wise to take direct title to the securities received in a securities lending transaction in order to avoid any uncertainty as to the lender's rights to such securities in the event of the borrower's bankruptcy. In such circumstances, it would appear to flow from GASB's analysis of the status of the lender's rights to the securities, that such securities must be reported as assets on the balance sheet.

Letters of Credit as Collateral Letters of credit are not reported as assets in the balance sheet.

Borrower Rebates The total rebates paid over the entire year are reported as an expense. Understandably, lenders will be concerned about this line item because the addition of rebates to the expense line item will make their funds look expensive to manage. Rebates should be reported by the lender as interest expenditures or expenses.

Fees to Lender's Agent Agent fees together with all other expenses billed to the lender, aggregated over the entire year, must be reported as expenses. GASB Statement No. 28 expressly states that such expenses should not be netted against income from the investment of cash collateral, any other related investments, borrow fees, or other fees.

Borrow Fees Where a lender holds securities as collateral and the borrower pays a fee for the privilege of borrowing securities, such fees are reported as income. Once again, such fees must be reported in the aggregate over the entire financial year of the lender.

Income from the Investment of Cash Collateral Such income, aggregated over the entire year, must be reported as income.

Pooled Funds or Separate Entities Accounting practices should follow those of the lender. GASB requires that government funds that pool their assets with other government funds for the purpose of lending should allocate lending income and associated expenses (rebate, fees, etc.) above on a pro rata basis.

Disclosure in the Notes
The following items must be disclosed in the notes to the financial statements. Lender's agents may find it efficient and appropriate to prepare a standard form of disclosure statement appropriate to its program, contractual relationships, and monitoring capabilities.

Contracts The notes must disclose the source of the legal or contractual authorization to lend securities.

Contract Violations The notes must disclose any "significant" contract violations. GASB has not provided any guidance on the meaning of a "significant contract violation." This may include, for example, lending to borrowers not authorized by the lender, deviations from investment guidelines or a failure to hold adequate collateral.[5]

General Program Description   The notes to the lender's financial statements must contain the following description of the lending program in which they participate: (1) general description of securities lending transactions during the period covered by the financial statements; (2) type of securities lent; (3) form of collateral received; (4) whether the government has the right to pledge or sell securities held as collateral; (5) the applicable collateral margin; (6) any restrictions on the amount of loans that may be made; (7) any loss indemnification provided to the government by its lending agent; and, (8) the carrying amount and market or fair values of the loaned securities at the balance sheet date.

Investment Maturity Mismatch   Government entities must disclose whether the maturities of the investments made with cash collateral match the maturities of the securities loans. It is unclear from the GASB statement whether this applies if the lender has invested its cash collateral in a commingled fund. If the lender's cash is managed in a separate account, the reporting requirement is more straightforward.

Credit Exposure to Individual Borrowers   The notes must also contain a statement as to whether the lender has any credit exposure to the borrowers calculated as the difference between the amount owed by the borrower to the lender (including the market value of the loaned securities, including accrued interest, unpaid substitute payments, or other distributions on the loaned securities and loan premiums or fees) and *the amount owed by the lender to the borrower* (including the cash collateral, rebates, securities held as collateral, including accrued inter-

---

[5] The author encourages the reader to contact GASB independently to verify the meaning of the term "contract violations." In verbal conversations with GASB staff members, the author has been advised that this should be interpreted as violations of the parameters under which securities may be loaned as set forth in the enabling statute, if any, that governs the lender. The author is concerned that the term may have a broader meaning, such as any violations of either the lender's contract with the lender's agent or any violations of the lender's agent's contract with the borrower.

est, the face value of letters of credit and unpaid income on collateral securities). If the lender is over collateralized and has no credit risk then a mere statement of that fact will suffice. If the lender has credit risk exposure, then the amount of such exposure must be provided. As a consequence, we need a method for calculating credit exposure and reporting thereon to the lender.

Losses Disclosure is required of any losses on securities lending transactions resulting from the default of the lending agent or any borrower, together with any amounts recovered on losses disclosed in previous statements.

Custodial Credit Risk

Government entities are required to report on the risk associated with investment securities that are not held in the possession of the government. The requirement to make such reports is contained in GASB Statement No. 3. This Statement was created in an effort to alert government entities to the risk associated with the potential for the insolvency of a custodian. In brief, GASB Statement No. 3 created three custodial categories for the classification of such risk. Which of the three categories is applicable depends upon who the custodian is, whether the assets are segregated, and whether such securities are held in the government entity's name.

Collateral that Should Be Reported All collateral that is reported on the balance sheet should be reported and classified by category of custodial credit risk. This would include (1) uninvested cash (2) securities in which cash has been invested in separate accounts (3) loaned securities, the collateral for which is not required to be reported on the balance sheet, and (4) securities held as collateral where the lender has a right to pledge, sell, or otherwise dispose of securities held as collateral. With respect to item (3) above, the loaned securities should be classified with respect to the custodial arrangement for the collateral.

Cash invested in commingled investment pools does not have to be categorized. As a result, lenders may favor commingled vehicles over separate accounts. The schedule of investments by category of custodial credit risk will require disclosure of the fair value of all uncategorized investments. Funds that maintain a dollar per unit value are reported at a dollar, despite the fact that there may be losses within the fund.

The Categories The categories set forth in GASB Statement No. 3 are as follows:

> *Category 1:* The custodian is the government's agent and is not the counterparty or the counterparty financial institution's trust department. The custodian holds the securities in the government's name.
>
> *Category 2:* The custodian is the counterparty financial institution's trust department or the counterparty's agent and the custodian holds the securities in the government's name.
>
> *Category 3:* The custodian is the counterparty, regardless whether it holds the securities in the government's name, or the custodian is the counterparty financial institution's trust department, or the counterparty's agent and the custodian do not hold the securities in the government's name.

Even though lending agents view themselves as an agent acting for the lender, for the purposes of GASB Statement No. 3 and the classification of custodial credit risk, GASB views lending agents/custodians as the counterparty. The categories most likely to apply to typical lending programs are:

> *No category:* Investments in commingled funds such as bank short-term investment funds, mutual funds, investment trusts, or other similar pooled funds.
>
> *Separately managed accounts:* For the purposes of GASB Statement No. 3, lending agents would be viewed as the counterparty in circumstances where the agent acquires the investment securities for the lender and the trust department of the lending agent is not involved in the transaction. As a consequence, investment securities purchased with the lender's cash collateral should be classified in custodial risk

category 3. Lending agents who find this custodial risk category unpalatable to its lending clients may wish to explore setting up a trust relationship for the investment of cash collateral and requiring that the investment be managed through the lending agent's trust department.

Loans of securities collateralized by securities and tri-party lending programs: Securities on loan which are collateralized by securities are assigned to the category which is relevant to the collateral. This is an exception to the GASB Statement No. 28 requirement that normally it is the collateral which is assigned to the appropriate custodial risk category. In the case of securities loans collateralized by securities, it is the loaned securities themselves and not the collateral that is assigned to a custodial risk category.

Similarly, where collateral is held by a third-party custodian, the loaned securities are assigned to the custodial risk category appropriate to the collateral. In such case, unless the collateral is held in the name of the lender, the applicable custodial risk Category 3.

Accounting and Reporting for Cash Invested in Commingled Pools

As discussed earlier in this chapter, GASB Statement No. 28 requires that cash collateral invested in commingled pools is reported at the value of the units issued by such pool to the government entity. In March 1996, GASB issued a proposed statement on the accounting treatment of investments held in external investment pools.[6] The proposed statement covers a number of accounting issues, among them, the accounting treatment of interest bearing investment contracts, debt security instruments, the issue of financial statement for government sponsored collective investment pools, and other accounting issues relevant to the reporting of investments held by government entities. Of interest to participants in securities lending programs is the requirement that government entities report their investments in external investment pools at fair market value.

---

[6] Proposed Statement of the Government Accounting Standards Board, *Accounting and Financial Reporting for Certain Investments and for External Investment Pools* (March 13, 1996).

The proposed statement allows for an exception for "2a7 like"[7] pools which would be accounted for at the unit price for such pool. A "2a7-like" pool is defined as funds that may not necessarily be registered with the SEC but has adopted a policy to operate in a manner consistent with such rule. In particular, the proposed statement refers to criteria set forth in Rule 2a7 that permit the adoption of amortized cost pricing, such as rules on portfolio diversification, types and quality of investments, restrictions on the term to maturity, and the dollar-weighted average of the portfolio divestiture considerations in the event an investment is down graded or defaults, and action to be taken in the event of a significant deviation from a dollar per unit valuation.[8]

GASB's concern is that government entities may, through funds which are exempt from registration with the SEC,[9] employ amortized cost pricing and effectively hide losses or a decline in the market value of the units issued by the fund. The concerns raised by the industry, however, is that Rule 2a7 may be too restrictive, and that other criteria exist that may also justify the use of amortized cost pricing and dollar-per-unit valuation of investments.

The proposed statement is in the comment phase at the time of this writing, and GASB received a number of comments regarding the appropriateness of the selection of the criteria of 2a7 as determinative of whether a government pool would be permitted to employ amortized cost pricing and whether investments in externally managed pools would be reported at market or their unit price. In response to industry comments, GASB is currently considering whether criteria broader than the 2a7 concept may be appropriate as a standard for the accounting treatment of collective investments.

FASB SFAS NO.125

As discussed earlier in this chapter, FASB approached the topic of lending of securities from a very different perspective. Concerned with cir-

---

[7] The proposed statement refers to Rule 2a7 of the Investment Company Act of 1940 (17 C.F.R. s. 270.2a7).

[8] See page 11 of the proposed statement.

[9] Such funds would include bank short-term investment funds, private placements, or funds created exclusively for the investment of monies of a state or any political subdivision (see s. 2b of the Investment Company Act of 1940).

cumstances under which an entity may, notwithstanding a transfer of control to certain assets, retain sufficient rights to such assets that would justify maintenance of the assets on the balance sheet, FASB developed criteria for distinguishing, in the securities lending context, sales from secured borrowings.[10]

Entities Affected by SFAS No. 125

FASB rules have broad application and affect every non-government entity. Organizations subject to SFAS No. 125 that would be participants in securities lending programs include mutual funds, insurance companies, endowments, charitable organizations, corporations, non-government pension plans, and other similar organizations.

Effective Date

SFAS No. 125 applies to loans of securities occurring after December 31, 1996. Unlike GASB, the Statement expressly states that "earlier or retroactive application is not permitted."[11]

Accounting for Transfers

FASB acknowledges that loans of securities and repurchase transactions are difficult to categorize because they have attributes of both sales and secured borrowings. The exposure draft proposed that transfers of assets under securities loans or repurchase agreements would be treated as secured borrowings if the transaction was "assuredly temporary." That concept was initially defined as transactions having a term of under 90 days or, if longer, such transactions had to be subject to a ready right of recall and daily mark to market. The industry, during the comment period, protested that the 90-day criteria was artificial and

---

[10] During the comment phase of SFAS 125, the industry argued strongly in favor of secured borrowing treatment of loaned securities. FASB struggled with the notion of whether loans of securities should receive secured borrowing treatment (i.e., where the loaned securities remain on the balance sheet) or whether sales treatment, with a corresponding removal of the loaned securities from the balance sheet, would be more appropriate. Had FASB adopted sales treatment of securities loans, the effect on the industry would have been drastic. The balance sheets of entities participating in securities lending programs would look drastically different from those of non-participants and would force realization of gains or losses on the balance sheet even though the lender's intent was to participate in a loan and not sell the securities.

[11] SFAS No. 125, Summary.

created a cumbersome accounting barrier. SFAS No. 125 abandoned that notion and opted for a requirement that the transferor maintains effective control over the asset where it has the contractual right and the contractual obligation to reacquire the transferred securities[12] and the transferor receives collateral sufficient to fund substantially all of the cost of repurchasing identical replacement securities.[13]

Dollar Rolls

The exposure draft would have treated dollar rolls as sales, because secured borrowing treatment was conditional upon the right of the transferor to receive, upon termination of the loan, securities identical to those initially transferred. Dollar rolls typically involve transfers of mortgage-backed securities and are structured to allow for the return of substantially similar securities to those originally transferred. SFAS No. 125 requires that dollar rolls be accounted for as secured borrowings, notwithstanding that the transaction allows for the return of substantially similar, but not identical securities.

Collateral

The treatment of collateral is very similar to the treatment adopted in GASB Statement No. 28. The criteria adopted by FASB is whether the recipient has the right to control and repledge or transfer the asset and whether the asset can be used to generate income. Cash collateral, therefore, must be placed on the balance sheet, as well as securities held as collateral where the holder has a right to sell or repledge the asset. The obligation to return the cash collateral to the transferor should be recorded as a liability and the transferor records the cash as a receivable.

The secured party must also recognize collateral as an asset where it sells or repledges the collateral on terms that do not allow repurchase or redemption of the collateral on short notice by substitution or termination of the contract.[14]

---

[12] SFAS No. 125, Par. 151, p. 67.

[13] The Statement notes that the interpretation of the term "substantially all" will require an exercise of judgment, but states that collateralization at 98% of the value of the transferred securities and marked to market daily would meet the criteria.

[14] SFAS No. 125, par 169, p. 73.

Disclosure

The level of disclosure is not as extensive as that required by GASB Statement No. 28. SFAS Statement No. 125 requires that the entity disclose if it has entered into securities lending transactions and its policy for requiring collateral or other security. FASB has not commented on other disclosure items considered important to GASB, such as the occurrence of an event of default, net credit exposure, or indemnification offered by the lending agent.

Fees, Rebates and Other Expenses

The exposure draft initially would have required that fees, rebates payable to the borrower, and other expenses be indicated on the expense line. The industry raised concerns about whether this requirement would place mutual funds, for example, at a distinct disadvantage in their calculation of expense ratios. SFAS Statement No.125 abandoned any requirement with respect to the treatment of fees and rebates.

EXPENSE OFFSET ARRANGEMENTS FOR MUTUAL FUNDS

As a final afterthought, while the SEC has not made any major pronouncements with respect to the accounting treatment of securities lending transactions as a whole, it is worth noting that the SEC recently released a requirement affecting securities lending by registered investment companies and the treatment of expense offset arrangements. Mutual funds and other lenders of securities may negotiate with their custodian as reduction in custody fees in return for a higher percentage of the income from securities lending transactions.

The amendments to Rule 6-07 of Regulation S-X require funds to include as expenses the amount of reduction in fees arising from such offsetting arrangements and require that the expense line reflect the true cost of services that fund would have paid in the absence of an expense offsetting arrangement. The SEC acknowledges, however, if the reduction in fees is due to a negotiated rate between the fund and the custodian, then the custody fee would not have to be increased to market levels.

CONCLUSION

The accounting treatment of securities lending transactions has changed dramatically over the past few years. We have seen a period of intense scrutiny of the securities lending business from all regulators, not only the accounting profession. The industry has evolved from uncertainty over ownership of cash collateral where attorneys and accountants scratched their heads over whether the lender owned the cash collateral or it merely was a secured creditor and the borrower retained ownership rights to the cash. We now find ourselves in the situation where cash collateral and other forms of collateral clearly have a place on the balance sheet and the lender has distinct disclosure responsibilities with respect to the investment of cash and overall participation in securities lending programs.

Chapter 16

The Role of Carry in the Equity Markets

Robert S. Sloan
Director, Global Manager of Equity Finance
CS First Boston

The underlying concept of securities lending is one that is very simple: the holder or portfolio manager rents his securities to another party who in turn pays for the right to borrow. The holder receives all rights and distributions, except voting, as if the shares had not been lent. For the holder of securities it is the best of all possible worlds: he maintains all the exposure that he desires, there is total flexibility in managing the portfolio, he receives collateral to insure against a counterpart's insolvency, he receives a considerable incremental return for the lending of his shares, and he is able to offset many of the costs that he may have to incur, such as staffing, administrative, or custody. There is nothing remarkable about the cash flow that is involved in securities lending

What is it about securities lending that is at the base of almost all derivative transactions, financing transactions, and involved in almost all hedging vehicles that can cause so much confusion from such simplicity? Why is it that fixed income repo financing has evolved so differently from the equity side of the business? Why does the fixed income side of the securities lending universe seem to have a consistent structure across all Wall Street Firms? Yet, the equity finance business is found in many different forms and structures — with little uniformity.

If one looks at many fixed income desks, it is easy to see that the repo desk is at the hub of a trading floor. All activity is centered around the concept of *carry* — the difference between the interest rate pick up on an asset and what it costs to finance that asset. Look at balance sheets and income statements of many Wall Street firms and one can see that these firms make a lot of money by financing their positions more cheaply.

The repo desk is the center of activity. When a primary dealer is participating in an auction of government bonds, the repo desk plays an essential part in financing the roll and executing many trading strategies. If the option desk is looking at pricing a forward dated option, carry is an essential part of understanding the pricing of the deal. In fact, the price in the repo market has a direct bearing on the forward pricing of the option. If a customer has a portfolio of high yield securities and is looking for leverage, the repo desk can provide liquidity for the customer. The repo desk functions as the spoke in the wheel for almost all fixed income activities: government auctions, option pricing, corporate bond financing, and customer leverage.

The repo desk is also organized to fund the firm's inventory. This was the original intent of the repo desk. The leverage that exists today was unheard of only a short time ago. Some 20 years ago positions were of limited size. The billion dollar plus positions of today were just unthinkable. Commercial paper was considered something of a new and unsteady product. The fact that firms today can leverage so many times one dollar of capital shows how well firms have marketed the idea of a secured loan on an overnight basis. It also shows that firms have realized that it is unhealthy to rely solely on commercial paper for financing. Drexel went under because they could not monetize their junk bond positions. They did not develop an outlet for financing their inventory.

Looking across Wall Street one can see that the desks are organized in a pretty coordinated fashion. There are traders for different categories of securities: securities that are "special;" securities for different categories of bonds, e.g., European, agency, and mortgage; and securities that are fungible for money and can be used to finance the firm. There are product managers, salespeople, traders, and large organizations that support their activities.

The existence of a forward curve for interest rates and a general level of interest rates that underpins all products makes the uniformity of a funding desk more unlikely than in the world of equities.

Much of the equity products that are considered today are based upon the premise that there is a forward curve for equities. This means that the individual dividend streams for each stock can be said to replicate the coupon or implied curve of interest rates that exist in the fixed income market. Because of the very nature of equities and bonds, the resulting impact that the above concept has on the development of the financing businesses is important to distinguish: the cash flow of a company as expressed in its dividend payout is said to be equal to the overall level of interest rates in conjunction with the activity of the overall economy or the coupon attached to a particularly rated issue. Obviously the volatility of the company's cash flow as expressed in dividends will generally be much more than that of the overall level of interest rates and much more than a fixed coupon.

Why is this concept important when speaking about the structure of an equity finance group on Wall Street? It is important because of the fact that the disorganization of the equity financing desks — some are in banking, some are in operations, some are part of trading, and some are independent units — means that the true pricing mechanism for equity products has yet to be sufficiently explored. And that means that there is a wealth of opportunity yet to be had in all equity finance markets. Because the desks are differently organized, and because the actual carry pricing is in an OTC market, there is really no established forward curve; therefore, the pricing of many of the products comes down to stock borrow risk. The premium paid or collected is a direct function of a market that is not listed on any screen and has a universe of stocks that are special. In fact, I am all for recharacterizing the fee paid to or received from clients to a premium. The job of a stock loan desk is to serve as protection for the hedge which is established in the market. The borrower of the stock is going to pay something for the protection of his position. That is why I think that there is some insurance aspect to the stock loan market that is unrecognized. The price of borrowing the security is actually a way of recognizing a financial actuary done on a portfolio.

The very nature of most equity businesses also works to confuse the issue. Most equity houses are structured in such a way that emphasizes the deal and distribution aspects of investment banking. Deals are underwritten, sold to the investment community, and traded in the secondary market. The introduction of derivatives has brought the ideas of time, carry, and credit to the world of equities. There are many equity products which go by other names but are in fact nothing more than standard, time-tested fixed income strategies. For example, index arbitrage is no more than stock repo, swaps are definitely repo, and synthetic converts are reverse repos. There are many 3-month equivalent securities that are called by other names in the equities market. There is a definite and unrecognized fixed income aspect to the equity world which is now just beginning to get some light. It is with the above consideration to seeing how carry fits into the overall scheme of securities lending that one should pursue a lending or financing program to increase incremental yield.

Index

EURO BROKERS INC.
THIRD PARTY SECURITIES
LENDING PROGRAM

Are you getting the maximum performance from your Securities Lending Program?

By choosing Euro Brokers Inc. we can offer you:
- A high percentage of securities on loan ensuring maximum revenue
- A favorable revenue split
- An experienced staff with an enviable track record
- The ability to lend domestic and international securities
- A finite program. We tailor our program to meet the needs of the customer by running each program separately with no co-mingling, no STIF fund and each customer receiving the attention and results that they deserve.
- Our own proprietary system that can be tailored to each customers' needs.

If you are a:
Public Fund
Insurance Company
Pension Plan
Foundation
Bank

And you own any of the following:
U.S. Government securities
U.S. Corporate Bonds
U.S. Equities
Non-Dollar Government Securities and Equities

Euro Brokers Inc. would like to further discuss the benefits of its third party lending program. Please call George Martello at (212)749-7170 or Wayne Kuhnel at (212)748-7539.

InformationManagementNetwork

Leading-Edge Summits On

Securities Lending & Repurchase Agreements

Table Of Annual Programs:

US Beneficial Owners' Securities Lending Summit	Arizona	4th Sunday in January
European Beneficial Owners' Securities Lending Summit	Scotland *or* Ireland *alternating annually*	Early September
REPO Investors' Summit	Hilton Head Island	Late June

Additional Comprehensive Events Include:
Asset Securitization
Consultants' Congress
Corporate Pension Funds
Endowment & Foundation Investment Management
Fire & Police Investment Management
Fixed Income Portfolio Management
Indexing Summit
Public Pension Funds
Stable Value Symposium

For complete information:
Tel (800) 235-3466 • Fax (800) 575-6311
E-mail: imnreg@aol.com

Securities Finance | Securities Lending | Repo | Prime Brokerage

"SFI *helps clients*

To find out more about how SFI might be relevant to you or your organisation

achieve better

contact Mark Faulkner or Charles Stopford Sackville in complete confidence.

results quicker"

Consultancy | Recruitment | Counterpart Selection | Risk Management | The Symposium

Securities Finance International

Ten Wilkes Street Spitalfields London E1 6QF
Telephone +(44) 0171 377 2977 Fax +(44) 0171 377 2919
Email SFI@sfi-ldn.co.uk Website http://www.sfi-ldn.co.uk

A lasting commitment in securities lending.

You know UBS as a leading player in securities lending. But leadership means more than size and scale; it means quality of service too. We believe that strong customer relationships are the cornerstone of success: with UBS as your counterparty, you get a commitment to building a long-term relationship, rather than concentration on short-term profitability. This approach to business, combined with our triple-A rating and global 24-hour capability, are the reasons that UBS can offer an outstanding securities lending and repo product. For a long-term partner in securities lending, look no further than UBS.